Running an
Agile Software
Development Project

Running an Agile Software Development Project

Mike Holcombe
University of Sheffield, United Kingdom

A JOHN WILEY & SONS, INC., PUBLICATION

Published by John Wiley & Sons, Inc., Hoboken, New Jersey
Published simultaneously in Canada

For general information on our other products and services or for technical support, please contact our
Customer Care Department within the United States at (800) 762-2974, outside the United States at (317)
572-3993 or fax (317) 572-4002.

Wiley also publishes its books in variety of electronic formats. Some content that appears in print may
not be available in electronic formats. For more information about Wiley products, visit our web site
at www.wiley.com.

Library of Congress Cataloging-in-Publication Data:

Holcombe, W. M. L. (William Michael Lloyd), 1944-
  Running an agile software development project/by Mike Holcombe.
      p.   cm.
  Includes bibliographical references and index.
  ISBN 978-0-470-13669-0 (cloth)
 1. Computer software—development.   2.   Agile software development.
3. eXtreme programming.   I.   Title.
  QA76.76.D47H647 2008
  005.1′1--dc22   2008009444

Printed in the United States of America
10 9 8 7 6 5 4 3 2 1

Contents

3. Foundations: People and Teams Working Together   41

4. Starting an XP Project   73

5. Identifying Stories and Preparing to Build   119

6. Bringing the System Together as a Coherent Concept   153

7. Designing the System Tests   181

8. Units and Their Tests   215

9. Evolving the System   **239**

10. Documenting and Delivering the System   **251**

11. Reflecting on the Process   269

12. Lifestyle Matters   281

Appendix   291

Bibliography   305

Index   309

Preface

This book is a radical departure from the usual book on software engineering and design methodologies. Its purpose is to put software development into a context where *professional* skills are developed as well as the technical skills. At the end of a project based around this book, students should be much more like real software professionals than before, ready to embark on a career where professionalism, a quality orientation, and an understanding of the business context are better developed than ever before.

The target audience is computer science and software engineering students in their second or third year or in a master's program who have already covered the basics of programming and design and who have had some experience of building a small piece of software. Software developers who have graduated and are about to embark on their first commercial project will also find the topics of interest. Those interested in starting up their own software house might also find some part of this book useful.

The contents have evolved over 15 years or so during which time I have been teaching software engineering through practical project work involving *real* business clients. In the second year of our computer science and software engineering degree programs, students are put into small teams and spend one third of their time during a 12-week period building a business solution for their client—this is the Software Hut module. Typically, we have 3 or 4 clients and up to 20 teams of 4 to 6 students. Teams compete to build the best solution, and each client will then choose this from several that are supplied. The competitive aspect is generally positive, and the clients have always had several excellent software systems to choose from and use in their businesses. This long practical experience has shown me that much of what is written in academic software engineering books and taught in university courses is largely irrelevant to practical *real-world* software development.

Academics tend to abstract away the *messy bits* and treat software development in an idealized and essentially trivial manner. Many of the techniques and notations promoted in academe just do not work in real life. There is little rigorous scientific evidence for their utility in practice, and they are derived from a naïve understanding of the very real pressures that exist in business. This lack of understanding of the business world is now proving to be a serious issue—a handicap, even—in terms of recent computing graduates getting good jobs in the IT industry. In the United Kingdom, only 28% of IT graduates found graduate-level jobs in the IT industry (this includes IT posts in industry and commerce generally).[1] Many traditional

---

[1] e-skills.com, the UK government board responsible for the IT sector, has identified this fact for 2006.

programming jobs have been outsourced to developing countries, and the IT industry now needs graduates with much more business understanding: Technical programming skills are less critical, and many companies are happy to recruit graduates from other disciplines and train them up in the relevant technical material. However, computing graduates who do have these business skills are highly sought after and currently are gaining very highly paid jobs on leaving university.

About 13 years ago, I introduced an extension to the Software Hut. This is for fourth year master's degree students. It is a commercial software company called Genesys Solutions.[2] This company runs all year, and the students spend one third of their time in it. The students actually run the company. It has its own premises and equipment. The students negotiate contracts, prices, and delivery with clients and then work in a number of development teams to deliver. There is a marketing department and a systems administration department to maintain the infrastructure. Such a company has to deal with maintenance contracts as well as new developments, and it is vital that this is borne in mind by the developers, especially as the workforce at Genesys changes every year, and the original developers may have left the company when maintenance is needed. This company has been a great success—it seems to be unique in the world. Customers often return for extensions to existing software and new developments. The University of Sheffield has recently spun the company out. It is now a fully fledged and legally registered commercial company called epiGenesys. (http://www.epigenesys.co.uk).

The intention of the book is to use the new ideas from the so-called *agile methodologies*, particularly the approach known as *extreme programming*, or *XP*, as the vehicle for teaching *practical* project development skills. XP is a rapidly evolving set of ideas that can be applied in many different application areas; we focus here on the use of XP practices in the development of some real software for a business client, perhaps from a local company or another part of the university. The book is based on 20 years of experience of teaching in this way and managing such projects. In all, I have managed around 100 projects involving a couple of hundred teams, of which most have tried to use XP in the past 7 years. I have learned a great deal from this and have adapted XP to fit in with the demands of such *fixed-period* projects. Some may argue that I am demanding too much from students, but I am convinced that well-motivated students will be able to perform very well using these ideas; they not only can deliver excellent software to their clients, but also they will learn much more than from any other typical course on software development, which will concentrate on lots of lectures and artificial exercises. As so many people comment, success in the software industry is much more dependent on personal and teamwork skills than it is on technical knowledge. If you are unable to work effectively in a team, then you will be of little use to a software development company whatever technical knowledge you have. These sorts of projects will teach you a great deal about yourself and, the realities of teamwork and of dealing with real clients. One of the key challenges you will face is getting yourself organized and planning and working in an effective way. I have tried to give practical suggestions and mechanisms for doing

[2]See http://www.genesys.shef.ac.uk.

this. At the end of such a project, you will be amazed at what you will have achieved. The appendices contain examples of systems built by my students.

The book will also address the connections between IT development and business pragmatics through the use at the end of each chapter of *Conundrums*. These are based on real scenarios that either I have faced or have been experienced by business colleagues. In many cases, these explore the dilemmas between following the established philosophy of academic software engineering and the realities of businesses driven by the need to make money.

Some basic principles governing the book's philosophy are as follows:

1. It assumes that the readers will be engaged in a *real* rather than an academic software project. This means the project is for an external business client, and this factor will expose the students to the very real problems of requirements capture and the need for the highest quality software if the client is to be able to use it in their business. Most team-based projects are designed around problems posed by the instructor and often lack credibility with students, most of whom respond enthusiastically to the challenge of building something useful for a client.

2. It assumes that the readers will be reading it as members of a software development team and will be able to undertake the key activities together.

3. It aims to develop self-learning (and lifelong learning skills in the readers); this is a *problem-based learning* approach, and it is expected that the students will have the need to supplement their reading by consulting the literature, textbooks, articles in the professional press, and so forth. This is not intended to be an exhaustive and self-contained book on software engineering and software project management. I am convinced that, given the responsibility, students will rise to the challenge and develop intellectually and personally far more from this approach than from traditional educational approaches.

4. The book is not a large tome; it emphasizes the XP philosophy on minimal but informative and reliable documentation, and much of it is taken up with real examples from commercial agile projects.

5. Unlike existing XP books, this one deals with some of the practical details and provides effective methods and models for achieving high-quality software construction in an "agile" manner. Life is never as simple as most writers seem to imagine; sticking to *pure* XP is rarely going to work in most projects, but adapting it to suit the context—both in terms of clients and developers—has proved extraordinary effective.

6. There is an accompanying Website, http://agile.genesys.shef.ac.uk, for instructors/coaches that provides practical advice on how to motivate students, organize real group projects, and deal with many of the problems that arise in a simple and effective way. This is based on more than 15 years of running real software projects with student teams.

7. No specific programming language is used because particular projects will require particular implementation vehicles, but some reference is made to the language Java.

Some may claim that I am asking for too much documentation, too many models, too much systematic testing, and so forth. Everything that is discussed here is here for a reason and is often prompted by problems we have had with projects—delivering late, poor-quality systems, maintenance problems, and so on. Delivering high-quality software in a timely fashion is a big challenge, and these techniques have worked well.

Many people have helped me with this book; first, all my students who have taught me so much over the years. In particular, Francisco Macias, Sharifah Seyd-Abdullah, Chris Thomson, Phil McMinn, Alex Bell, and all the students from Genesys Solutions and the Software Hut over the years.

I must also thank my academic colleagues Marian Gheorghe, Andy Stratton, Helen Parker, Kirill Bogdanov, Tony Simons, and Tony Cowling for helping me with many aspects of the work but especially Marian, Helen, and Andy who have played a large part in making our real student projects such an amazing success.

A number of XP industrial experts from around the world have looked at drafts of this book, including Ivan Moore, Tim Lewis, and Graham Thomas. Fellow academics and collaborating researchers from a number of universities who have also been a great help include Mike Pont, Giancarlo Succi, Michelle Marchesi, Bernard Rumpe, Leon Moonens, Andres Barravalle, and Jose Canos.

Kent Beck has taken a detailed interest in the book and in what my students have been doing. He is a key influence and is always trying to keep me from being too conventional!

Amanda Watkinson, Jonathan Collett, and Vernon Green, senior developers at IBM, have been mentors for Genesys students for a number of years, and they have contributed a lot of important advice and support that is reflected in many aspects of this work.

I would also like to thank a number of anonymous reviewers whose comments on drafts have helped to improve the book immeasurably.

Finally, I must thank my wife Jill whose tolerance and support were invaluable.

MIKE HOLCOMBE

Sheffield, United Kingdom
May 2008

Chapter 1

What Is an Agile Methodology?

SUMMARY

Rapid business change requires rapid software development. How can we react to changing needs during software development? How can we ensure quality (correctness) as well as fitness for purpose? What are the requirements that an agile process should meet? What are the problems and limitations of agile processes?

1.1 RAPID BUSINESS CHANGE: THE ULTIMATE DRIVER

It has often been said that the modern world is experiencing unprecedented levels of change in technology, in business, in social structures, and in human attitudes. Of course, this is a complex and poorly understood phenomenon, but I know of no sources that disagree with the basic axiom that the world is changing fast and that fact is not, itself, about to change. Some may prefer that the world not be like that, and others may believe that this phenomenon is unsustainable in the long-term—the world will simply run out of resources or collapse into social anarchy and destruction.

At the present time, however, rapid change is a key factor of both business and public life. The other important truism is that computer technology, and software in particular, is a vital component of many businesses and organizations. It is clear, then, that the developers of this software have a problem. The pressure to develop new software support for rapidly changing processes is causing serious problems for the software industry. Traditional software engineering has repeatedly failed to deliver what is needed at the cost and within the timescale that are required.

This is caused by some structural and attitudinal problems associated with traditional software engineering. Deep thinkers about this problem have come up with a number of—what may seem to be paradoxical—insights into the problems. Key texts such as Pressman (2001) and Sommerville (2006) present a broad survey of traditional software engineering that documents many of the current approaches. Other thinkers such as

Gilb (1988) and more recently Beck (1999) are beginning to question the way in which software engineering has been carried out.

Thinkers such as Beck recognize that everything about our current software processes must change. On the other hand, their proposed solutions partly involve a number of well-tried and trusted techniques that have been around for years. It is not just a matter of shuffling around a few old favorite techniques into a different order; rather, it is a new combination of activities that are grounded in a new and very positive philosophy of *agile* software development.

1.2 WHAT MUST AGILE METHODOLOGIES BE ABLE TO DO?

We note that any agile software development process has to be able to adapt to rapid changes in scope and requirements, but it has also to satisfy the needs for the delivery of high-quality systems in a manner that is highly cost-effective, unburdened by massive bureaucracy, and that does not demand heroics from the developers involved. Thus, we will try to specify the basic properties that a successful agile software development process must satisfy.

1 The first issue is the ability to adapt the development of the software as the client's problem changes.

2 The second issue derives from the need to allow for the future evolution of any delivered solution.

3 The third issue is that of software quality: How do we know that the software always does what it is supposed to do?

4 The fourth issue is the amount of unnecessary documentation and other bureaucracy that is required to sustain and manage the development process.

5 The fifth issue is the human one, which relates both to the experiences of the developers in the development process and to the way in which the human resources are managed.

Coupled with these is a need to have a clear business focus for any software development project and application.

We will look at all of these in turn.

1.3 AGILITY: WHAT IS IT AND HOW DO WE ACHIEVE IT?

When we embark on a software development project, the initial and some would say the hardest phase is that of determining the requirements—finding out, with the client, what the proposed system is supposed to do.

It might start with a brief overview of the business context and the identification of the kind of data that is to be involved, how this data is to be manipulated, and how these various activities mesh together with each other and with the other activities in the business.

Many techniques exist to do this: Ways of collecting information, not just from the client but also from the intended users of the system, will be needed in this initial stage. Sifting through this information, making decisions about the relative importance of some of the information, and trying to set it into a coherent picture follow. Again, a number of different approaches, notations, and techniques exist to support this.

Having achieved some indication of the overall purpose of the system, the way that it interfaces and interacts with other business processes will be the next issue. We are trying to establish the system boundary during this phase.

From this we construct a detailed requirements document. Some examples of actual documents will be given in a later chapter. Such a document will be structured, typically, into functional requirements and non-functional requirements. Both are vitally important. Each requirement will be stated in English, perhaps structured into sections containing related requirements and described at various levels of detail. The client may well be satisfied at this point with what is proposed. However, it is always difficult to visualize exactly how the system will work at this stage, and our understanding of it may not be right.

Now we would embark on some analysis, looking at these key operational aspects, identifying the sort of computing resources needed to operate such a system and considering many other aspects of the proposed system. After analysis we get into the design phase, and it is here where we describe the data and processing models and how the system could be created from the available technical options.

This stage is often lengthy and complicated. Rarely will the developers be able to proceed independently of the client although there may be pressure on them from managers to do so. There will be many issues that will arise during this process requiring further consultation with the client. This is often not carried out, and the developers start making decisions that only the client should take. We see the system starting to drift from what it should be.

At the end of this process, we will have a large and complicated detailed design that may or may not still be valid in terms of the client's business needs, which may be evolving.

If we go back to the client at this stage, we may very well find that the business has moved on and the requirements have changed significantly. The traditional development methods, such as the waterfall method, cannot handle this challenge effectively. Because of the investment in the design, there may be a reluctance to change it significantly or to start again.

The waterfall model envisions a steady and systematic sequence of stages starting with the capture and definition of the requirements, the analysis of these requirements, the formalizing of a system and software design, the implementation of the design, and the testing of the software. Finally we have delivery and after-sales, which covers a number of different types of maintenance: perfective maintenance where faults are removed after delivery, adaptive maintenance, which might involve building more functionality in the system, and maintenance to upgrade the software to a different operating environment.

It will always be necessary, and sometimes possible, to backtrack around some of the stages, but the emphasis is on a trying to identify the requirements in one go. The diagram in Fig. 1.1 tries to illustrate the approach.

The need to respond more quickly to the changing nature of the customer's needs does not sit easily with this type of model.

The first two key issues are, therefore, to find an approach that retains a continual and close relationship with the client, and to find an approach to development that does not involve the heavy overhead of a long and complex design phase.

If this is achieved, then the development process might be more able to adapt to the changing requirements.

There are a number of other approaches to software development that have attempted to address these issues. The spiral model (Sommerville, 2006) describes this approach (Fig. 1.2). It involves a series of iterations around the *requirements capture or specification–implementation–testing or validation–delivery and operation* loop together with periodic reviews of the overall project and the analysis of risks that have been identified during the course of the project.

It attempts to recognize that for many projects, there is an ongoing relationship with the customer that does not end with the delivery of the system but will continue through many further stages involving correcting and extending or adapting the product. In these cases, there is no such thing as a *finished product*.

Rapid applications development and evolutionary delivery are similar sorts of approaches that are built around the idea of building and demonstrating, and in the latter case delivering, parts of the system as the project goes along.

Such approaches can be successful but differ in many ways from the approaches taken by the current agile or lightweight methodologies, one of which we are considering here. One issue is the length of an iteration cycle; in agile approaches, these are very short.

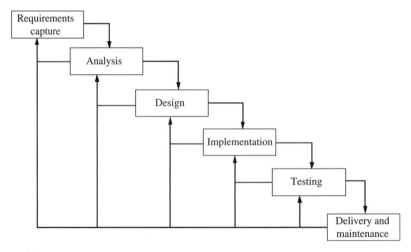

Figure 1.1   The waterfall model of software development.

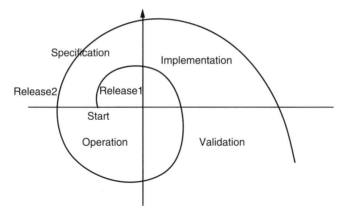

Figure 1.2   The spiral model.

There have been many analyses of failed software development projects. Failures in communication, both between developers and clients and between and among developers, seem to be some of the most common causes of problems. In the traditional approach, the various documents (requirements documents, design documents, etc.) are supposed to facilitate this communication; however, often the language and notation used in these documents fails to support effective communication. UML (Unified Modeling Language) diagrams, for example, can often be interpreted differently by different people.

1.4   EVOLVING SOFTWARE: OBSTACLES AND POSSIBILITIES

Even if we are able to deliver a solution that is still relevant, it may not remain so for long. Things are bound to change, and there is thus a need to see how we can evolve the software toward its new requirements. Some of the old functionality is likely to remain, however, so it would be inefficient to throw it away and start again. How can we develop a method whereby changes can be achieved in the software quickly, cheaply, and reliably? Agile techniques are an attempt to answer some of these questions.

Many systems will involve a database somewhere, and this is one of the key issues when it comes to obstacles to evolution. Traditionally we use a relational database structure and a relational database management system to manage it. Much time is spent building and normalizing the data model. When circumstances change, however, the data model may not still be appropriate. What can we do about this? It may not be a straightforward matter to reengineer this data model. It may not be possible to just insert a couple of new fields or a new table or two. It is likely that the whole data model will have to be substantially reengineered, and this could be expensive.

What are the requirements of a software engineer when faced with the problem of adapting an existing or proposed system to deal with some new requirements?

In the case where there is an existing system that forms the basis of the development, the first thing to do is to gain a clear understanding of what the current system does. This can be achieved, to a certain extent, by running the software and observing its behavior. A complete knowledge, however, will only be achieved by looking at the design in some detail. The design may not be reliable, and so we have to look at the source code. If this is written in a clear and simple fashion, then it will be possible to understand it well. If we could do this with a clear structure to the requirements document, we may have a chance of understanding things.

If the original system was built in stages, gradually introducing new functionality in a controlled manner, we may be able to see where features that are no longer needed were introduced, and we can explore how we might evolve the software gradually by introducing, in stages, any new functionality and removing some of the old. Throughout, we need to consult the client.

For projects that require a completely new system to be built, then time needs to be spent on identifying the business processes that will be supported by the new system, along with information about how current manual processes operate, if there are any. The more that is known about the users and their needs, the better.

Thus we need the system to be built in such a way that the relationship between the requirements and the code is clear; and the code itself to be clear and understandable.

1.5 THE QUALITY AGENDA

The quality of software is a key issue for the industry although one that it has had great difficulty in addressing successfully.

For real quality systems, we have to address two vital issues: identifying the right software to be built and demonstrating that this has been achieved.

In terms of the types of faults that are often made in software development, we can identify two important types of faults: *requirements faults* (we tell the computer to do the wrong thing) and *operational faults* (the computer wrongly does the thing we told it to do).

Neither problem is easy to deal with. The first task is made more difficult by the possible changing nature of the business need and the consequential requirement to adapt to a changing target. This is one of the key objectives of an agile methodology. However, it might be possible to find a way of adapting and altering the software being built to reflect the developers' changing understanding of the client's needs, but it is quite another to be sure that they have got the changes right. Here is where a strong relationship between the developers and the business they are trying to develop a system for is needed. It also requires a considerable amount of discussion and review both between the developers and the client and among the developers but also among the client's staff; they really do have to know where their company is going.

Hence an agile methodology must be able to deal with identifying and maintaining a clear and *correct* understanding of the system being built. By correct we mean something that is acceptable to the client, a system that has the correct functional and non-functional attributes as well as being within budget and time.

To satisfy such requirements, the agile methodology must provide support, not only for changing business needs but also for giving assurance that these are indeed the real requirements. In order to do this, there has to be a continuous process of discussion, question asking, and resolution based on clear and practical objectives.

The second quality issue is that of ensuring that the delivered system meets its requirements. Here there are serious problems with almost all approaches. Despite the best intentions of many, testing and review are aspects of software engineering that are either done inadequately or too late to be effective.

An approach to improving quality in a model like the waterfall model is called the *V model* (Fig. 1.3). Here each stage in the process provides the basis for testing of a particular type. We will discuss more about testing later. Some of the terms may seem unfamiliar at this stage; they are also not always distinct. However, the idea that, for example, the requirements could be used to define some of the acceptance tests, and so on, is a useful indication of what might be a practical approach to ensuring quality.

In most development projects that are not completely chaotic, some attempt is also made to carry out reviews of the work done. This might be the review of requirements documents, designs, or code and should involve a number of people examining the documentation and code provided by the developers and inspecting it for flaws of various types. The developers then have to address any concerns raised by the review. Human nature, being what it is, is such that developers are often reluctant to accept other people's opinions. In many cases where serious problems have been found, the developers will try to adjust and work around the problems rather than carry out significant reworking. In fact, one often sees the situation where the best solution is to start again with a component but the resistance to doing this is often profound. This just compounds the problems and is very hard to overcome. If a developer has spent a week or longer on some component that is then found to be seriously flawed, they are

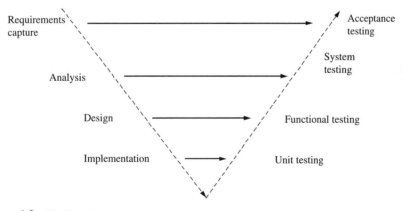

Figure 1.3   The V model.

likely to resent having to start again. This is a potentially serious quality and efficiency problem. In many companies, software developers spend most of their time developing their code on their own with little discussion with others, and when flaws in their output are found, a lot of time has been wasted.

An agile methodology, therefore, needs to address this issue of review and testing and to provide a mechanism that will provide confidence in the quality of the product.

Another quality aspect is the correctness of the final code. This is usually addressed by testing whereby the software is run against suitable test sets and its behavior monitored to establish whether it is behaving in the required manner. For this to work we need two basic things: we need to know what the software is supposed to do, and we need to be able to create test sets that will give us enough confidence that the code does do what it is supposed to do.

The role of testing in the design and construction of software is a misunderstood and underdeveloped activity. An effective agile methodology must provide a clear link between the identification of what the system is supposed to do and the creation and maintenance of effective test sets. Furthermore the testing must be fully integrated into the construction process so that we avoid the massive problems and expense that arise when the testing is done last.

It also allows us to introduce key *design for test* considerations driven by the realization that the way the system is constructed will affect the ease and effectiveness of the testing. Some systems are almost impossible to test properly because of the way that they have been built. This is well-known in hardware design (microprocessors, etc.) but is not something that seems to exercise software engineering much.

There are many myths about software quality and what the position really is. Little empirical research has been carried out analyzing the quality of software systems. What has been done has often uncovered some uncomfortable news. In terms of the operational faults—leaving aside the problem of capturing the wrong requirements—the evidence is pretty gloomy.

Hatton (1998) in a series of studies discovered the following: Using *static* deep-flow analysis across many different industries and application areas, he measured the consistency of several million lines of software written in various languages: C, Fortran 77, C++, and so forth.

He also measured the level of *dynamic* disagreement between independent implementations of the same algorithms acting on the same input data with the same parameters in just one of these industrial application areas.

On average there were 8 serious faults per 1000 lines for C programs and 12 for Fortran; 10% of the C population would be deemed untestable by any standards.

Object-oriented languages were worse, not only in the density of faults but also in the time it took to correct them—findings also supported by the work of Humphreys (1995).

Many of these faults relate to technical issues in the implementation; the programs compile but do not work in a predictable or correct way. Variables are used before being properly declared, memory overflows, and so on.

The key to managing these problems is to *test thoroughly all the time*.

1.6 DO WE REALLY NEED ALL THIS MOUNTAIN OF DOCUMENTATION?

Most nonchaotic software development methods are *design led* and *document driven*. We need to examine the purpose of all this paperwork (it might be stored electronically, but it still amounts to masses of text, diagrams, and arcane notations).

Let's look first at the issue of design: what is it for and where does it fit in a development project?

Design is a mechanism for exploring and documenting possible solutions in a way that should make the eventual translation into working software easy and trouble free. If there is an analysis phase, then typically this will establish the overall parameters of the project and will result in a (usually fixed) set of requirements and constraints for the project. The design phase then takes this information and develops a more concrete representation of the system in a form that is suitable as a basis for programming.

The desire for agility means that the analysis phase is likely to be continuous throughout most of the project if it is to be able to adapt to changing business need. If an agile approach is to work, the nature and role of analysis must change. Therefore the role of design will also be an issue. How can we deal with the rapid changes that analysis might throw up if the design is proceeding by way of a large and complex process that is trying to identify, at a significant level of detail, issues that will eventually be the responsibility of programmers to solve? Large, complex designs are almost impossible to maintain in this context. Some tool vendors will emphasize the benefit of using computer-aided software engineering (CASE) and other tools that might provide support for the maintenance of the design, but many programmers dislike these systems, which are often imposed by the management, and some programmers may feel that their creativity is compromised.

Creative programmers will also be tempted to solve problems that arise during implementation that were not predicted by the analysis or design phases without updating the design archive. This is a real problem in many projects that may only come to light during maintenance when it is discovered that the design differs from what the system actually is. In other words, the code does not work as the design documents indicate in some, possibly crucial, areas. Thus maintenance is carried out by reference to the code, which is the key resource, and the design may not be used or trusted.

Thus why is it there? The design is a resource that has cost time and money to create, and yet it may not seem to provide any reliable value. It might actually damage projects because of the difficulties of ensuring that the design can evolve as the business needs change. It is possible that the existence of a large and complex design may encourage developers to resist changes to the system asked for by the client. If this happens, and I believe that it often does, then the client is not going to get the system they want. A standard technique is to tell the client that it would be too expensive to change things and this often works, but it is a short-term solution. The client is going to be less than satisfied at the end. An agile process needs to be able to deal with this issue.

Thus is design a key part of an agile process? It has to be made much more responsive to a project's changing needs and it should also provide a precise description of the final code, otherwise it is merely of historical value. Design notations can help us to clarify and discuss our ideas, and from that point of view they are useful. Bearing in mind that design documents might be misinterpreted by people who were not involved in the development, for example those carrying out maintenance in subsequent years, we should not place all our reliance on these documents. We will also need to document the code carefully and also the test sets; these will help a great deal in understanding what the software does when the original team has dispersed.

Another aspect that also relates to the human dimension is that creative people—and good programmers are creative—do not work to their best ability if they feel dominated by bureaucratic processes and large amounts of seemingly irrelevant documentation. It's a natural feeling and applies in all walks of life. If you feel that churning out lots of unnecessary paperwork gets in the way of your ultimate desire—building a quality system to satisfy your client—then you may not put your best effort into creating all this stuff. Good morale, as we shall see next, is vital for good productivity. If nobody needs it, why generate it?

1.7   THE HUMAN FACTOR

People are individuals with their own desires, values, and capabilities. Software engineering is a people-based business, and the morale of the team is a vital component in the success of the project. Too often, organizations organize themselves in hierarchical structures whereby those who are above you feed down instructions perhaps without any serious explanation, and those below you suffer from you doing the same. It is often difficult to feel valued and to know what is really going on—as opposed to what the managers think is going on.

To obtain the best work from people, we have to consider them as intelligent and responsible individuals and to show interest in their views and an awareness of their objectives. This calls for skilled and sensitive management. This does not mean that the management system abdicates all responsibility and we are left with a chaotic approach where everyone just does their own thing.

What is needed is a system that focuses on the key issues, involves everyone to the greatest possible extent, jointly identifies the constraints and parameters applicable to the project, and provides an open mechanism for discussion, decision making, and the taking of responsibility. Over many years of supervising and managing projects, I am convinced that this is the most effective way. It is not without problems, there will always be problems, and sometimes individuals are just unreasonable and threaten the joint endeavors of the team. In my experience the team, if given the responsibility, will deal with the issues effectively. In the few instances where I have had to intervene, the solution has been negotiated quickly and effectively. There are a number of management devices that can work: yellow cards and red cards as used in football (soccer) may be useful; the use of a *sin bin* might also be considered for unreasonable colleagues. It has to be a group decision rather than the manager's to be most effective, however.

Agility requires cooperation from the development teams; they need to be able to adapt to changing circumstances without feeling threatened or pressured. A flat and inclusive management structure seems to be able to deliver this.

We shouldn't forget the needs of the clients. They are the other people in the loop, and one way to ensure that they are kept happy is to keep them informed and to have excellent lines of communication between the development team and the clients and users. Clients also worry about progress because they may be held responsible for project failure or other consequences caused by problems beyond their control. Many clients are skeptical about the reassurances given to them by developers using traditional approaches to software engineering where the only things to show for months of work are incomprehensible diagrams and paperwork. Providing pieces of functioning software, albeit prototypes in some methodologies, provides some confidence that things are progressing. It also provides a mechanism for feedback from a real implementation rather than from vague abstractions.

The issue of *end-user programming* could be raised here. One of the most ambitious goals of this is to provide users with no programming experience with the facilities to build their own applications, the argument being that they know their business better than the programmers and analysts and thus they should be in a better position to know what they want. If we can give them an environment that enabled them to build their application easily, then this would overcome some of the problems.

Things aren't quite as simple as this, however. Some clients find it difficult to articulate what they want or to step back sufficiently to understand their business processes adequately to create a coherent business model and thus an application to support it.

However, there are some possibilities. In a way, spreadsheets are an example of the sort of application that many business people can create and use, although it is easy to make errors in the way these are set up and the formulas in the cells defined. It does present a possible way forward, however.

Another example is the work of Bagnall (2002) who built an experimental end-user system called Program It Yourself (PIY). This was founded on a particular approach to identifying the business model for an e-commerce site that was based directly around concrete things involved in the business, products, prices, and so forth. In trials with naïve users (i.e., nonprogrammers), he found that they could build useful and maintainable systems based on the use of an XML Hunter (2000) database supporting a user-friendly GUI that implemented a clear business model. Similar systems for other business domains should be possible.

1.8 SOME AGILE METHODOLOGIES

There are a number of possible contenders for the description of an agile methodology. We will look at some of the more popular ones, leaving extreme programming until the next chapter where we will look at it in more detail. This account is not exhaustive but is meant to provide some ideas of the different directions in which agile development is going.

1.8.1   Dynamic Systems Development Method

The dynamic systems development method (DSDM) (Stapleton, 1997) is an approach that uses an iterative process based on prototyping that involves the users throughout the project life cycle. In DSDM, time is fixed for the life of a project rather than starting with a set of requirements and trying to keep going until everything has been done—or we have all given up! Thus resources are fixed as far as possible at the start, and this can provide a more realistic planning framework for a project. This means that the requirements that will be satisfied are allowed to change to suit the resources available.

There are nine underlying principles of DSDM, the key one being that fitness for business purpose is the essential criterion for the acceptance of deliverables. This philosophy should ensure a clearer focus on the purpose of the software rather than on technology for technology's sake.

1.8.1.1   The Underlying Principles

The following principles[1] are the foundations on which DSDM is based. Each one of the principles is applied as appropriate in the various parts of the method.

1 Active user involvement is imperative. Users are active participants in the development process. If users are not closely involved throughout the development life-cycle, delays will occur, and users may feel that the final solution is imposed by the developers and/or management.

2 The team must be empowered to make decisions. DSDM teams consist of both developers and users. They must be able to make decisions as requirements are refined and possibly changed. They must be able to agree that certain levels of functionality, usability, and so forth, are acceptable without frequent recourse to higher-level management.

3 The focus is on frequent delivery of products. A product-based approach is more flexible than is an activity-based one. The work of a DSDM team is concentrated on products that can be delivered in an agreed period of time. By keeping each period of time short, the team can easily decide which activities are necessary and sufficient to achieve the right products.

4 Fitness for business purpose is the essential criterion for acceptance of deliverables. The focus of DSDM is on delivering the essential business requirements within the required time. Allowance is made for changing business needs within that time frame.

---

[1]These are taken from the DSDM site: http://www.dsdm.org.

5 Iterative and incremental development is necessary to converge on an accurate business solution. DSDM allows systems to grow incrementally. Therefore the developers can make full use of feedback from the users. Moreover partial solutions can be delivered to satisfy immediate business needs. Rework is built into the DSDM process; thus, the development can proceed more quickly during iteration.

6 All changes during development are reversible. To control the evolution of all products, everything must be in a known state at all times. Backtracking is a feature of DSDM. However in some circumstances, it may be easier to reconstruct than to backtrack. This depends on the nature of the change and the environment in which it was made.

7 Requirements are baselined at a high level. Baselining high-level requirements means "freezing" and agreeing on the purpose and scope of the system at a level that allows for detailed investigation of what the requirements imply. Further, more detailed baselines can be established later in the development, although the scope should not change significantly.

8 Testing is integrated throughout the life cycle. Testing is not treated as a separate activity. As the system is developed incrementally, it is also tested and reviewed by both developers and users incrementally to ensure that the development not only is moving forward in the right business direction but also is technically sound.

9 Collaboration and cooperation between all stakeholders is essential.

DSDM is independent and can sometimes be used in unison with other frameworks and development approaches, such as extreme programming (XP).

1.8.2 Feature-Driven Design

Feature-driven design (FDD) (Coad, 1999) begins by developing a domain object model in collaboration with domain experts that is then used to create a *features* list. This is used to produce a rough plan, and informal teams are set up to build small increments over short, say 2-week, periods.

There are five processes within FDD:

1 Develop an overall model.

2 Build a features list; these should be small but useful to the client.

3 Plan by feature.

4 Design by feature.

5 Build by feature.

A *feature* is a client-valued function that can be implemented in 2 weeks or less. A *feature set* is a grouping of business-related features.

We illustrate the process in Fig. 1.4.

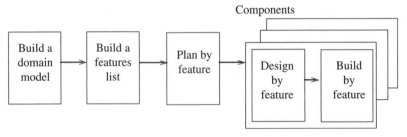

Figure 1.4 Feature-driven design.

1.8.3 Crystal

Communication is a key aspect of Crystal (Cockburn, 2001) by considering development as "a cooperative game of invention and communication." Crystal aims to overcome many of the problems caused by poor communication between all the stakeholders, particularly developers, customers, and clients.

Cockburn looks at a software development project as a bit like an ecosystem "in which physical structures, roles, and individuals with unique personalities all exert forces on each other."

The approach highlights intermediate work products that exist in order to help the team make their next move in the *game*. These products help team members to orient themselves in the project and to remind members of important issues, decisions, goals, and so forth. They also help in prompting new ideas and potential solutions to problems. These products do not have to be complete or perfect but should help to guide and motivate team members. As the game progresses, these products help in the management of it. "The endpoint of the game is an operating software system . . . ."

As we can see, the approach is more of a management framework rather than a set of explicit technical practices. There exist some policy standards and guidelines on the numbers of developers and how to assess the critical attributes of projects.

1.8.4 Agile Modeling

"Agile modeling is a collection of values, principles, and practices for modeling software that can be applied on a software development project in an effective and light-weight manner" [http://www.agilemodeling.com].

An agile modeling (AM) approach (Ambler, 2002) can be taken to requirements, analysis, architecture, and design. The idea is that whatever modeling approach is taken, whether as use case models, class models, data models, or user interface models, the emphasis should be on a lightweight but effective approach to the modeling. The model should not become the purpose but just the vehicle for understanding the customer's needs better. Because the models are light weight, they are easier to adapt or are even thrown away if they become obsolete through requirements change.

AM is often combined with notations from UML and for example the rational unified process (RUP), but the full bureaucratic treadmill often associated with these processes is reduced. AM is not a complete software process; it doesn't cover programming, software delivery, or testing activities, although testability is considered through the modeling process. There is also no emphasis on project management and many other important issues. However, AM is very sympathetic to the principles of XP that we examine in Chapter 2 and it is possible to combine AM with some of the more complete agile processes such as XP, DSDM, or crystal. In this book, we will combine a type of agile modeling with XP.

1.8.5 SCRUM

SCRUM is a management process that can be applied to a number of different activities, not just software development. Introduced in 1995 (Schwaber, 2002), it has had some success in a number of projects.

A project is divided into features with an assigned project value and estimated effort or cost. *Sprints* are time-boxed plans corresponding with iterations. Daily *scrum* meetings—which are short and focused—are held to monitor progress. At the end of each sprint, a review meeting is held to consider the quality of the features produced. Different stakeholders and actors are identified including the product owner, the scrum master, and the team members.

There have been successful approaches that combine SCRUM with other agile methodologies; for example, SCRUM might be used for the overall management of a project, which could include marketing and support activities, while an agile software development method is used for the production.

SCRUM has been applied to a distributed development project across several countries (e.g., Sutherland, 2007).

1.8.6 Summary Table

These different approaches have different strengths and weaknesses, but all adopt parts of the agile philosophy. There are a number of other approaches such as lean software development (Poppendieck, 2002 http://www.Poppendieck2002.com). We briefly summarize some of their properties in Table 1.1. In the table, "+" indicates a strong aspect featured in the approach, "−" means that this aspect is not emphasized in the literature, and "?" indicates that this can be featured but not always, and critical support for this is not a fundamental part of the method.

Some of these approaches are really more like philosophical perspectives on software development rather than a complete set of techniques and methods, some are general approaches to managing and planning software projects, and some are tied into an existing design-based approach such as UML. All have their strengths, and which ones will succeed in the industry over the next few years is dependent on many things.

Table 1.1   A Summary of the Features of the Agile Methodologies in This Chapter

Feature	DSDM	FDD	Crystal	Agile modeling	SCRUM
Clear business focus	+	+	?	−	+
Strong quality/testing focus	?	−	−	−	?
Handles changing requirements	+	+	?	+	+
Human-centered philosophy	?	?	+	+	?
Support for maintenance	?	−	−	−	−
User/customer-centered approach	+	+	?	+	?
Encourages good communications	+	?	+	?	+
Minimum bureaucracy	?	?	+	+	−
Support for planning	+	+	+	−	+

There is a shortage of scientific evidence about the benefits and weaknesses of these approaches. There are plenty of case studies, experience reports, and opinions available—in the proceedings of conferences on agile development and on Web sites that abound. However, no extensive comparative trials have been carried out in an industrial context except those undertaken in the Sheffield Software Engineering Observatory (http://observatory.group.shef.ac.uk/) where the approach described in the next chapter has been compared with a traditional design-led approach.

In the next chapter, we will focus on extreme programming, XP (Beck, 1999) and see that it will provide all of the desirable features that we have identified. It also gives much clearer guidance on how to achieve them. Some of the other agile approaches, such as DSDM and SCRUM, are proposing to adopt some of the XP ideas in a kind of hybrid approach.

1.9   REVIEW

The issues that an agile approach to software engineering must address can be summarized in the following six properties:

1 a clear business focus;

2 the ability to plan and adapt the development of the software as the client's problem changes and to provide feedback on progress;

3 the need to allow for the future maintenance and evolution of any delivered solution;

4 the assurance of the quality of the delivered software;

5 the reduction of the amount of documentation and other bureaucracy that is required to sustain and manage the development process;

6 the emphasis on the human dimension must be a key aspect both for the developers and the clients.

Consult the agile modeling manifesto for another perspective on the issues discussed above.

EXERCISE

Consider the Agile Manifesto reproduced here from the following Web page: http://www.agilemanifesto.org/principles.html.

> *We follow these principles:*
>
> *Our highest priority is to satisfy the customer through early and continuous delivery of valuable software.*
>
> *Welcome changing requirements, even late in development. Agile processes harness change for the customer's competitive advantage.*
>
> *Deliver working software frequently, from a couple of weeks to a couple of months, with a preference to the shorter timescale.*
>
> *Business people and developers must work together daily throughout the project.*
>
> *Build projects around motivated individuals. Give them the environment and support they need, and trust them to get the job done.*
>
> *The most efficient and effective method of conveying information to and within a development team is face-to-face conversation.*
>
> *Working software is the primary measure of progress.*
>
> *Agile processes promote sustainable development. The sponsors, developers, and users should be able to maintain a constant pace indefinitely.*
>
> *Continuous attention to technical excellence and good design enhances agility.*
>
> *Simplicity—the art of maximizing the amount of work not done—is essential.*
>
> *The best architectures, requirements, and designs emerge from self-organizing teams.*
>
> *At regular intervals, the team reflects on how to become more effective, then tunes and adjusts its behavior accordingly.*

Think about these principles and reflect on your own experiences in software development, what you have been taught about the process. How do these principles relate to these issues? If you have been involved in a significant development project, what processes did you follow?

CONUNDRUM

The following scenario is based on a real-life business situation that arose in the late 1990s.

The Internet is opening up, and many businesses are now connected. Banks are beginning to consider if they could provide online access to their business customers. One bank considers two strategies.

(A) The bank's IT director suggests that they put together a *quick and dirty* Web site that allows customers to submit transactions through their browser, to get this up and running, and to try to develop a connection with the "back-office" legacy mainframe database system.

(B) The bank also gets a report from some outside consultants that suggests they should reengineer the legacy back-end and build an integrated Web front-end to provide a powerful user-friendly e-banking system engineered to a high standard.

Which strategy would be best and why?
See Chapter 11 for a discussion of this dilemma.

REFERENCES

S. ANCHA, A. CIOROIANU, J. COUSINS, J. CROSBIE, J. DAVIES, K. AHMED, J. HART, K. GABHART, S. GOULD, R. LADDAD, S. LI, B. MACMILLAN, D. RIVERS-MOORE, J. SKUBAL, K. WATSON, S. WILLIAMS. *Professional Java XML.* Wrox Press, 2001.

M. BAGNALL. The Dyna Cat System. http://www.dcs.shef.ac.uk/intranet/teaching/projects/archive/ug2002/pdf/ugmab.pdf.

S. AMBLER. *Agile Modeling.* John Wiley & Sons, 2002.

K. BECK. *Extreme Programming Explained.* Addison-Wesley, 1999.

P. COAD, J. DE LUCA, E. LEFEBRE. *Java Modelling in Color.* Prentice Hall, 1999.

A. COCKBURN. *Agile Software Development* (A. Cockburn and J. Highsmith, eds.). Addison Wesley, 2001.

T. GILB. *Principles of Software Engineering Management* (S. Finzi-Wokingham, ed.). Addison-Wesley, 1988.

L. HATTON. Does OO sync with the way we think? *IEEE Software*, 15(3):46–54, 1998.

W.S. HUMPHREYS. *A Discipline for Software Engineering.* Addison-Wesley, 1995.

D. HUNTER. *Beginning XML.* Wrox Press, 2000.

R.S. PRESSMAN. *Software Engineering: A Practitioner's Approach.* McGraw Hill, 2000.

K. SCHWABER, M. BEEDLE. *Agile Software Development with SCRUM.* Prentice Hall, 2002.

I. SOMMERVILLE. *Software Engineering*, 8th ed. Addison-Wesley, 2006.

J. STAPLETON. *DSDM: The Dynamic Systems Development Method.* Addison-Wesley, 1997.

J. SUTHERLAND, A. VIKTOROV, J. BLOUNT, N. PUNTIKOV. *Proc. HICSS.* 2007.

Web Sites

http://www.Poppendieck2002.com.

Chapter 2

Extreme Programming Outlined

SUMMARY

The fundamental principles and the 5 values and the 12 activities involved in extreme programming (XP) are introduced. These are reviewed and discussed in the light of some current experiences in applying XP in industry.

2.1 SOME GUIDING PRINCIPLES

Before we get into the details of the main approach taken in the book, an evolution of extreme programming (XP), which incorporates many of the aspects described in the agile methods discussed in Chapter 1, we will consider some of the issues from a broader perspective.

Software development is a human activity, and we must ensure that the human dimension is at the center of our thoughts when we discuss ways to make software more effectively.

There is a social dimension in which groups of people (developers, customers, managers) collaborate together to achieve a common aim—the development of a software solution to a business problem. However, it is not just the achievement of this that is important. We all develop and learn as individuals and groups, and this has to be at the forefront of things as well.

There are a number of social principles that apply here. No project is without its challenges, and any group of people comes with its dynamic relationships. If we are aware of these from the start, then we will be able to both benefit from their positive aspects and manage any possible negative ones.

We should consider how people think and feel about things—their work, their environment, their relationships, their hopes and fears. People experience many different emotions and have many different needs. Recognizing that people are individuals and respecting that is a key pillar upon which XP is built.

Thus people want to succeed in their work, to enjoy what they do, to feel a sense of achievement, to learn and improve their knowledge and technical skills, to be able to relax with colleagues, and to manage their responsibilities without the stigma of failure.

From a technical point of view, there are many issues to be considered.

Fundamentally, we are engaged in the development of something of value, a product that may have some economic benefit: it pays our wages and contributes to the company's profits; it benefits our customers by providing them with enhanced capacity to achieve their business objectives. However, it may not be business based in the narrow interpretation of the term but enables clients to do their work better (many of our customers are charities or public sector organizations, which are not necessarily profit driven).

Thus we need to think about value and its costs in time and money in a holistic way, and these will be at the core of our work.

A key mechanism for keeping these three things together is to proceed in very small steps. In this way, one can see how well one is doing, and if we can combine this with a view of where we are going—accepting that this may not be totally clear at all times—then we can make progress.

Adding value and demonstrating this should be the objective throughout. We can see how this is achieved if we maintain a constant relationship with each other—developers, customers, and managers—all the time. To do that we need to *communicate*: to talk to each other, to show each other what we have done, to discuss where we are going, to reflect on what has been achieved in an honest way, to help each other if things go wrong, to keep relationships in a positive state. Sometimes we should think about developing and maintaining these relationships outside of the work environment through social and leisure activities.

A dominant theme is the *flow* of activities. We will focus on building frequent small releases of code that can demonstrate some value to the project; we will reflect on what has happened frequently and regularly; we will respond to setbacks in a positive way that enhances our understanding of the development process and of our professional and personal capabilities; we will promote discussion and sharing of perspectives and knowledge; and we will try to improve ourselves, our team and our organization bit by bit.

These fundamental principles lead to a set of values that will form the basis of XP: good communication, simplicity, feedback, courage, and respect.

2.2   THE FIVE VALUES

Before we get into the more detailed description of what XP is all about, we need to understand the fundamental values that are its reason for existence and the reason for its success.

These five basic values of XP are shown in Fig. 2.1.

2.2.1   Communication

Almost all the research that has been attempted into the great software engineering disasters has concluded that breakdowns in communication between developers

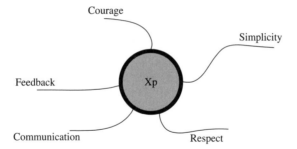

Figure 2.1   The values of XP.

and client, among the clients, and among the developers play a major role. In a sense, computing is all about communication from human to computer to human, and thus the very essence of our subject requires that we address this in a fundamental way.

XP tries to emphasize this factor by building a rich collection of procedures and activities that emphasize effective communication among *all* the stakeholders.

Stakeholders include

Customers: managers, financial directors, marketing departments, and so forth

Users: administrative staff, general public, and so forth

Developers: programmers, managers, financial directors, marketing, and so forth

Media and other organizations who may take an interest

Let us look at some of the most important areas where communication is vital. The first one doesn't involve the developers at all. Consider a company that wishes to have some software developed to support its business activities. The first and most vital requirement is that they can decide what the principal objective of the software that they need is. This requires them to understand their business, its context, the strategy of the business, and so on. For this to be done successfully, there has to be good communication among the principle players in the company, the directors, managers, operators, and possibly their clients and business backers. Many software disasters have been caused by failures at this level. Perhaps the company has not thought through its business objectives properly: Is the proposed software either needed or providing the most *business value*? It is often the case that the reason for the software becomes obscured, perhaps the principle project *champion* in the company leaves or changes their role in the company. Someone else might take over this responsibility and may either be unaware of the motivation for the development or unsympathetic to it.

It is therefore vital that the company is clear about why it wants the software developed, has analyzed its operations sufficiently well to be able to justify it on business grounds, and that there is a knowledgeable champion for the development who is well connected with *all* the stakeholders in the company. We will rely on the existence of these parameters during our project. If something is wrong here, then there is a strong chance that we will be building the wrong system, a waste of time for all concerned.

Naturally the phrase "business value" may have a number of interpretations—it can affect organizations that are not commercial companies (charities, non-profit organizations, etc.). The point about the term is that there is some benefit to the organization—it makes them more efficient; produce better-quality outcomes; improves the experiences of their workers, customers, or some other stakeholder. It does not always have a clear financial benefit, and it is important to take a holistic view of things.

The next issue to address is the communication among developers and the client. This is also vital. It is no good having one meeting at the start of the project and then to meet again when the supposed solution is delivered. This is bound to be a disaster unless the system is fairly trivial in nature. So much can change in the business between the start of the project and the final commissioning of the solution that there has to be much more regular communication between these two parties.

The communication needs to provide several benefits. First it has to provide a continuous or, at least, frequent renewal of the business requirements that are being addressed. As has been pointed out earlier, business needs can change rapidly, and the purpose of the software could change with them. We must be aware of what is happening in the business and the way that things are changing. This agility depends heavily on the communication mechanism between clients and developers (also between developers and among the clients' business partners).

As well as receiving this information from the clients, the developers need to keep the client informed of how they are doing. There is nothing more frustrating for a client than not to know how things are getting on. They are paying for all this, and there will be many other demands on their money. Regular feedback on progress and demonstrable signs of progress are needed.

The third aspect is the communication between the developers. This is often sadly lacking in traditional development regimes. The communication process here involves keeping all the team involved in the planning of the project, keeping everyone up to date with progress, with objectives, and with the changing nature of the target. This is very difficult and usually results in some of the team becoming disengaged and de-motivated if it is not addressed. The human side of the management of the team becomes crucial. Giving people respect and responsibility provides a good basis for the development of rich and productive communication processes within the team. Several XP practices contribute directly to this goal, as we shall see.

2.2.2 Feedback

Feedback is closely related to communication; they are two dimensions of the same phenomenon.

We need to establish very rich mechanisms, as we saw above, to keep the client informed and involved in the project. This is to ensure that we are building the right system for the business and that we are making clear progress toward the joint objectives of all concerned. Thus there needs to be a mechanism for the client to see real results of the developers' efforts and to try to relate them to his or her business activities and needs. Traditional design-led approaches rely on producing large amounts of often incomprehensible documents to do this. This is a ponderous and ultimately unrewarding endeavor. Regular increments of software can help this but can cause a distraction if the quality is poor and the client is sidetracked into doing the testing that should have been carried out by the developers and having to report faults and bugs. It is no good delivering a prototype or an increment of the solution if it is unreliable and fails to meet the client's quality expectations. We must avoid this—previous approaches such as rapid applications development (RAD) sometimes failed in this respect because it was based on the rapid development of, possibly arbitrary, increments rather than on the rapid development of *high-quality* increments *that add business value* to the client's business.

Within the development team, we need to ensure that everyone knows what is going on, where the project has got to, and how their work fits into the *big picture*. They also need to know how good their work is and how good the work of all the others is. Building on the work of others when you have doubts about its quality is always a frustrating process. We need to avoid this. It is no good relying on the occasional review meeting. Although these are necessary and often productive, they can also be a source of great problems.

Imagine the following scenario, typical of most traditional development projects. The managers have allocated you some aspect of the development to code up. You might receive some textual descriptions or requirements of what is needed, you might receive some design documents, and it is your task to deliver some code by a deadline, perhaps a week or longer. Thus you go to your machine, which may well be separate from or shielded from others working on the project. You then spend the next few days trying to get your head around what it is that you are supposed to do. After a while, the manager gets fed up with your questions and requests for clarification—probably he or she doesn't know the answer, maybe the client should be asked, but everyone is too busy for that. Thus you struggle on and eventually manage to deliver the code by the deadline.

There is then a review or inspection meeting where your code is looked at by others: managers, other programmers, and so on.[1] At the review they start criticizing your code. You have sweated over this and have done your best yet they complain about many things. You misunderstood a requirement, but when you asked them about that very thing they either didn't know or told you to sort it out yourself. At points where you showed initiative, they criticize you for failing to follow some, previously unknown, house convention or requirement. Criticizing your detailed code may involve taking your algorithms apart and suggesting that they would have used "better" ones. Perhaps some smart guy knows about a clever way to do what you did with half the effort. I could go on. Suffice it to say that you are soon on the defensive and getting angry or demoralized. They want big changes, and you

---

[1]This would only happen in a so-called well-organized company; in many, review is not a formal process, and the only reviews take place during integration testing when vast amounts of time and money are spent on the futile task of trying to find and fix bugs.

would prefer to try to fix the problems by some judicious *tweaking* of the code. In many situations, the best solution is to start again having obtained a better understanding of what is wanted and what the "best" solution might be. However, human nature often conspires against this, and the tweaking approach is often adopted. Anyway, it is probably too late to do anything else with the deadline approaching.

We have to find a better way.

2.2.3 Simplicity

How many times have you used some software where there were complicated and confusing features that *got in the way*? If this is the case of computing experts, how much more is it the case for ordinary users?

Many projects get into trouble because the developers get sidelined into doing something that is technologically novel or "clever" when, in fact, the feature in question is just not really needed. Clients can be seduced by such "enhancements," too, and could agree to some new fancy feature being added when it makes no sense to do so; it adds nothing to their business capability. These extra features are a potential threat to the success of the system. They introduce unwanted complexity into the system, especially if the delivery deadline is fast approaching, as the work on the new feature will, probably, be at the expense of more thorough testing of the software. Some call this *feature creep*.

Einstein once said that "any solution should be as simple as possible but no simpler."

We need to adopt the same attitude. Every aspect of the system should be considered; can we really justify the time and effort in adding some supposed enhancement? However, if the reason for adding a layer of complexity is a good one, for example in order to make the software more robust by trying to trap inappropriate data input, then we have to do this. But we must have suitable tests to demonstrate that we have done it properly.

2.2.4 Courage

This means having the confidence to do things that might otherwise be considered risky. Much of the philosophy of XP derives from abandoning some of the traditional ways of software development, ways that are widely taught and widely used in industry. It takes some nerve to turn one's back on all this expertise and experience.

One aspect of courage that XP and other agile approaches promote is the enthusiasm for change, in particular a willingness to adapt to the clients' changing needs as the project develops. This does take some courage as it may involve changing some of our previous work; there is a natural tendency to resist change in traditional approaches under these conditions. The ability to relish new challenges is part of the underlying philosophy of XP.

Extreme programming, like an extreme sport, is software development without the normal constraints. Like climbing mountains without a rope, building software without a design seems, at first sight, to be suicidal. Why it isn't is the subject of much of this book. There are constraints, and the practices of XP are meant to be followed.

Rather than being an informal and unregulated exercise it is in fact highly disciplined. You will have to learn how to enjoy the disciplines and to revel in the practices until they become second nature. It is only by making them automatic and natural that you will then gain the confidence to attack any software project with the certainty that you will succeed as well as anyone could.

We will see that there is coherence and a rationale about the key set of values and practices of XP that will support us in our endeavors.

Confidence is one thing, but overconfidence is another. You are not always right; others may have a valid point of view, too. As we have observed, learning how to argue from a position of knowledge has to be moderated with the ability to compromise and agree when others have the best argument. In the end, it is important that those involved negotiate an acceptable outcome.

2.2.5 Respect

The most important issue about any joint, team-based activity is the relationships between the participants. Many of the problems that arise in software development projects are "people issues" rather than technical ones. People issues are generally about relationships—between developers in the team and between team members and clients, users, managers, and others in the immediate working environment. Of course, relationships with those close to you and your family can have an impact on a project as well.

In order to deal with these, you have to treat each individual with respect—allow them to express their point of view, discuss things with them calmly, and actively delegate responsibility for doing things in a reasonable way and to trust them to get on with it. The two complementary facets of responsibility and trust are very important. XP is supposed to be a human way of doing things that is built on both these pillars. If you respect someone, you will also trust them and then give them responsibility.

2.3 THE 12 BASIC PRACTICES OF XP

2.3.1 Test-First Programming

Before writing any code, programmers build a set of tests. These tests are run—of course they will fail as no code has been written. Why would one do this?

To get used to testing continuously—at the end of a session, at the end of the day, whenever a small piece of code has been built.

All the test sets are run: this means all the relevant unit tests, testing classes, and methods as they are coded; all the functional tests, testing at the integration level and derived from the planning game and subsequent discussions with the client; and all the non-functional tests.

The test sets are the most important resource and are continually enhanced.

The customer can help to supply some tests, they understand the business processes in their organization, and these, if they are to be replicated or involved in the system being built, will provide a wealth of potential test material. Functional tests are derived from the planning game (see later) using techniques defined in subsequent chapters. The quality of these tests is crucial, and the methods described will provide test sets of outstanding power.

In a sense, the test sets replace the specification and the design. They present us with a rapid feedback mechanism that tells us if the code is "correct."

If any tests fail, the code must be fixed.

This sounds very plausible as it is known that strong testing delivers quality systems. However, is it realistic? Testing and debugging as activities are Cinderella subjects both in universities and industry. There are few courses dedicated to the subject, and when programming is taught, testing is generally ignored. Programmers are often left to their own devices in terms of what techniques to use. Here, though, testing is fundamental; the development process is centered around testing, and this is what gives us continuous feedback on how we are doing. But there are tests and tests. Any fool can write test cases, but only the smartest developers can write really good ones. Furthermore, we have to design the tests before we start to code. This presents another problem as many test techniques, for example, the so-called White Box testing, relies on having the code structure available. These types of testing are based on finding test values that will exercise the program graph, for example traversing every path in the code, accessing every decision point, and so forth. Many of these techniques can be automated by using the code as a basis for the generation of the test but the code is not written.

In terms of functional testing and acceptance testing, the tests are often created on a fairly informal basis from whatever requirements are available. There is almost no knowledge of how good the tests are. Many developers will stop testing when the rate of discovery of defects slows down—this does not mean that *all* fundamental flaws have been discovered.

We will address this issue of testing fundamentally in this book.

2.3.2   Pair Programming

Two people, one machine. This is a key feature. Organize the project so that when any work is being done it is done in pairs. One person will be using the keyboard and the other will be looking at the screen with them both discussing what they are doing.

All code must be written in this way. This is a process of continuous review and ensures that mistakes are made less frequently and the reasons for doing something in a particular way are open to discussion throughout. In fact, it not only applies to coding; all aspects of an XP project should be like this, pairs of people working together, pooling their expertise and intellect and sharing information. Planning and discussing the project with the client should also involve as many of the team as possible.

The pairs swap around regularly; swapping roles within a pair and swapping developers from one pair to another gives a much greater understanding of what is being done in the project.

It is also an excellent mechanism for learning: Your partner may be an expert in some aspect of the project or the techniques being used, and you will then benefit from this. Perhaps they know the programming language better than you; you are bound to benefit from such a pairing. Perhaps you have some skills that you could transfer to others. Even if you think that you know all about something, the process of trying to explain it to someone else can be very beneficial to improving your own understanding. Everyone should benefit; part of your motivation is thus to become multiskilled and to enhance your technical knowledge quite apart from completing the project successfully.

Success does need to be built upon mutual respect among the team. You will get to know all of the team because different pairs will form up regularly and so communication throughout the team is enhanced. Pairings will change at suitable points in the project: perhaps someone has some specific knowledge that someone else needs to learn; perhaps the change will be driven by availability of personal. Ideally, everyone should have the opportunity to work with everyone else during the project.

One interesting observation of the difference between XP projects and traditional ones is that the XP teams are always talking to each other. When you walk into an XP site this is very noticeable, there is a lot of noise compared with the traditional lab where everyone is silently staring at their screens and very little talking is going on, and what talking there is may not be relevant to the project.

2.3.3 On-site Customer

This is recommended, if it is possible, as it will enrich the communication between the client and the development team. The customer/client has the authority to define the system functionality, set priorities, and to oversee the direction of the project. Of course, it might be difficult to actually have the client in the development team at all times and it may not even be desirable. If the key issue is to be able to respond to sudden changes in business need, then the client needs to be well connected back to the business in order to achieve this. I prefer a very close relationship, regular visits and meetings both at the site of the development team but also at the business site. Team members need to familiarize themselves with both the operating environment and a representative sample of the users of the system if they are to fully understand the issues involved. This could be better than a permanent presence of the client in the development team.

One of my projects hit problems when we delivered part of the system only to discover that the role of the *actual* users did not correspond with what the client thought; he did not understand some of his business's processes. We had to go back and rebuild the system. We wish, now, that we had spoken with more people in the business, in the presence of the client, of course, and thus been able to identify the business processes better. This project dates from before we adopted XP.

It is an old adage that the client never knows what he or she wants, and this is often the case. We have to question the clients and all the stakeholders in the business carefully and rigorously if we are to move toward identifying exactly what the business needs are and how they can be supported.

We can use many ways of trying to bridge the gap between what the client thinks they want and what the development team thinks the client wants. It may not be based solely on writing things down: videos of potential users working, recordings of interviews with stakeholders, and studies of similar systems used by other organizations including competitors are also valuable sources of information.

Excellent communications between the development team and the business should reduce the volume and cost of documentation as well as ensure that the right system is being built.

As with pair programming, this aspect of XP encourages intense face-to-face dialogue.

2.3.4 The Planning Game

The customer provides business stories, and estimates are made about the time to build software to implement the stories. We will see later how to approach the issue of identifying stories. The essence is to identify small pieces of meaningful functionality and to describe these on a small card in such a way as to illustrate the sequences of interactions that are involved in the story process.

Stories, which are about small pieces of working software, should be developed over a short time (a week is a good target) and need to be customer focused (the customer must understand them and their place within the overall system).

From time to time—maybe around monthly—a review of the business objectives should be carried out with the customers and users.

From this information, which should be clear and understandable to the client as well as the developers, we construct test sets that will be applied to any implementation that is supposed to implement that story.

Designing the test set for this purpose is a technically challenging task and one that is crucial; if we get it wrong, then we are in trouble. Some authors suggest that the client should determine the stories. This must be inadequate; if testing and test set generation is a key professional activity, then the task should involve people with professional skills in testing—the development team should develop an understanding of systematic system testing. The client needs to be involved and to identify many of the cases that have to be addressed, but for the really rigorous testing that we need to use, more sophisticated input is needed. This does not mean that the development team cannot do it. They can and the techniques described in Chapter 6 and beyond will address this.

For each story, we also need to identify any non-functional requirements (see Gilb, 1988) that are stated or implied in the initial project description. This could relate to usability, efficiency, and so forth, and accurate metrics for measuring these and criteria for deciding when they have been achieved need to be agreed upon. This is a system level rather than a unit level exercise although the way the units are built will influence the results of these tests.

Thus we have tests that are determining whether the functionality is correct and tests that will establish whether the non-functional requirements are also satisfied. Neither should be forgotten or skimped.

For each story, we need to try to identify the cost of implementing it, how long will it take, and how many people it will need. This is a difficult and error-prone activity, only experience will help and it is thus *really* important that you record your initial thoughts and compare them, later, with the reality. There is a tendency to be too optimistic—there may be problems ahead with the use of the technology chosen, the supply of data needed to build the system, as well as revisions to what the client wants. All of these things confuse the estimation process. Only by recording carefully what you think will be the cost of implementation at each stage and seeing how it changes over time will you develop the experience to make more reliable judgments in the future.

Once a collection of meaningful stories has been agreed upon and the cost estimated, then the customer decides which stories provide the most business value. This has to be done with a clear measure of the way these benefits can be measured and in consultation with the other key players in the business.

The programmers then implement the chosen stories.

Of course, things won't always go smoothly. It is important to build in some slack to use if problems arise that could impact on the progress of the project.

2.3.5 System Metaphor

Thus, now we have some stories to build, so how do we get started? The test set generation process, which focuses on the business processes in the stories and how these might be integrated into a solution, will provide us with some clues. As part of this we are, maybe implicitly, building models of the behavior of parts of the system. This is an important resource and so we will already know quite a lot about the system-level, functional requirements needed.

We now try to organize a collection of classes and methods that will achieve the functionality described by the stories under development. As we will see below, we need to keep in mind that we will integrate these stories into stand-alone and deliverable chunks of software and so our decisions here should reflect that. There is something of a trade-off in terms of how much effort is invested in defining a metaphor and the amount of flexibility needed to deal with changing requirements. Initially, the metaphor may be rather vague as you research the problem with your customer. Soon parts of it will become more firm, and these can then be documented more precisely.

The programmers define, perhaps, just a handful of classes and patterns that shape the core business problem and solution. This is like a primitive architecture. There are many ways to try to do this, one may wish to utilize some existing patterns or libraries in order to re-use existing resources.

If this is the case, however, it is important that (a) you fully understand what is being re-used and (b) the reuse is natural and provides the sort of software components that really do help with the story.

We will make no assumptions about the quality of the re-used components. If they have been produced through an XP approach, then there will be full test sets available that you can use, extend, and adapt for the new stories. If not, then it is vital that they are fully tested and the test results properly analyzed.

The system metaphor will be used as a means of communication between programmers and customer. The notation chosen to represent it, therefore, has to be understandable and representative of what you are trying to do.

This area is still a subject for research whether you are using XP or not, and sensible notations and approaches are much sought after and rarely found. We will return to this issue later.

We have been trying to find a simple diagrammatic method that shows how the system hangs together, which illustrates the flow of the processes, is understandable to both developers and customers, and can adapt to changing requirements. Our research into the cognitive processes involved in design and requirements modeling have shown that the generalized machine model, the X-machine, works extremely well. In our recent industrial projects, we have used it extensively and the results have been very encouraging. We will discuss this in Chapter 5.

2.3.6　Small, Frequent Releases

Release early and release often; that is the philosophy. Once we have produced an implementation of a story that provides some coherent business benefit, we deliver and install it in the client's business. This then provides the users opportunities to look at it and to provide feedback through the client to the development team. In many cases, there are simple interface improvements that can be made or it might lead to a greater awareness of how the whole system might support the business. This might cause some revisions of the project scope and requirements and is thus valuable to the development team. The release might be reengineered to suit the new understandings.

Thus we do not regard these releases as prototypes; each release is real, each release is functionally useful, each release implements more stories, each release is thoroughly tested.

2.3.7　Always Use the *Simplest* Solution That Adds Business Value

As we have mentioned before, it is often tempting to develop something that is more sophisticated than is needed. We must avoid "bells and whistles," that is, unnecessary features that, although they might be smart, technologically impressive, or just plain fun to build, are not actually needed.

Always ask—does the customer really need this feature?

For the programmer, this philosophy could be embodied in the practice of using, for example, the minimum number of classes and methods to pass the tests. There are some dangers here, however, and they will be looked at in Section 2.3.11. Simplicity of code does not always correspond with simplicity of function, as we have observed.

2.3.8 Continuous Integration

Code is integrated into the system at least a few times every day. All unit tests must pass prior to integration. All relevant functional tests must pass afterwards.

This could be done every few minutes if that is possible. Some of the work can be automated, particularly running tests. Working code is committed to a CVS (Concurrent Versions System) or similar repository.

This is a major source of confidence that the team is getting somewhere. Rather than trying to integrate all the software (classes, etc.) together at the end, we integrate whenever we can. Adding trusted new stories to the current state of the system that is also well tested requires the running of all the previous functional or system test cases. If everything passes, then we know that we have built a system to supersede the previous version; it works and delivers something useful to the client.

We can deliver it for further feedback and go on to the next set of stories (Fig. 2.2).

It is sometimes recommended that only one pair should be responsible for integrating all the code into an operational system. The integration process must be done carefully if we are not to undermine much of what has been achieved previously. Whoever does it should do it in the full knowledge and agreement of the entire

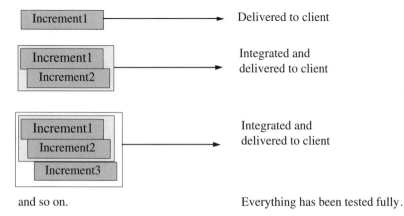

Figure 2.2   Incremental delivery.

team at a time that is appropriate to the project. Letting anyone in the team carry out system integration whenever they feel like it will lead to chaos and many different versions of the core system. Successful integration can be achieved by having a project directory structure that gives authorized team members sole write access to the directory with the latest version of the running system.

2.3.9 Coding Standards

These define rules for shared code ownership and for communication between different team members' codes.

They should involve clearly defined and consistent class and method naming protocols that everyone is familiar with.

Everyone should use the same coding styles. These need to be agreed upon at the start of the project; they will be dependent on the context of the project, the programming language used, and the existing resources available.

Similar conventions should apply to the way that test sets are defined and to the user story cards. These need to have a set format, and we discuss this later.

The benefits of clear conventions should be obvious. The source code, the stories, the metaphor, and the test sets are the major project descriptors; they replace the design. They therefore must not fall into the same trap that much of the design notations suffer from. They must be well understood and relevant for the job in hand.

It is worth exploring the use of XML and of suitable tags in these sources to enhance understanding, to structure thinking, and to allow for the use of suitable semantics extractions tools and query mechanisms.

2.3.10 Collective Code Ownership

All the code belongs to *all* the programmers. Anyone can change anything.

This is a controversial aspect of XP and seems to go against common sense and current practice. But we are dealing with a situation here where there are much richer communication processes, where all the team members are fully involved, through pair programming, with all aspects of the project. The common use of code standards will also mean that each team member should be able to understand any piece of code, what its purpose is, and how it fits into the overall plan of things. If someone changes some code, perhaps to make it better in some way, then this should be apparent, and if others disagree then they can change it back.

Because the code does not *belong* to any one person, there is no one to get defensive and possessive about it. This should lead to a more relaxed but at the same time a more consistent awareness of what is happening in the project.

Because there are house rules for writing and documenting code and for communicating between teams, we should be able to benefit from this inclusive approach to the project resources.

2.3.11 Refactoring

Refactoring is defined to be the *restructuring code without changing its functionality*.

Its use is mainly to *simplify* code—make it more understandable, and thus more maintainable. This is vital. We have no design, although we have observed that the design may not be accurate or that useful for maintenance, something has to take its place and be more effective. These are the stories, the test sets and the code.

Refactoring (Fowler, 2000) could involve a number of improvements:

Moving (extracting) methods used in several classes to a separate class

Extracting superclasses

Renaming classes, methods, functions

Simplifying conditional expressions

Reorganizing data

Some basic support for refactoring is supplied by a *refactoring browser* of which there are a number supporting different programming languages.

You may have noticed that there is an issue here regarding the unit tests. If we have unit tests defined for each class and the class structure changes because of some refactoring, for example, extracting a method into a new dedicated class, then there is a mismatch between the new set of classes and the set of unit tests. What this means is that we should also refactor the tests to preserve the relationships between the classes and their tests.

At the systems level, the refactored system should still pass the functional (systems) tests because the functionality of the system should not have been affected by the refactoring. For the sake of maintenance, however, the link between classes and unit tests should be kept, if at all possible.

2.3.12 Forty-Hour Week

Tired programmers write poor code and make more mistakes. Because much of the software industry is reliant on the heroics of individuals working around the clock to meet deadlines, it is hardly surprising that mistakes are made. We need to get away from this treadmill approach.

The way that XP is organized helps to eliminate stress caused through unrealistic timescales, lack of knowledge and understanding about what is going on, worries about the quality of what is being built, the timeliness and usefulness of the solution for the client, and the concern that so much time has been spent on design that the final coding and integration will present a mountain to climb, with testing left to the end and neglected.

Thus, XP is supposed to minimize this stress with its emphasis on communication, feedback, quality, incremental builds, and the rest. It should minimize the need for overtime and remove the panic. In comparative experiments I have undertaken with real projects being carried out by competing teams, XP and traditional, it was quite clear that the stress levels and the panic are much reduced using XP. XP adherents claim that it offers a more sustained approach to development, one that allows a steady pace and an improvement in quality as well as greater job satisfaction. There is some circumstantial evidence that this might be the case.

Because it can be seen that much more progress is being made, working for fewer hours is now a feasible strategy.

2.4   CAN XP WORK?

We have briefly described the original values and practices of XP. They seem to make a lot of sense, but do they work in real projects? The first thing to say is that this style of software development may not be suitable for all types of application and industry. Very large projects involving hundreds of developers will be extremely difficult to bring to a successful conclusion whatever method of working is employed. It may be that some of the elements of XP will be useful in these situations—test first is an obvious one—but only time will tell. Certainly, current methods are problematic as a perusal of the trade literature and its articles about recent failed projects will testify. Another important point is that the XP approach is evolving all the time as we learn from experience. There is probably less emphasis on these 12 practices as specific activities that have to be engaged with in a dogmatic way but rather an emphasis on the principles underlying them and their adaptation to the specific context of an agile development. We have adapted and strengthened some of these ideas as we shall see shortly.

In some business contexts, it will be difficult to apply all the practices fully. For example, not all software development is of a bespoke nature. Many software houses build speculative or generic software for a particular market, and there is no client who could take the role of an on-site customer. There is a community of potential purchasers and users. However, it is possible to adapt XP successfully for this situation, and a number of companies have been very successful at doing so. A good model is to set up a separate quality assurance (QA) department, which plays the role of the customer as well as carrying out some of the acceptance testing including some of the non-functional requirements testing. For this to work, the QA group must be very well connected with potential customers and know their business needs extremely well.

Another issue is with companies carrying out bespoke development on a *fixed-price contract* basis. Here it does not make sense to have a highly dynamic requirement that is subject to continuing change. Accountants and lawyers on both sides will not accept this. It is important to have the requirements capture phase ring fenced so that after a certain period of the contract, the requirements are more or less fixed. It may be possible to make small cosmetic changes later on but the key functionality has to be defined and will be the subject of a formal contract. Because this is a fixed-price contract, the amount of time and resources available to the suppliers will also be limited, and this is vital if they are not to get into financial difficulties. Thus the on-site customer may only be on-site during the initial requirements capture stage and then at prototyping and incremental delivery times. In practice, it is this type of contract that we will be focusing on in this book. Your time is limited to a semester or whatever, and so the fixed-price approach is the best. It will require rather more planning and organization as you only have a limited amount of resource—time and labor—at your disposal.

Some software houses have long-term open contracts with their customers. Their role is continual software development, perhaps of a major system that supports a changing list of functions, and so there is a lot of scope for a continual and close relationship between the customer and the developers. An "on-site" customer is then both practical and desirable. In a large software project involving several teams, then some of these might have a purchaser/supplier relationship with each other. Thus internal customers can be treated as on-site, and the use of XP in a large project might be feasible.

The business context for an organization employing XP will have an effect on the way XP is implemented. For example, following the financial scandals in some large U.S. corporations, accountants and lawyers are likely to be much more cautious about committing to expenditure without any contractual or documentary evidence about a software project. Thus a clear and well-defined requirements document may have to be produced in an XP project. A collection of scrappy story cards will not be sufficient. Even within a software company, it will often be necessary for managers to have evidence of clearly planned and resourced projects. The way in which XP adapts to these pressures, which some may resent, will be critical to its future success.

2.5 THE EVIDENCE FOR XP

There has been a lot of research into whether agile developments actually deliver what is claimed. In particular, some of the practices discussed above have been considered to see if they work. In many cases, the detailed experiments involve students carrying out tasks in a laboratory setting. Unfortunately, these experiments often lack credibility in the sense that it is not possible to generalize their finding to real industrial settings; in other words, the results lack external validity. Also, by taking the individual practices and considering them in isolation from the other practices may also fail to provide evidence for the benefits of XP and other "complete" agile methodologies.

2.5.1 Evidence for Test First

The evidence for the benefits of a test-first approach is mixed. The first thing to say is that it is actually quite difficult to carry out—nearly all of the approaches to teaching introductory programming that are found in universities tend to downplay testing—if it is considered seriously at all. Thus many programmers find the idea of writing a test set before they start coding unnatural. This makes it difficult to carry out comparative experiments without having to undertake some extensive training on the technique.

Janzen (2005) found that the design of the software was "better" (smaller and less complex units), whereas Siniaalto (2007) found that the quality of the design was poorer. There are a number of other examples of inconclusive results (e.g., Muller, 2003).

One comment that is worth making is that the time that tests are written and used is only one of a number of factors that might affect the benefits of doing test first; another is the type of tests created. Testing is very dependent on the capabilities of the test sets to detect faults and so influences the ultimate quality of the software under test. Simple measures such as test coverage can provide some insight into the quality and effectiveness of a test set, but things are more complicated than that. Test design is discussed in more detail in Chapter 7.

2.5.2   Evidence for Pair Programming

Williams (2000) presented some evidence for the benefits of pair programming. The approach has been criticized on blogs such as hacknot.info, and other experiments by other researchers (Nawrocki, 2001) have produced different conclusions. In practice, pair programming is not for everyone as some people's personalities are such that they seem to be unable to cope with the intense relationships with their partners that are needed. Our experience has been that, in the right context, that is, a real project with a real customer and combined with the other XP practices, pair programming works for most people—many of whom become very enthusiastic about it.

2.5.3   Evidence for XP

There is again a problem in identifying conclusive and convincing evidence about the benefits of XP. Carrying out comparative experiments in an industrial setting is always going to be a problem, and much of the evidence is based on simple experiments involving students. Macias (2003) found a small benefit in a comparative study involving small industrial projects. Abdullah (2003) found that the more XP practices used, the better the quality of the software, again in small industrial projects. Abdullah (2006) also found that there was evidence that teams using XP experienced a higher level of well-being than did teams using a design-led approach involved in the same projects.

There are many critics of XP, and the book *Extreme Programming Refactored: The Case Against XP* (Stevens, 2003) takes a number of aspects of XP and criticizes them. Some of the criticism is based more on the exaggerated claims of some who were not adopting the full set of practices; other issues need a more detailed consideration. Part of the rationale of this book is to consider these issues in the light of our experiences over 7 years with hundreds of XP projects, their programmers, and their clients.

2.6 PREPARING TO XP

The purpose of the rest of this book is to provide you with the insight and the support to make a real agile project, based on the XP principles, an enjoyable and successful experience. Nothing can be guaranteed, of course, but whatever happens, many lessons will be learned, and at the end of it you may be in a much better position to answer the question: Does XP work?

EXERCISE

This exercise assumes that you are about to start working in a small group of four or five people on a software development project. It is intended to provide an early experience of some of the XP practices. It is recommended that the exercise is done in a college laboratory or terminal room where it is possible to discuss what you are doing without disturbing other users.

Objectives

To introduce the idea of pair programming and to carry out a simple pair programming activity, which also relates to the activity of writing unit tests. It also tests out communication within the team and points toward the use of coding standards.

Method

Form into a pair.
Change round on the machine every 20 minutes.
Each pair will develop a simple Java program that does the following:

> *takes as input a list of characters representing team members and a number representing work sessions and outputs something equivalent to a 1 × 1 table with columns indexed by the number of sessions and lists of pairs so that both pairs are present in each session.*

Example 1

Input: {A, B, C, D, E} (a five-person team and six sessions).

Table E1

Session	1	2	3	4	5	6
Pairs	{A,B},	{A,C},	{D,E},	{B,C},	{D,E},	{E,A},
	{C,D},	{D,E},	{B,C},	{A,E},	{A,B},	{C,D},
	{E}	{B}	{A}	{D}	{C}	{B}

Output:
Thus in the first session, A and B pair up and C and D pair up and E operates on their own.

Example 2

Input: {A, B, C, D} and five sessions.

Table E2

Session	1	2	3	4	5
Pairs	{A,B}, {C,D}	{A,C}, {B,D}	{D,C}, {A,B}	{B,C}, {A,D}	{B,D}, {A,C}

Output:

It is not required that the program has to display the results in such a table, just lists will do.

The first task is to write the test cases. This is not particularly easy as there is usually very little emphasis on testing and writing tests in programming courses. Later we will see how to do this in a more systematic way, but for the time being write down simple test sets that provide two things: input values and the corresponding outputs.

You need to develop a test environment based on your test cases and JUnit. Log onto www. XProgramming.com and find the JUnit software for Java. This was written by Kent Beck.

Download this into your account and read the accompanying documentation.

Change round on the machine every 20 minutes.

Prepare some brief notes—just sufficient so that you can make sense of how it is used.

Now start the coding.

Run your tests even if you have not finished coding.

Debug as needed.

Continue coding and testing.

Don't forget to change places every 20 minutes or so.

Now read up the Java coding standards (peep ahead to Chapter 8 or look at http://www.dcs. shef.ac.uk/~wmlh/Java.pdf).

Review the code to see if the coding standards are met. If not, refactor, that is adjust, the code to ensure compliance. Retest the code.

Discuss how you find pair programming. Talk about its good points and those aspects that you found difficult, annoying, or wasteful.

For the other practices, discuss how you might be able to adopt them—what are the difficulties; how might they benefit you?

CONUNDRUM

Your client has already built a prototype system and wants you to develop it further so that he can then market it. He needs to demonstrate something fairly soon to his business backers in order to persuade them to put more money into the development of the system.

The original system is very poorly written, the database is badly structured, the code is all over the place, and it is going to be a nightmare to maintain.

Should you (a) carefully document the functionality of the system and start reengineering it before adding new functionality? or (b) carry on building the prototype based on what has already been done?

A discussion of this dilemma is to be found at the end of Chapter 11.

REFERENCES

S. SYED-ABDULLAH, M. HOLCOMBE, M. GHEORGHE. Practice makes perfect. In *Extreme Programming and Agile Processes in Software Engineering*. Lecture Notes in Computer Science, Vol. 2675. Springer, 2003.

S. SYED-ABDULLAH, M. HOLCOMBE, M. GHEORGE. The impact of an agile methodology on the well being of development teams. *Empirical Software Engineering*, 11(1):143–167, 2006.

K. BECK. *Extreme Programming Explained*. Addison-Wesley, 1999.

M. FOWLER. *Refactoring—Improving the Design of Existing Code*. Addison Wesley, 2000.

T. GILB. *Principles of Software Engineering Management* (S. Finzi-Wokingham, ed.). Addison-Wesley, 1988.

D. JANZEN, H. SAIEDIAN. Test-driven development concepts, taxonomy, and future direction. *Computer*, **38**:43–50, 2005.

F. MACÍAS, M. HOLCOMBE, M. GHEORGHE. A formal experiment comparing extreme programming with traditional software construction. In: *Proceedings of the Fourth Mexican International Conference on Computer Science* (ENC 2003), Tlaxcala, México, Sep. 8–12, 73–80, 2003.

M. MULLER, F. PUDBERG. 'On the Economic evaluation of XP projects'. ACM SIGSOFT. Engineering Notes. Vol. 28, Issue 5, 2003.

J. NAWROCKI, A. WOJCIECHOWSKI. European Software Control and Metrics (Escom), 2001. Available at http://www2.umassd.edu/SWPI/xp/pairprogramming/Nawrocki.pdf.

M. SINIAALTO, P. ABRAHAMSSON. Does TDD Improve the Program Core? Alarming Results from a comparative case study. CEE–NST 2007, Ponzan, Poland, October 10–12, 2007.

M. STEPHENS, D. ROSENBERG. *Extreme Programming Refactored: The Case Against XP*. Apress, 2006.

L. WILLIAMS, R.R. KESSLER, W. CUNNINGHAM, R. JEFFRIES. Strengthening the case for pair programming, *IEEE Software*, **17**:19–25, 2000.

Web Sites

http://www.xp.programming.com.
http://www.extremeprogramming.org/.
http://c2.com/cgi/wiki?ExtremeProgrammingRoadmap.
http://www.hacknot.info/hacknot/action/showEntry?eid=50.

Chapter **3**

Foundations: People and Teams Working Together

SUMMARY

Group work and software projects

- The role of personalities in successful projects
- How to set up and maintain a successful team
- Carrying out a skills audit
- Choosing a way of working
- Speed training
- Finding and keeping a client
- Day to day activities
- Keeping an archive
- Some basics of planning
- Dealing with problems
- When things go wrong—appreciative enquiry
- Risk analysis

3.1 SOFTWARE ENGINEERING IN TEAMS

Almost all software that is produced commercially is developed with teams of people. The teams might be structured into programmers, testers, requirements engineers, and so forth. The teams probably have some hierarchical arrangement with managers, team leaders, subteams, and so on. A team could be a small one, perhaps two or three people, or it could involve hundreds. A team may all be working in the same place or it could be scattered over different locations, even countries. What is common to all these manifestations is that they share a general objective, the production or development of some quality software product.

Learning how to work effectively in a team is thus a vital part of one's education as a software engineer. Many universities and colleges provide some place in the curriculum where a team project is set up and you have to participate with colleagues in a design project. In many of these activities, the professor or instructor will set some problem and you try to solve it, learning along the way from the many experiences you share, good and not so good, which relate to the way your team worked.

There are many sources of advice about how to make the most of a team but there are no easy rules or procedures. A team comprises a group of distinctive and independent personalities; we cannot generalize very easily about how these personalities will interact and how the team will progress. However, there are some simple basic rules that seem to work, and the purpose of this chapter is to describe some of these.

3.2 PERSONALITIES AND TEAM SUCCESS

The role of individuals in a software development team is an important and poorly understood area. Software development is usually a cooperative and team-based endeavor that may involve diverse groups of people who have to communicate effectively with one another, cooperating and solving complex problems under pressure. Some of the most vexing difficulties involved in software development projects are of a social or political nature. By their very nature individuals are individual, they possess complex personalities, express a variety of attitudes, and believe in a variety of values. Different people have different personalities, and their psychological makeup can have an impact on the success of a team. Problems such as personality clashes, nonparticipation, and the phenomenon of one group member doing all of the work can be very serious problems and are often detrimental to the team's performance. If such problems are not dealt with early on in the process, there is a real danger that the team will become totally dysfunctional.

This section is about recent research on the matter and tries to highlight a number of things to think about. By considering how you and your team colleagues share different personality characteristics and how this might impact the project outcome, you may be able to achieve a more successful experience both in terms of the projects having successful outcomes and in terms of your own enjoyment and career progress. Awareness of differing personality types will help to promote understanding and a more harmonious team working throughout the profession, enabling software engineers and managers to gain an insight into how opposing views have developed and what they represent based on personality profiles.

The behavior of teams has been a subject of study for many years and has mainly focused on factors such as task design, group composition, internal and external processes (conflict, communication), and group psychosocial traits (i.e., group norms). Some of the research has been based on the interactions of different personality types in a team context, and we will refer to some of this here.

In many teams there are different roles carried out by the various team members, and this has been studied by Belbin (1981) and Elam and Walz (1988).

Elam and Walz's work looked at team dynamics during the requirements analysis phase of a software project. The aim of their research was to gain an understanding of the processes that occur during software development team meetings. They were particularly interested in recording the interpersonal conflict that went on within the team. A number of other researchers have looked at personality in a software engineering context.

If one of the purposes of the XP approach is to make software development more human-centered, then it would be worth investigating whether the problems observed in other team-based activities are replicated in XP. Some educationalists have looked at how personality type relates to how the teaching of XP appeals to different personality types and whether some personalities are more suited to play specific roles in XP teams.

One major issue in all team activities is that of disruption caused by argument and disagreement. Karn and Cowling (2005) have considered this in the context of both XP teams and more traditional teams. Their research is founded on a popular and well-researched technique for characterizing individual personalities based on the work of Jung, a leading psychologist of the twentieth century.

The *Myers–Briggs Type Indicator* (MBTI) classifies people in terms of four different personality dimensions. The MBTI is used to assess an individual's personality style on four dimensions: social interaction, information gathering, decision making, and dealing with the external world. Millions of people take the test each year, many as part of recruitment and assessment exercises by many employers, and it is widely recognized as a useful way to characterize some aspects of human psychology. Other applications include team building, improving customer service, reconciling group differences, career planning, adapting to change, analyzing troublesome behavior between employees, and facilitating competitive strategic thinking. It is not the full picture, however, and we should be cautious about treating it as definitive. There are alternatives to the MBTI that are used.

There are four elements of the MBTI that are based on *opposites* in personality terms:

Introversion–extraversion (social interaction)

Sensing–intuition (information gathering)

Thinking–feeling (decision making)

Judging–perceiving (dealing with the external world)

Individuals are regarded as having a combination of these four broad characteristics; however, many will have characteristics that are not exclusively of one of these types but are a combination, thus someone may have some extrovert characteristics and some introvert ones. Myers–Briggs argued that one process, whether it be sensing, intuition, thinking, or feeling, must have clear sovereignty over the others and be given opportunity to reach its full development in order for a person to maximize their effectiveness. A balanced personality needs adequate (not equal) development of a second process, not to rival the dominant process but to act as a welcome auxiliary.

The MBTI identifies the clarity of preference of these four dimensions of attributes and provides a measure of the relative position of each individual's makeup in terms of the four dimensions.

Most of the terms used in the MBTI framework are relatively easy to grasp.

The *extrovert* is outward-going and relates to external things and objectives.

We all know people who have strong extrovert tendencies—they are the *life and soul of the party*—always getting involved with other people, not frightened of strangers, and so forth.

The *introvert* is often shy and reticent and is primarily concerned with his or her own thoughts and feelings.

There is a general belief that many computer scientists and programmers are of this second type, perhaps *loners* in some sense—more at home with their own world rather than with that of other people. Of course, this is not generally true although some people are attracted to computers as a substitute for interacting with other people.

The next category defines *how* people perceive (gather) information.

Sensing people rely on their senses for information.

Sensing means that a person believes mainly information he or she receives directly from the external world. This is what they trust most—believing what they see or hear—what is real rather than imaginary. They tend to be methodical.

The *intuitive* relies more on their intuitions, these are derived from their unconscious rather than from the external world. Inspiration is a vital part of their makeup.

The difference between rational, logical behavior and the more emotional relationships with people are the next dichotomy. This dichotomy is concerned with how people come to make decisions.

The *thinking* person is impersonal; they are interested in the truth and prefer to view the world in terms of things being either true or false.

This is a natural attitude among programmers as they have to exhibit these characteristics in the design of a program; however, they also need some empathy for the users of the program, and failure to have this can lead to problems later.

A *feeling* individual is more responsive to personal relationships and values, where issues may not be entirely black and white. They are often more sympathetic when dealing with people and seek compromise rather than conflict.

Thus, such a person may well be better placed to deal with requirements gathering and usability issues.

The final dimension is concerned with how people reach and implement conclusions based on the foregoing processes, gathering information and analyzing it and making *decisions*. It is the difference between a perceptive and a judging attitude. Thinking–feeling is more relevant to how one comes to make a decision rather than the processes of expressing it to the external world.

A *judging* person will evaluate the available information and reach a definite conclusion.

We have all met such people—they usually have an opinion—often things are analyzed carefully so that the answer is clear and justifiable to them.

A *perceiving* person will hesitate to reach a conclusion because of the concern that further information or issues remain undiscovered.

These sorts of people are more likely to appreciate the complexity of an issue, they may recognize the nontechnical aspects—the social or psychological dimensions of a software solution.

Everyone will combine all of these traits in various proportions. Because building software is a complex task with many key factors—demanding skills from across these four dimensions—it is important that any team is able to demonstrate a good balance of these.

The MBTI test identifies where on these scales an individual is positioned—abbreviations are used to provide a shorthand descriptor.

I = introversion and E = extroversion

S = sensing and N = intuitive

T = thinking and F = feeling

J = judging and P = perceiving

Thus, INTJ means someone with strong tendencies to introversion, intuition, thinking, and judging, and ESFP is an extrovert, sensing, feeling, and perceiving individual. In theory, there are 16 basic combinations.

For each test, the relative strengths of the attributes is indicated in percentage terms and indicates the strengths of the different attributes. This is an indicator where

40% or higher (30 for T/F): very clear preference is shown

31% to 39% (21–29 T/F): clear preference is shown

11% to 20%: moderate preference is shown

1% to 10%: slight preference is shown

An example is I, 52%; N, 33%; T, 22%; J, 62%. Such a person has a strongly introverted character with a clear preference for intuition, a lower level but still a clear preference for thinking, and a strong preference for judging.

Why don't you find out what your index is? This can be measured through your participation in an online test based on the MBTI developed by Human Metrics, a consortium of psychologists: http://www.humanmetrics.com/cgi-win/JTypes1.htm.

There is no cost and it is entirely confidential—it might help you to reflect more on your strengths and weaknesses if your are aware of your MBTI.

My type is ENFJ: moderately extroverted, very intuitive, moderately feeling, a clear preference for judging. The strength of these preferences is 11, 75, 12, 33, respectively.

The general consensus seems to be that it takes a variety of skills and personalities, but this is not the opinion of all of the researchers in this area. Others argue that optimal teams will have a typical engineering profile. Engineering students are concentrated heavily in the IN quadrant, also featuring the two ENT types and ISTJ. There is a strong emphasis on N and J.

3.3 OBSERVATIONS OF TEAM BEHAVIOR IN XP PROJECTS

Karn and Cowling (2006) observed a number of meetings of XP teams involved in commercial software development projects, both meetings just involving the team working together and meetings of the team with their clients.

Initially, the researchers recorded everything that they observed during these meetings and then classified the contributions that each member of the team made according to a simple set of possibilities.

Example Team 1

Id	MBTI type	E-I %	S-N %	T-F %	J-P %
1A	INFP	I 44	N 33	F 44	P 22
1B	INTP	I 44	N 22	T 11	P 33
1C	ENTJ	E 44	N 33	T 44	J 44
1D	ENFJ	E 11	N 22	F 11	J 22
1E	INTJ	I 33	N 67	T 56	J 1

This team had a good mix of personality types and worked well together. There were no dominant personalities and the levels of disruption were minor. Karn states:

As an INFP, 1A focused on feelings and human conditions and attempted to avoid rushing to any impersonal judgments. 1C as an ENTJ with clear preferences had a natural tendency to organize and direct the team. 1C was decisive, knowing what needed to be done, and was confident when assigning roles to team-mates. 1E's type is INTJ. 1E was the person most likely to answer any technical query or deal with any problem in this area. 1E was aided and abetted in this by a hardworking though subservient colleague in 1B. The final member of this team 1D is an ENFJ. 1D had very good people skills and sought to bring out the best in team mates.

Example Team 2

Id	MBTI type	E-I %	S-N %	T-F %	J-P %
2A	INTP	I 78	N 78	T 44	P 33
2B	INTJ	I 11	N 11	T 78	J 44
2C	INTJ	I 56	N 33	T 33	J 44
2D	INFJ	I 11	N 33	T 33	J 56
2E	ENTJ	E 1	N 33	T 11	J 11

This team had a rather skewed profile of personality types, and many problems were caused by this.

From Karn's observations:

2A was very analytical and often caused annoyance by correcting others in a sharp manner. Another team member 2D admitted that "2A was good with ideas, and proved to be very useful to the team." 2C also stated that "at times the team seemed to be like a one man band," and said 2A's contribution was "crucial.". . . The over reliance on 2A was due in part to the personality type of the other members of the team, as the three INTJs were naturally cautious when coming forward with new ideas and leading the discussion. . . . Misunderstandings led to over reliance on 2A which led to poor quality or missed deadlines. . . . Lack of debate was not a problem for this team; they were often aware of problems yet instead of acting on them preferred to leave things to 2A. . . .

The end result of all of this was that there was no working system at the end of the project, this was made worse by the fact that important documentation was incomplete.

A possible conclusion from this sort of work is that a "balanced" team comprising a mix of personality types might be best. On several occasions it has been noted that having too many similar types of people can lead to either major disruptions or to *groupthink* situations where there are not enough constructive arguments. Groupthink refers to the situation—often found when one of the team plays a very dominant role—where there is little discussion of alternatives and everyone "toes the party line."

We have seen that different individuals have different strengths and weaknesses and a good combination of people will probably be best able to deal with all of the key aspects of a software project—which is much more than design and implementation but also involves client liaison, understanding user characteristics and motivation, and the social organizational environment within which the software is deployed.

In the following extract notes from a meeting between a client and a XP development team, we see the range of issues discussed—technical, conceptual, and financial. The project was eventually successful but there were many problems along the way—many caused by the client wanting to change to "cheaper" technologies at points in the project, this causing considerable rework and delays.

From the Genesys Archive: a team meeting.

Genesys Team Meeting

Courtesy of John Karn

Not all members of the team were present at the start. A then explained that the team has come up with some requirements and gave them to the client to take away. B had drawn the architecture on the board and the team appeared to be very organized. B then explained the problems associated with text messages and wanted to allow users of the system to use the Web as well.

A then said that the team has captured all of the system so far. She also suggested eliminating names from subscription. The only details she believed were necessary were age, location, and sex. She couldn't see any real use for name. The client disagreed, he believed that people needed to be addressed by some sort of handle. *A* argued that this will take up too much space in a text message. She said there are two aspects to the project: register and communicate. There is also a problem with many different types of name. *A* believed that people could be identified by number alone as this will be in every message. The client pointed out that some people have more than one phone. *A* then had a discussion with *B* and they talked about people having a unique, default number. Then *B* suggested identifying people by nickname and number as numbers can change. *A* then argued that messages will be sent only to the main phone to which *B* suggested another table for secondary numbers. *A* then informed the client that there will be redundant data in the DB. The system could be sending messages that are not delivered. *B* then said that after a certain number of messages have bounced then it is time to move the phone from the main DB into an archive.

A said the interface will be simple for a mobile phone and can then be expanded for a Web interface. *B* said that the reaction to the DB was the key to the entire project. He said simplicity is very important. *B* then said that the primary number will receive more than 90% of the messages and that all people will have a main phone. The client said that some people will use different phones for making calls and sending texts.

B suggested giving people another option for the primary phone such as add number. This will give people the option of registering another phone. *F* then said the users can change their details through the Web.

The client said the system should ask for data such as first name, last name, and nickname. *F* says this will be checked and a response validated to the user. *B* said that users will need their mobile phone number and their password to log onto the Website. *D* then raised the issue of people messing around with other phones such as taking a friend's phone and subscribing to all of the groups. The client said that every text sent by the system must give the user the option of unsubscribing. *D* labored this point but according to the client it would not be a problem as the unsuspecting user would be able to leave the system at any time.

B then said that simplicity is the key to the project. Do not make users enter more information than is absolutely necessary. Also make sure that the correct market is targeted.

A then asked an important question about legal aspects. There can be no illegal content in messages. She asked if it was necessary for the system to have a disclaimer. The client didn't believe that this was necessary as the system will be very controlled with regard to what companies can send users.

A then said that in order to test the system, the team will need a mobile phone from the client. This seemed to be okay. One problem was that four members of the team were totally silent almost throughout the meeting. *A* then announced that the team will start testing Web sites in the prototyping stage.

A then said that the team has discussed using PHP but decided that ASP would be more reliable. This was a team decision. The client agreed and laughed and said that PHP was like something out of the ark. He assured the team that they can use any software they want. A said this was good news. She also said that the marketing team's price for the project was way out. The client didn't look too happy about this and said he would talk to Mike about it.

B then said that the DB must be updated by the users. The DB must keep records about who has responded to what. A said that the querying capabilities are very important. F then said that each user will have their own data and that the project is all about data manipulation. The campaigns cover very different areas. A then asked if the administrator required the capability to go in and change any user details by hand. The client said that data belongs to individual users and that removing data is okay but modifying data is detrimental. F then asked if companies can modify their data. He wanted to know the exact registration procedure for companies.

Then a serious problem arose. The client pointed out that one of the team members could be fired if they were employees and not students. The client was fuming because he received a phone call from someone asking him about work. He was angry because someone must have told him this number. He said this was a clear breach of confidentiality. He said that such actions could wake other people up and give the initiative to other companies. He said there could be a job in this at the end of the project if the students are successful. He warned the students that it is a business now and they need to be professional. Then F stated in a loud voice that there is no proof that any one in this team had given out the client's number. The client laughed and said it must be. F pointed out that it could be from anyone within Genesys or even an external person could have passed on the clients details. The client didn't believe this.

B then stepped in and managed to bring the meeting back on track when he stated that the team is still deciding which technologies need to be used. He said the team will sort working pairs out and go from there. B then said the primary mobile phone is crucial. He then discussed going against the client and not having three names. F said the team should contact the server because they feel the client is not telling the truth. He said he doubts if the team can use any technology.

F also complained about the DB getting bigger. A said this project might not be done within the year. F accused the client of lying and said it was dangerous to allow him to modify any information in the DB.

In this group, *A* is playing a major leadership role—*A* is technically strong and has some vision of how the project should develop. *B* is also showing leadership and some creativity and is engaged in a discussion with *A*. Team member *F* is being more negative and at one point judgmental, with *D* playing a subordinate questioning role. Two other members present were silent.

Id	MBTI type	E-I %	S-N %	T-F %	J-P %
—	ISFJ	I 34	S 44	F 24	J 22
—	ENFJ	E 22	N 78	F 11	J 33
—	INTJ	I 67	N 11	T 22	J 33
—	INFP	I 44	N 22	F 28	P 36
—	INTJ	I 33	N 22	T 44	J 44
—	ENTJ	E 88	N 67	T 74	J 56

From this extract, we can see how some of the different characteristics of the individuals in the team are combining to explore many issues in the project. Members *A* and *B* made a good partnership with *B* acting in a managerial role trying to resolve differences in the team. *A* worked hard and emphasized loyalty and respect for others within the team. *A*'s introversion combined with sensing and judging produced a stable and empathetic climate in the team. *B* favored N which was a good complement to *A*'s S as intuitive types need sensing types to provide elements of reality and sensing types need the creative influence of intuitives. The table provides some detailes of the team's MBTI scores, which have been made anonymous.

F was sometimes a little boisterous, and this was not always productive and some-times generated negative feelings toward the client—respect was sometimes lacking in this individual. *F* did work hard throughout the project, but his approach to work strained relations with some of the others. *F* and *C* did not work well together, and others in the team needed to intervene at times, especially *B*. *C*, by virtue of being an INTJ, was intuitive and easily bored, needing constant stimulation to be engaged with the project; of an introverted nature, he was often rather distant and disengaged.

Of course, our personalities cannot be changed to a large extent—we have to live with what we are—but a knowledge of each person's strengths and weaknesses can be used, from a management point of view, to optimize the team's performance to a certain extent.

An important point to consider is that psychological types are essentially an individual's preferred style of approaching and dealing with the world, and there are no right or wrong ways of accomplishing this. As such, personality research should not be used as an excuse or justification of the superiority of one type over another or as a way to eliminate or discourage people from working in software development teams if they do not meet expected or prescribed personality profiles. With that said, a better understanding of personality preferences can lead to a greater appreciation of individual differences and will provide team members and managers with greater opportunities to create an optimal working environment.

3.4 SETTING UP A TEAM

In this section, we will look at how teams may be put together for a project. This may not be an issue as your employer or instructor may allocate you to a team without pro-viding any choice in the matter. This is a reasonable reflection of what happens in industry, so one can't really complain. It would still be useful to understand the makeup of the team and to recognize its strengths and weaknesses. The previous section may provide some insight on how different combinations of people can work together or not. If we can recognize our limitations and plan accordingly, we may be able to avoid many problems.

However, if you are asked to form yourselves into teams, here are some pointers to doing that.

Suppose that we are trying to form a team of four, five, or six. We need to look for a blend of personalities and skills that will knit together and produce an effective force. The nature of the project may determine some of the parameters but let us assume that all the potential candidates for the team are reasonably well prepared in terms of having progressed satisfactorily through the programming, design, and more specialized courses and training needed for the project.

The key requirement is for the team to be people who get along reasonably well with each other, and knowing that you have a team with a good blend of characteristics, personality, skills, and attitudes will provide a sound basis for success.

For those involved in a university project, finding somewhere that they can meet also may be an issue. In all cases, making sure that all the team members have a similar interest in doing well in the project—partly because of the desire to get a good grade in the exercise or bonuses—will be important. Poorly motivated team members are a threat to the team's success; agile methods may help because of their possibly more human approach, which tries to support motivation.

A software project involves a number of key activities, and it is important that there are members of the team who can make useful contributions to these activities. We need some good programmers but there are many other things to be done in the project. We need people who have abilities to organize, to plan, to negotiate and communicate—with, for example, the client—and there is always the need to document clearly and systematically various important things.

No single person will come to the project with all these abilities to a high level, but most people will be capable of most to some extent. Extreme programming emphasizes the equal involvement of all team members in all the important activities, and so the project will be a framework within which all team members will develop significant skills across the board. You will learn both technical material and skills as well as how to cooperate, communicate, organize, resolve problems, deliver a successful product, and mature as a software professional in a way that is just not possible in other types of learning.

In situations where there is an odd number of team members, it makes pair programming awkward to organize. It doesn't really work with three people around a machine, so the best way to operate if you have a team of five is to have two pairs doing programming, testing, and debugging and the other person can do a variety of tasks such as reviewing code, documents, and models, system testing, preparing documentation and manuals, and so forth. The important thing is to keep changing the pairs around, involve everyone equally in contributing to the project, and to keep talking to each other.

Doing a *real* project with a *real* business client is very different from what you usually experience at university where the projects tend to be artificial and very different from real industrial projects. Doing a real project will change you forever, your perspective on life, on your colleagues, and on the process of working together. Your understanding of the profession of a software engineer will be transformed, as will your job prospects, as future interviewers will be really impressed by your experiences in doing real software development; it will set you apart from the rest of the applicants as someone with extra skills and experiences and value for their business.

A skills audit is another important feature of any team-building exercise. It may only happen in an informal way, you gradually learn what your colleagues know and can do. It is best, initially, however, to try to write down what your strengths and weaknesses are and to share this with the rest of the potential team. See if there are people with a good selection of the skills needed. If most of your team is good at programming but not very good at talking to people or organizing documentation, then that should be a cue to try to recruit someone with these skills. The deal is then that the extreme programming approach will help them to develop those skills that they are weak in. Extreme programming is all about multiskilling and learning all the key skills needed in software development to a high level.

Table 3.1   A Skills Log

Skill and preferences	Excellent	Moderate	Limited	Wants to learn more
Programming in Java	Pete, Mary	Joe, Oscar	Jane	Jane
Programming in PHP	Jane		Oscar	
Communications skills	Oscar, Joe	Mary, Jane	Pete	Oscar
Organizational skills	Mary	Pete, Oscar	Joe, Jane	Joe
Documenting skills	Jane, Oscar	Mary	Pete, Joe	Pete
Solving problems	Mary	Joe, Oscar, Pete	Jane	
Presentations	Joe	Pete, Jane	Mary	Oscar

Itemize your group's relevant skills or at least your own assessment of them in a table such as Table 3.1.

This is only a rough guide and the definition of the skills and levels is bound to be vague, but it does give you some basis to plan out your project and also a simple benchmark to compare with at the end of the project. One would hope that there is a significant improvement across the board by the end of the course.

3.5 DEVELOPING TEAM SKILLS

There are many activities that can help in developing a team spirit and, with it, an effective way to work as a *team* rather than as a group of individuals.

In this exercise, we will assume that there is a team of six. It is based on a real project undertaken by Genesys. (Genesys is the commercial software development company run by students within the University of Sheffield.)

Scenario 1 should be given to two members, scenario 2 to two different members, and scenario 3 to the remaining two members.

Each pair should spend 15 minutes discussing, in private, their scenario. Then all the team should get together to discuss the following:

1 What does the client want?

2 Is it feasible, given the resources (time) available?

3 How should it be designed?

4 What technology should be used?

5 Who should do what?

Scenario 1

The client is a retailer of mountaineering equipment and wishes to have an e-commerce site for his business. He currently has a paper-based system and has to manually update his wholesaler orders when items are sold. He would like to take payment through the Internet and offer some other value-added features to his customers.

Scenario 2

The client is a retailer of mountaineering equipment and wishes to have an e-commerce site for his business. He currently has a chaotic manual system—most of the information is kept in his head. Payment for items would be by credit card, and customers will be able to upload mobile phone videos of their climbing exploits for others to see.

Scenario 3

The client is a retailer of mountaineering equipment and wishes to have an e-commerce site for his business. He currently has a database system and is thinking of using a stock control system that would connect automatically to his suppliers. He wants the site to be visually exciting and better than those of his rivals.

All of these descriptions have been given by the client to different people, and the task is to try to find out what is actually needed. What you may find is that some of the aspects—such as the video feature—will be taken up enthusiastically by the members who read scenario 2 and they may try to push the others down this route but others may see it as a less important feature in comparison with the basic Web site and purchasing facility.

The discussion will need to reach agreement on what is a sensible scope for the project—some arguments may ensue about the technology as whatever is chosen may prevent the development of some of these peripheral features at a later stage.

In fact, nothing should be concluded until a thorough business analysis has been carried out—this is discussed in a later chapter. Some danger signals that might need to be heeded will be considered then.

The point about the exercise is for the team to come to some agreement about what is really needed. A practice run in this simulated situation might help deal with problems in a real project.

Questions to ask yourselves:

1 Did any one person try to dominate the discussion?

2 Were there arguments that were difficult to resolve amicably?

3 What did you do about conflicting or ambiguous information in the scenarios?

4 Did anyone push for a specific technology in an unreasonable way (it is far too early to discuss technology because we have no real idea about the context, the volume and nature of business, etc.)?

In a real project, you will probably be able to resolve some of the issues by discussion with the client. The analysis of how the group dealt with the exercise could be a useful pointer to issues about the team that need to be watched.

3.6 TRAINING TOGETHER

Members of the teams will be assumed to have developed technical skills—programming, testing, and so on. The purpose of the training described here is to provide a rapid introduction to XP in a team context.

We run this exercise every year in Genesys once the initial materials about XP and the Genesys environment and tools have been discussed. It takes 6 continuous hours, with only short breaks, in 1 day and is meant to build team structures and practices quickly rather than provide an in-depth understanding of XP.

Genesys Speed Code Challenge 2006

October 11th. 11.00–17.00

A Web-based management tool for organizing playlists of music tracks.

Tracks (songs) will have a title, singer, genre, and length (time).

Conditions:

  1 Work in your teams;
  2 Use you team space—in the lab and the Intranet (if possible);
  3 *Languages*: Java, MySQL;
  4 *Tools*: Eclipse, svn, ADEPT, JUnit;
  5 *Deliverables*: Story cards, Unit tests, incremental builds, X-machines, system tests, final build.

Target system: *GenPlay*

Functions:

  1 add a new song;
  2 delete a song;
  3 query for songs on artist and genre; Advanced feature—if time permits
  4 generate a random sequence of songs to last for a given (user specified) length of time.

All this to be done between 11.10 and 5.00 on Wednesday October 11th, 2006.

Exercises like this can demonstrate where teams might need to improve their working methods. If a team does not complete the task in the time, then more training should be given and further assignments like this given. We use it as a diagnostic test—teams that do well will start on the commercial projects straightaway.

3.7 FINDING AND KEEPING A CLIENT FOR A UNIVERSITY-BASED PROJECT OR A SMALL BUSINESS START-UP

It may be the case that your instructor has found a suitable client with a realistic problem for you to tackle or you are starting a real project with your first employer. If you are still at university, ideally the client should not be in your academic department but from outside, either from an external business or other organization or perhaps from another department within the university. It may be more realistic for your instructor to organize a collection of projects that involve a member of the staff of the department acting as a client. Much can be learned from this experience, but a real client provides that unpredictability that XP should be able to handle.

If you have to find your own client, and this is perfectly possible, then there are a number of avenues worth exploring.

Check out your family and friends. It is likely that you know someone who has a small business or who works for a local organization. See if they would like some high-quality software developed exclusively for them at a nominal cost.

Contact the local chamber of commerce or similar business organization.

Approach local charities: these often have interesting and useful problems and cannot always afford to get professional software created for them.

Talk to staff in other parts of the university: this is always a rich source of good projects, in my experience.

Examples of systems that could be useful include: databases for business dealing with customers, orders, and other relevant information; Web pages with some useful functionality, perhaps allowing customers to request products, catalogues, or to supply information such as customer details, market surveys, and so forth; planning tools that might enable an organization to organize its resources better, time tabling some of its activities in a more effective way:

There are many other applications that you could consider.

Once you have identified a potential client, it is important to establish the following: *Is the client prepared to give enough of their time to meet you and identify what it is they require in detail as well as to evaluate your software over the period of the project?*

As we shall see later, extreme programming requires a very close interaction with the client; if the client cannot afford the time required, say a couple of hours a week for a semester, then look for another client. If the client does not operate locally, this could also be a problem.

Having identified a client and a potential problem, see your instructor to find out if they think it is appropriate for your capabilities. Your instructor may have originally intended you to do a team project that he or she had made up. Argue the case that it would be much better for you if you could do a *real* project instead. It would also be much better for your client. Even if you are not totally successful in building a complete solution, your client would have learned a lot about their own business or organization simply because your questions would have made them think about what they do in a fresh light. They might use your work as a basis for a contract with a commercial software house. It may be possible for an incomplete system to be completed by some of the team during the vacation. Everyone will benefit, even your instructor. It is so much better if your efforts are directed at building something that will be useful to someone rather than something that, once it has been marked, will be thrown away!

You will also learn so much about dealing with a client, about delivering a quality solution, and about planning and organizing yourself because you will be better motivated compared with the traditional sort of projects that professors dream up. You cannot learn many of these things from lectures or books, you must learn by doing it all *for real.*

Once you have a client and a project, it is vital that you make efforts to keep them both. Regular feedback to the client is essential, so regular meetings must be held. When you attend these meetings, make sure that you approach them in a professional way. Think smart and look smart. Give your client confidence that his or her investment will be worthwhile and they will get something out of the exercise. Never break appointments; if some other crisis occurs, it is vital that the client is warned if it is necessary to change a planned meeting.

Always describe what you have achieved since the last meeting. Always appear interested in the client's business, and express some confidence about how the project is going but do not exaggerate progress. Honesty will ultimately pay.

My experience has been that clients really enjoy the activity, many have never been a client for a software development project before, and they are getting some useful insights that may be valuable in later years. They also generally like working with bright and enthusiastic young people. Thus for them it will be both an enjoyable and a productive experience. It should be the same for you.

3.8 THE ORGANIZATIONAL FRAMEWORK

We will now assume that you have been allocated to a team or have organized one yourself and have a client waiting. Before rushing into the project, it is important to get a few things organized. We now describe a few simple, and perhaps obvious, things to do. Do not underestimate these factors; many projects fail because of the simplest and most stupid of mistakes and omissions.

Learn as much about your team members as possible, their names, addresses, phone numbers, e-mail addresses, and so on. It is vital that you can contact everyone easily because you may be working on the project in a variety of locations, not just the usual laboratories. This is something that is different than most industrial practice where the team occupies the same premises all day and every day. See if everyone will sign up to a working agreement that identifies the responsibilities and expectations of all the team members, for example.

Agree on the location for the first meeting and make sure everyone turns up on time. This is important if one wants to be treated professionally, as your client will want to do; if you do not behave in a professional way, why should anyone treat you like a professional? This is the first test, if a team member does not make it to an important and agreed meeting and they do not have an excellent reason, then this is a major threat to the project and to all of the team's grades. The team agreement should emphasize the obligation on all team members to attend all meetings. If the culprit does not listen to reason, then discuss things with the instructor or manager.

Teams can work well in a variety of ways. Sometimes it is worth agreeing on having a team leader who takes over the responsibilities of organizing and chairing meetings, of leading the planning and other key coordinating activities. If everyone is happy with this solution, then this can work. My recommendation, however, is for the role to be shared, each member of the team taking over the running of the team for, say, 2 weeks at a time. Thus everyone gets an opportunity to develop their leadership skills and to take responsibility for the team's progress. This is more in keeping with the democratic nature of extreme programming.

It is important to establish an effective method of working. First of all, you will need to hold planning and progress meetings. Depending on the timescale and your other activities, there might be several of these each week. The current project leader should chair the session. There should be another team member to act as secretary—this could be the person who will take over as project leader after the current one. Formal minutes should be taken at the meeting. This requires the following information about the meeting to be recorded: date, location, attendance, absences (with reason); and then the record of the meeting.

See Fig. 3.1 for an example of a template that works.

Each item of discussion should be numbered and a brief description of the item made. Any conclusions and decisions taken must be recorded together with any further actions agreed upon. These must describe *what* is to be done, *who* is to do it, and *when* it must be done by.

All this is absolutely vital if the project is not to suffer from confusion and recriminations.

Each team should appoint an archivist. This role can also be shared around the team. The key requirement is that someone is given the responsibility to maintain a complete and accurate record of the plans and meetings of the project. This person should set up a suitable filestore on some server where all the team has access so that anyone can consult the archive to see what the status and history of the project is. We will later discuss the archiving of other, more technical documents, requirements documents, test cases, code, and so forth. The regime for these documents is different, however. Some members other than the archivist may deposit if the team decides this.

Another important activity is the recording of the amount of time each team member spends per week on the project activities. This should be recorded on a weekly time sheet for the team. Examples will be found in a later chapter.

It is vital that we record accurately the time we spend on projects.

First, it enables us to track our individual performance and helps us to identify where we are making progress and where we may still have improvements to make as we undertake various types of activity in the software development process. This is vital for apprentice software engineering and, in fact, should be something that we do throughout our professional lives. The personal software process (Humphrey, 1996) can provide a framework for this.

Second, it will help us to collect data from which we can predict how much effort future activities might take. Estimating the resources (time, people, etc.) needed for the development of software is notoriously difficult. Many decisions are made in an *ad hoc* manner and usually lead to disaster or, at best, to a very inefficient and expensive process. We have to learn to do better. As we will see later, planning is an important part of extreme programming.

GENESYS

Minutes of group meetings.

Group no. or name ....

Date of meeting [dd/mm].......

Time of meeting [hh:mm].......

Place of meeting................

Present...

Absent (reason)...

Agenda item	Discussion:	Action by:	Deadline:
1			
2			
3			

Figure 3.1   A template for the minutes of a meeting.

Finally, the documentation can be used in reviews and evaluations of the team, during assessments, and so forth.

An example is given in Fig. 3.2.

A major issue for software projects is that of ensuing that all the team members are using the latest version of every document or program. To assist in this, many organizations use a version control system such as CVS. We use *Subversion* together

GENESYS

Minutes Date: 1st November 2002

Time: 13:00   **Location**: Genesys Lab

Chair: GJ   **Secretary**: JD

Present: Team K Proceedings

Item	Point	Action
	Decided that GJ to produce the monthly report, to include a rough plan for the rest of the semester based on discussions so far. Noted that this plan will be open to change over the next few weeks. Everyone else to continue with either database reconstruction or mapping the interface (see point 2).	
	After considerable discussion, it is decided that half the group will work on the database and half the group on the interface. As follows: Database: SK, JD, BS Interface: RN, GJ, MB The group will work together mainly on the interface once the database has been restructured.	
	Database people are to look at the existing tables and put them onto a diagram. Restructure the database and normalize it. Interface people will begin to map the site.	Team K

Next Meeting: 13:00 Mon 04/11

Next Chair: JD

Next Secretary: MB

Figure 3.2   Example minutes.

with the *Eclipse* development environment. Eclipse is a framework for programming that can be tailored to your needs through the use of specific plug-ins to support many things that software developers do.

These are tools that you should check out to see how they might be used in the project. There are other options.

Information about Subversion is available from http://svnbook.red-bean.com/. Eclipse is available from http://www.eclipse.org/downloads/, which provides a background and some downloads to try out. Genesys has produced some Eclipse plug-ins to support extreme programming (ADEPT): http://www.genesys.shef.ac. uk/eclipse/.

A useful management tool that includes easy-to-use management features designed by Chris Thomson can be found at http://ext.dcs.shef.ac.uk/~u0017/ sheffieldmanagement/.

3.9   PLANNING

The basics of planning include decomposing the overall task into a collection of smaller tasks; identifying the dependencies and relationships between these tasks; estimating the amount of resource (time and manpower) required to complete the tasks; setting delivery times for each task; and describing the plan in some suitable notation.

Plans will inevitably require review and alteration because the estimates made of the time needed to complete tasks is often wrong, further understanding of the project could lead to a different structure to the previous task decomposition, and because exceptional circumstances, such as illness, intervene. The regular meetings provide an opportunity to review and replan the project. Do not shy away from hard decisions in these meetings. It is very easy to pretend that everything is all right when it isn't. Equally one can get depressed about progress. Later in this book, we will look at planning again and examine how extreme programming can provide some answers to some of the problems met in planning and running software projects.

We now look at some planning techniques. There is software that is widely available for project planning; however, this is often much more complex than is needed here.

It is necessary to split each phase down into activities at a level where these can be assigned to individual team pairs or possibly a larger group of team members. It is then necessary to monitor how progress is made with each of these activities, and to do this one needs a schedule describing which activities are to be undertaken when. Some activities will be prerequisites for others, in the sense that one activity will depend on the output of a previous one. The techniques discussed here are widely used in industry in traditional projects. It is not clear if they are so useful for agile projects, but there is a big danger if we neglect this aspect. If, as in Genesys, there are fixed deadlines—when the students finish the course—it is vital that we can take a slightly longer look than might be popular in traditional XP projects. Ultimately, projects have to be delivered, there is an acceptable timescale for the client—who may have to answer to more senior managers—and we have to pace the project within an acceptable overall timescale.

3.9.1 PERT (Program Evaluation and Review Technique)

This is a technique that enables a schedule to be constructed that meets all the constraints of the prerequisites and identifies the *critical path* through the program. The critical path is the part of the schedule that determines the minimum time in which the whole project can be completed. It allows us to identify the activities that are most important in terms of their effect on the overall timing of the program, and hence to identify those that need to be monitored most carefully.

The basis of PERT is a graphical representation of the activities known as a PERT chart. This diagram consists of nodes to represent activities, which is annotated both with the name of the activity and with its duration (in whatever time units are being used: typically days, weeks, or months). Where one activity is a direct prerequisite for another, there is a directed arc from the earlier to the later node. There are also two special nodes: one for the start of the program and one for its finish. A typical example of such a graph is given in Fig. 3.3, which follows from the description of PERT in Boehm (1981).

In this chart (Fig. 3.3), we have taken a rather *simplistic* view of the XP process. There is likely to be a lot more iterations, and the chart will be much more extensive in most cases. The numbers refer to person-hours of work and are just crude estimates; we would expect the activities to be much shorter in a full-time XP project. This plan tries to take into account the fact that most student team members will have to attend other classes and activities outside of the project. This needs to be taken account of sensibly.

In constructing a PERT chart, it is often easier to start at the finish and work backwards rather than start at the beginning and work forwards; this way, we can try to ensure that all the prerequisites for a node are identified and added to the chart. Even so, it is common that such a chart may need to change as the project develops and additional nodes are identified or different activities are found to be necessary.

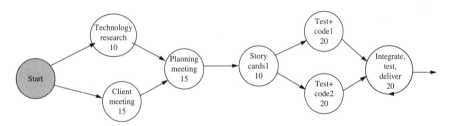

Figure 3.3   A PERT chart.

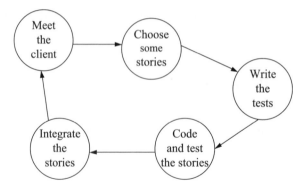

Figure 3.4   The weekly XP cycle.

In traditional approaches, once the chart has been constructed, it is used to determine the critical path; that is, the path for the project that will take the longest time. Here the situation is much more dynamic and fluid, and the role of the chart is merely to identify potential problems. In the example above, there is a potential issue in that the team carrying out the technology research might hold the rest up at the planning meeting. It might thus be sensible to involve more people in this aspect but not lose site of the problem that too many people working in an uncoordinated way is not only inefficient but is also a cause of potential team rows if some members believe that they have been wasting their time carrying out work that is not very useful to the project or has been duplicated by others.

A more natural way to illustrate an XP project, particularly the iterative cycle, is given in Fig. 3.4. This deals with the weekly cycle of activity, assuming that you can only meet the client once a week. If the client can be involved more than that is fine, but it isn't usually possible.

3.9.2   Gantt Charts

Whereas the PERT chart displays the relationships between the timing of the different activities, a complicated PERT chart can be difficult to read in terms of deciding which activities will actually be scheduled when during the periods that they can occur. For this reason, it is sometimes useful to derive from the PERT chart an alternative representation of the schedule known as a Gantt chart (Fig. 3.5). This in its simplest form consists of a column for each time period and a row for each activity, with a block drawn on the chart to indicate when that activity is scheduled to take place. One possible Gantt chart for the project illustrated in Fig. 3.3 is given below. It is clear from this that it is not particularly useful for an XP project.

There are a number of tools that help to create and maintain these charts. They may be worth investigating, but many are more complex than we usually require, and they do not fit the highly iterative nature of an XP project.

It would be better to produce a simple table of the weeks activities (Table 3.2).

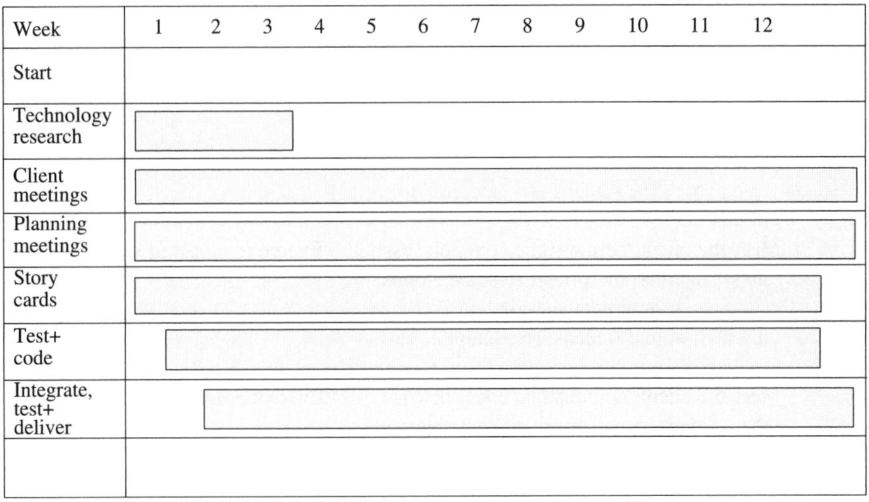

Week	1	2	3	4	5	6	7	8	9	10	11	12
Start												
Technology research	▭											
Client meetings	▭▭▭▭▭▭▭▭▭▭▭▭											
Planning meetings	▭▭▭▭▭▭▭▭▭▭▭▭											
Story cards	▭▭▭▭▭▭▭▭▭▭▭											
Test+ code	▭▭▭▭▭▭▭▭▭▭▭											
Integrate, test+ deliver	▭▭▭▭▭▭▭▭▭▭											

Figure 3.5   A Gantt chart.

Table 3.2   A Project Activity Table

Week	Activity	Comments
1	Meet the client, carry out some research, identify some simple stories, write some tests, write the code, produce some simple architectures, and screen ideas.	Mary and Pete to do the research, everyone else to do the other tasks.
2	Meet the client, discuss ideas, identify and prioritize some stories, estimate, test and code stories, further research, refine screens, etc. Integrate stories to date.	Swap round who does the research, everyone involved in everything else.
3	Meet the client, demonstrate code, discuss ideas, identify and prioritize some stories, estimate, test and code stories, further research, refine screens, etc. Integrate stories to date.	Everyone involved in everything.
4	Meet the client, demonstrate code, discuss ideas, identify and prioritize some stories, estimate, test and code stories, further research, refine screens, etc. Integrate stories to date.	Everyone involved in everything.
5	Meet the client, demonstrate code, discuss ideas, identify and prioritize some stories, estimate, test and code stories, further research, refine screens, etc. Integrate stories to date. Produce a summary requirements document (list of stories to be built, non-functional requirements, glossary).	Everyone involved in everything.

(Continued)

Table 3.2   (*Continued*)

Week	Activity	Comments
6	Meet the client, demonstrate code, discuss ideas, identify and prioritize some stories, estimate, test and code stories, further research, refine screens etc. Integrate stories to date.	Everyone involved in everything.
7	Meet the client, demonstrate code, discuss ideas, identify and prioritize some stories, estimate, test and code stories, further research, refine screens, etc. Integrate stories to date.	Everyone involved in everything.
8	Meet the client, demonstrate code, discuss ideas, identify and prioritize some stories, estimate, test and code stories, further research, refine screens, etc. Integrate stories to date.	Everyone involved in everything.
9	Meet the client, demonstrate code, discuss ideas, identify and prioritize some stories, estimate, test and code stories, further research, refine screens, etc. Integrate stories to date.	Everyone involved in everything.
10	Meet the client, demonstrate code, discuss ideas, identify and prioritize some stories, estimate, test and code stories, further research, refine screens, etc. Integrate stories to date.	Everyone involved in everything.
11	Meet the client, demonstrate code, discuss ideas, identify and prioritize some stories, estimate, test and code stories, further research, refine screens, etc. Integrate stories to date.	Everyone involved in everything.
12	Prepare for the final handover. At this stage, we should be doing only minor changes to the system, fixing problems, etc. Write basic user and maintenance documentation. Update the requirements document.	Everyone involved in everything.

Now we have to make an allocation of team members, usually pairs, to the various tasks identified. This could be done by a more detailed table. It is likely that this table will need to be revised on a regular basis as the project progresses. In most cases, the length of the project is fixed, and this provides a major constraint. You may have to compromise on what you are hoping to build: better to build a simple system that works than a fancy one that doesn't. Your client won't thank you for the latter!

These planning techniques are for a general view of where the project is going and how it might get there. In a later chapter, we will introduce a simple technique with a tool that helps you to track progress and plan in more detail. The plans discussed here are like software architectures—they are a top-level view of the project—more detailed day-to-day records and plans relating to the production of stories are the equivalent of detailed code.

3.10 DEALING WITH PROBLEMS

It is inevitable that things will go wrong from time to time. It is the teams that are able to deal with problems effectively that turn out to be successful. It is not about how clever people in the team are but the culture within the team. If this culture is one of cooperation, discussion, building consensus, and treating each member as an intelligent individual with a legitimate point of view, then resolutions can be found. If people are stubborn, arrogant, dismissive, and uncooperative, then it is much harder. Try not to lose one's temper, be patient and considerate to others, and discuss the issues on the basis of an informed knowledge of the matters under discussion rather than on the basis of prejudice and guesswork. Show respect for others.

3.10.1 Basic Strategies

Seek expert advice if the argument is about a technical point or the benefits of different strategies or approaches. Talk to the client as well. All these things can be sorted out if everyone is positive and prepared to give and take. Extreme programming is all about cooperation, communication, and treating people with respect and trust. All problems are soluble somehow even if the solution is somehow not what one would have hoped for—in some cases, the only practical way forward can be painful.

Try not to be upset if your argument is not the one that is successful in this process. Think about what has happened and see how you might benefit from the experience. Perhaps the way you handled your argument or yourself was counterproductive. Successful people in life reflect systematically on their experiences and learn from them, adapting their future behavior in order to ensure future success.

Sometimes you get into an argument where nobody is prepared to give way. This can happen if you are just working as a pair or it might occur with more people in the team involved. A simple suggestion from Miller (2002) might be useful. He discusses the issue in terms of pair programming, but the technique can be extended to bigger groups.

First, every person involved has to ensure that they understand the conflicting opinions.

Then each person is asked to rank his or her opinion on a scale of 1 to 3 with 1 meaning "I don't really care" to 3 meaning "I'll quit if I don't get my way." Thus 2 could be "I am interested in this argument and I am prepared to spend some time looking into it, I want to hear your point of view, but I will take some convincing that it is better than mine."

If there is a highest ranked option, then that is what is pursued until evidence emerges that it might not be the best.

If there is a tie, then you can pick a direction at random if the scores are low. If both views are ranked at 2, then more time is needed to research and analyze the issue. A trick here might be for each individual to try to make the best case they can for the *opposing* view. If that doesn't lead to a preferred option, then either ask a third party or spend a little time taking forward both ideas until a clearer position and, hopefully, a consensus emerges.

If you really hit a crisis and there seems no way out, seek arbitration. Find someone that everyone in the team respects, perhaps a tutor or professor, manager or mentor, and explain the issues to them and ask them to make a judgment. This might be a simple compromise that everyone was too uptight to see or it might be a ruling in favor of one side or another.

Sometimes differences are not as real as they seem and are mainly due to poor communication and a lack of understanding of what each other mean. These problems should resolve themselves if you try to listen carefully to what the others are saying, perhaps even writing it all down; this act often forces you to be a little more precise than before and can be the key to clarity on both sides.

3.10.2   When Things Go Really Wrong[1]

3.10.2.1   *Appreciative Enquiry*

This method is based on looking at the positives that can be linked with the team, avoiding negatives or apportioning blame; discussing weaknesses and an emphasis on what's wrong; avoiding taking the attitude that the team is failing and needs to be fixed. Try to appreciate what is best in all of us, what is best about the team, and what the team could achieve. Organizations have a tendency to emphasize negatives, to dehumanize and to monitor in order to control when they should be moving forward through constructive dialogue and collaboration.

David Cooperrider (1987) suggested taking *"the best of the past and present . . . ignite the collective imagination of what might be."*

How to do it.

1 *Discover: identify and appreciating the best of what is.* Find out all those things that are good about the team, things they are proud to have achieved, things that made them feel good.

2 *Dream: imagining what might be.* Look for all the aspirations that they share, what would they like to do or to be able to do, where would the team like to be.

3 *Design: discussing what should be.* Find some positive ways forward that would help to achieve the dreams, build upon our strengths, apply what works and makes us feel good to other parts of our work as a team.

---

[1]I am indebted to Kent Beck for bringing this approach to my attention.

4 *Deliver: changing to what will be.* Move forward with practical measures that everyone is comfortable with. Introduce change—changes in the way we feel about ourselves and our team members, changes in the way we communicate, changes in the way we work together—to achieve our dream.

In the context of XP this all makes a lot of sense. We have tried it in Genesys recently and will see how things go:

Genesys group F case study notes. October 2006.

All members present together with a member of the Systems Administration. In case of technical issues.

Background. The team had started on their project—there had been some delays in meeting the customer initially but things were moving along. Some members seemed to think that they were not fully involved and were frustrated and lacked motivation. A problem that had been highlighted was that some were unfamiliar with the programming language—in this case PHP—and would like to have some further training in this. The dominant personality was doing much of the work but some felt that their own contribution was low and progress was slow.

At the meeting we started by drawing out the positives only. Then we went on to the desires before agreeing a strategy for progressing things. This was achieved through gentle prompting using the 4 stages of appreciative enquiry. The designs were suggested by the team through discussion taking care to avoid making suggestions myself.

Discover. The speed code challenge was good—the team did well in this and worked together and enjoyed it—getting a system built and working in a very short time gave them a sense of achievement.

The client meetings were enjoyable and fruitful. Visiting the client's business was good.

The basic design of the Web site was implemented and everyone liked it.

Dream. It would be great to have meetings with the customer every 2 weeks and to show him all the progress that they had made.

We would love to know more about Linux—this was new to most of the team.

We would love to learn more PHP.

We would love to be able to build an attractive Web site that looked as if professional graphics designers had done it.

Design. We will ask the client for more meetings, invite him to the lab.

Systems Admin will give a tutorial about Linux.

We developed a strategy for learning about PHP through some tutorials witrh Systems Admin and hands-on pair programming using a good book on the language.

We will all learn some more about MySQL.

We will all find examples of Web sites that we like and discuss them and try to agree on what are the features that appeal and that could be incorporated in our client's site.

Deliver. This will take place over the next few weeks. We may have to review how things went in a few weeks.

I felt that it was a very positive meeting, the team seemed to be much more cheerful and they had developed some practical ways forward—building on the positive things that they had experienced over the time they had been together. We will see if it works!

Further comments: The first couple of weeks were positive with the team working much better together. Then it emerged that there was another aspect that had not been raised in their *dream* phase—getting a good assessment. This involves applying the Genesys XP process properly, including documenting stories, test sets, and so forth. We have to do this because maintenance of projects will often be done by the next cohort of personnel after this team has left. This issue led to a further discussion with the team and their realization that it was not enough to work together well, the work they did had to be of high quality, also. The team never did really integrate that well although appreciative enquiry helped to make some improvement to matters.

3.11   RISK ANALYSIS

Projects can always go wrong. One way to minimize the impact of this is to carry out a risk analysis. This involves an identification of the *hazards* (things that can go wrong) and their associated *risks* (estimates of the probability of those hazards occurring, and the likely severity of the consequences).

There are many hazards including

technical hazards: using the wrong technology (one that cannot be used to solve the problem) or one that the team is insufficiently experienced with;

planning hazards: the software being developed is too complex for the resources available and the project plans are far too ambitious;

personnel hazards: some of the team members are not capable of delivering, perhaps they are lazy and poorly motivated or perhaps their technical knowledge is weak;

client hazards: the client is too busy or lacks interest in the project, the client is trying to exploit the team by demanding too much for too little, the client's understanding of the operational environment is poor, and so forth.

These hazards relate to the project and its overall management. There are other hazards in the form of delivering an unacceptable final product. XP tries to deal with this by encouraging frequent releases and close client contact. Even this may still fail to prevent problems. Many failures are due to the non-functional attributes not being met (Gilb, 1988).

In order to prevent problems with the non-functional or quality attributes, it is important that these are identified clearly and precisely and a means for testing for compliance developed. Some people say that the functionality is the most important aspect of a solution and this is what should be concentrated on. The thinking is that issues such as performance, reliability, usability, and so forth, can be fixed later and that systems are often more efficient than one might expect. This could be a disastrous policy. It is not just about writing code that runs fast— it is also about making it usable, not just for the individual user in ideal circumstances but also for users in the operational environment. It is important that the team visits the client's business and sees the environment. Projects have failed because of misunderstandings about the sociology of this. These issues will be a concern of a later chapter.

We need to be able to estimate the likely range of variation in these attributes and realize that the risks to the success of a project come essentially from the possibility of actual attribute values finishing up outside the specified range. Thus, the risk to a project must be controlled, and we need to find solutions that will meet at least the minimum required levels for all the critical attributes.

Part of this risk control process therefore involves identifying which attributes pose the greatest risk to the project, and this comes in two forms. Some attributes will be mandatory and others merely desirable. Clearly, we need to focus on the former for most of the time. These critical attributes have to be monitored.

3.12   REVIEW

This chapter has tried to provide some practical guidance about how to organize your XP project team. Most of it is just common sense, but it is surprising how often these simple practices get forgotten in the heat of the moment. By forcing yourselves to act professionally, respect your teammates, and to document and plan your approach, you should avoid many of the common pitfalls that so bedevil software development projects.

Don't assume because you have been made aware of potential pitfalls and ways to avoid them that everything will be plain sailing. There will be problems, some of these will be down to poor organization, not planning the project properly and not delivering what is needed at a time and to a satisfactory level of quality. However, some problems may be beyond your control. Perhaps the client hasn't given you the correct information or hasn't reviewed your ideas quickly enough. Perhaps team members have been ill. There is not much you can do about the latter except try to adapt the project and reorganize the plans and team activities. Sometimes, however, problems arise because of personal differences and lack of interest or commitment among the team. There is no easy solution to this; discussion on the basis of a friendly meeting, perhaps held away from the lab, might be useful. Building a pleasant social atmosphere in the group can be helpful. One senior developer, who is often called in to rescue problem projects in his company, said "Projects must party," meaning that spending some time relaxing together, perhaps over a meal or a drink or some other outing, pays large dividends in terms of morale. Many problems in software engineering are human and social ones and should not be ignored.

EXERCISES

1. Meet with your team members and agree on a mode of working (where and when will you meet), decide on individual responsibilities (e.g., who is responsible for archiving the documentation, chairing meetings, maintaining the project plan, etc.).

2. Read one or more articles on project management—these are readily available. Research into the question: *Why do software projects fail?* Identify some of the possible pitfalls that your project might suffer from; what are you going to do to avoid these?
3. Develop PERT or Gantt charts or some other simple graphic for the project to cover at least the first few weeks.
4. Carry out some risk analysis—how can you control and minimize these risks?

CONUNDRUM

Your project involves programming in a language that is familiar to only one member of your team. Two others have a slight knowledge of the language but have never written anything serious in it. You are trying to do pair programming but the "expert" is getting frustrated because whenever she is paired with another team member, progress is very slow (because much of the time is taken up with explanations of what she thinks is obvious). She feels that it would be better if she worked on her own on the program and the other team members did other things, such as writing documentation and testing.

How should you deal with the situation?

For a discussion of this, see Chapter 11.

REFERENCES

R.M. BELBIN. *Management Teams: Why They Succeed or Fail.* Butterworth-Heinemann, 1981.

B. BOEHM. *Software Engineering Economics.* Prentice-Hall, 1981.

D.L. COOPERRIDER, S. SRIVASTVA. Appreciative enquiry in organisational life. *Research in Organizational Change and Development,* **1**:129–169, 1987.

J.J. ELAM, D. WALZ. A study of conflict in group design activities: Implications for computer supported cooperative environments. *Proceedings of the Twenty First Annual Hawaii International Conference on Decision Support and Knowledge Based Systems Track,* ACM, pp. 247–254, 1988.

T. GILB. *Principles of Software Engineering Management* (S. Finzi-Wokingham, ed.). Addison-Wesley, 1988.

W.S. HUMPHREY. *A Discipline for Software Engineering.* Addison-Wesley, 1996.

J.S. KARN and A.J. COWLING. A study of the effect of disruptions on the performance of software engineering teams. *Proc. ISESE2005.* Noosaheads, Australia, Nov. 17–18, 2005. IEEE, pp. 417–427.

J.S. KARN and A.J. COWLING. A follow up study of the effect of personality on the performance of software engineering teams. *Proc. ISESE2006,* Rio de Janeiro, ACM, Sep. 21–22, 2006.

R. MILLER. When pairs disagree, 1-2-3. In *XP/Agile Universe 2002* (D. Wells, L. Williams, eds.). Lecture Notes in Computer Science, Vol. 2418. Springer-Verlag, 2002, pp. 231–236.

Other Papers and Resources

R.M. BELBIN. *Management Teams: Why They Succeed or Fail.* Butterworth-Heinemann, 1981.

R.P. BOSTROM, K.M. KAISER. Personality differences within systems project teams: Implications for designing solving centers. *In Proceedings of the 18th Annual Computer Personnel Research Conference,* ACM, 1981, pp. 248–285.

P. COSTA, R. MCCRAE. Four ways, five factors are basic. *Personality and Individual Differences,* **13**:653–665, 1992.

A.J. Cowling, J.S. Karn. An initial observational study of the effects of personality type on software engineering teams. Presented at *Proceedings of the 8th International Conference on Empirical Assessment in Software Engineering (EASE 2004)*, 2004, pp. 155–165.

A.J. Cowling, J.S. Karn. An initial study of the effect of personality on group projects in software engineering. Department of Computer Science Research Report CS-04-01, University of Sheffield, 2004.

A.J. Cowling, J.S. Karn. A study into the effect of disruptions on the performance of software engineering teams. Department of Computer Science Research Report CS-04-17, University of Sheffield, 2004.

B. Curtis. Techies as non-technological factors in software engineering. *Proceedings of the 13th International Conference on Software Engineering (ICSE 1991)*, ACM, 1991, pp. 147–148.

J.J. Elam, W.D. Walz. A study of conflict in group design activities: implications for computer supported cooperative environments. *In Proceedings of the 21st Annual Hawaii International Conference on Decision Support and Knowledge Based Systems Track*, ACM, 1988, pp. 247–254.

L. Fernando-Capretz. Personality types in software engineering. *International Journal of Human-Computer Studies*, **58**:207–214, 2003.

A. Furnham. The big five versus the big four: the relationship between the Myers-Briggs Type Indicator (MBTI) and NEO-PI five factor model of personality. *Personality and Individual Differences*, **21**:303–307, 1996.

C.G. Jung. *Psychological Types*, Vol. 6. Harcourt Press, 1923.

I.B. Myers, P.B. Myers. *Gift's Differing: Understanding Personality Type*. Davis Black Publishing, 1987.

R.H. Rutherford. Using personality inventories to help form teams for software engineering projects. *In ACM SIGCSE Bulletin, Proceedings of the 6th Annual Conference on Innovation and Technology in Computer Science Education*, 33:73–67, 2001.

K.T. Stevens, S.M. Henry. Using Belbin's leadership role to improve team effectiveness: an empirical investigation. *Journal of Systems and Software*, **44**:241–250, 1999.

J. Teague. Personality type, career preference and implications for computer science recruitment and teaching. *In The Proceedings of the Third Australasian Conference on Computer Science Education (ACSE 98)*, 1998, pp. 155–163.

http://www.humanmetrics.com/cgi-win/JTypes1.htm.

Chapter **4**

Starting an XP Project

SUMMARY

Meeting the client or customer
- The first attempt at defining the scope of the project
- Some techniques for requirements elicitation
- Basic business analysis
- Functional and non-functional requirements
- Identifying dependencies and constraints
- The structure of a traditional requirements document
- An example of a real requirements document from a project
- Contracts

4.1 PROJECT BEGINNINGS

It is the first stage of the project, and you have now got a client and a brief. Initially, it all seems very daunting, and many students and novice graduates are pessimistic about being able to build something that looks very complicated with a technology or method that is unfamiliar. You will almost certainly succeed if the precautions that I have indicated in earlier chapters are taken. If there is a failure in a team, it is because of individual failures or a breakdown in communication; it is rarely due to the team being technically or intellectually unable to cope. It does depend, of course, on the project scope being appropriate, neither too hard nor too easy, and this requires some judgment and experience on the part of the tutor or manager.

We will assume that you are starting with a set of requirements that includes a reasonably simple initial phase, and you should confirm with your client and/or tutor whether there is a part of the system that is clearly within your capabilities and that can be addressed first in order to gain confidence. In fact, the extreme programming (XP) approach of building things in stages and getting them to work properly will soon build up your confidence.

Running an Agile Software Development Project. By Mike Holcombe
Copyright © 2008 John Wiley & Sons, Inc.

The initial project description may be nothing more than a paragraph, and it might seem to be too vague to allow you to start. Remember, however, that this description is just a starting point to your exploring, with the client, the client's business, its needs, and possible solutions and so there will be a lot of preliminary work to do to define the scope of the project and what a potential solution might look like.

This is not an easy stage of any project, and it is impossible to learn exactly how to do it in books and lectures; there is no substitute for trying it out and reflecting, as you go, on how the process proceeds.

The requirements for a system are a description of what the system must do and how well it must do it.

If we get this wrong, then the system we build will also be wrong.

It is very difficult to get right for the following reasons:

1 The client may not really know what he or she actually wants.

2 The developers may not understand the application/domain.

3 The client's business needs may change.

4 Even when you have produced a complete picture of the required system, this, itself, can lead to new requirements.

Most of all, the key to requirements is

Good communication: between clients and developers, among the clients, and among development team

Analysis: what is the client wanting to do

Inspiration: creating potential solutions to the client's problem

Detail: is every aspect covered and clearly documented

Practical: is it realistic, cost effective, timely

Above all: Does it add value?

Agile development approaches try to address these issues in a coherent and effective way.

4.1.1 Researching the Business Background

We will use *mind maps*—they can be used at many different levels to organize your thinking. For these purposes, business means any organization—so it will apply to the public sector and charities as well as to commercial concerns. We try to understand what the business is, what it does, its markets, customers, employees, suppliers, and so forth.

A *mind map* is a diagrammatic representation of a number of concepts or issues and a relationship between them. It is a technique for structuring and organizing information in a simple but effective way, particularly useful when identifying requirements but also in various other management tasks, for example, in trying to identify priorities and possible courses of action. It is one of a number of similar techniques such as cognitive maps or semantic networks.

Mind maps are diagrams consisting of nodes (sometimes represented as bubbles, with names and possibly annotated with various properties) and links between the nodes, which are also possibly named and annotated and which move outwards from the center toward nodes of increasing speciality.

Figure 4.1 demonstrates a sample analysis for a typical organization drawn using mind maps.

An important aspect of mind maps is their flexibility and adaptability for the task in hand; they do not have to meet some set of definite formal criteria, and so teams can use them for their own purposes. They could be used as an initial stage of thinking and, then, once things are clear and a course of action has been agreed upon, they can more or less be forgotten. If they are used when talking to clients, it is important that both sides understand how to use and interpret them—they are then very useful. They would not, normally, be regarded as a project artifact, although keeping a note of them might help in maintenance and reviews. Researchers have concluded that managers and students find the techniques of mind mapping to be useful, being then better able to retain information and ideas than by using traditional "linear" note-taking methods.

Mind maps can be drawn by hand, either as "rough notes," for example, during a meeting, or can be more sophisticated in quality. There are also a number of software packages available for producing mind maps (e.g., http://www.freemind.org).

4.1.1.1 How to Draw a Mind Map

1 Start in the center with an image of the central topic.

2 From this central point, draw lines out to the next level of concepts.

3 Select suitable key words and print them on the nodes and the lines leading to the nodes.

4 Each word/image must be alone and sitting on its own line.

5 The lines must be connected, starting from the central image. The central lines are thicker, organic, and flowing, becoming thinner as they radiate out from the center.

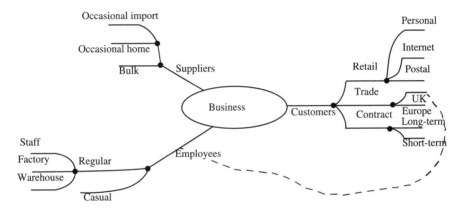

Figure 4.1 A simple mind map of a business.

6 Make the lines the same length as the word/image.

7 Use colors—your own code—throughout the mind map.

8 Develop your own personal style of mind mapping.

9 Use images, symbols, codes, and dimensions throughout your mind map. Use emphasis and show associations in your mind map.

10 Keep the mind map clear by using hierarchy, numerical order, or outlines to embrace your branches.

(See Buzan, Tony. *The Mind Map Book*, 2006.)

The idea of mind maps is to break down a general problem into a number of key concepts over a number of stages. Sometimes we might wish to identify a cross-link—such as some employees are also customers purchasing at trade rates. There is no correct mind map for a given problem, it will depend on the circumstances and the ideas of the individuals involved in the process. It is not meant to produce a definitive view but to act as a vehicle for discussion and eventual understanding.

4.1.2   Exploring the Outline System Description

The initial project description may be nothing more than a paragraph, and it might seem to be too vague to allow you to start. Remember, however, that this description is just a starting point to your exploring, with the client, the client's business, its needs, and possible solutions. There will be a lot of preliminary work to do to define the scope of the project and what a potential solution might look like.

This is not an easy stage of any project, and it is impossible to learn exactly how to do it in books and lectures. There is no substitute for trying it out and reflecting, as you go, on how the process proceeds.

Start with a brainstorm about the initial project brief and use *textual analysis*[1] as well as mind maps, again. To use textual analysis, we need to look closely at the phrases in this statement

---

Loony Tones Corp.

Through the web, the company sells ringtones and video clips for use on the latest generation phones and personal devices.

The company needs a regular supply of new products that are gathered from multiple sources.

A major concern is that some products are very similar to other products—the issues of copyright and illegal downloading are of major concern.

A system is needed that will check whether a ringtone or video submitted by a supplier, composer, and so forth, is distinctive and not a copy of existing material.

---

[1]The analysis of the roles of each word in the grammar of the text.

Are the statements clear or ambiguous? What further information do we need? All of the highlighted phrases need to be checked out.

Loony Tones Corp.

Through the web, the company sells **ringtones** and **video clips** for use on the **latest generation phones and personal devices**.

The company needs a **regular** supply of new products, which are gathered from **multiple sources**.

A major concern is that some products are **very similar** to other products—the issues of **copyright and illegal downloading** are of major concern.

A **system** is needed that will **check** whether a ringtone or video submitted by a supplier, composer, and so forth, is **distinctive** and not a **copy** of **existing** material.

Another example:

SmoothCorp is a company that sells smoothies. They want a system that will allow them to manage their products and sales efficiently. They sell a wide range of smoothies in various quantities and at prices that vary according to the type and size of the drink. The system should allow the company to easily change the products and prices and to permit trends and customer preferences to be identified. The system will also manage the customer base and be seamlessly integrated into the company's existing accounting system.

We need to make a number of things clearer.

What are the range of products and prices—how will these be described?

How often will the product range be changed and by whom?

What sort of trend data do they want to extract and when?

What customer information is needed?

What is this accounts package?

All of these questions will need to be answered in detail. The statement also gives us some leads into both the functionality of the system and the data it will use.

Look for *verbs*: These are words that describe activities—*doing words*—and they will tell us about some of the functions of the system (manage, change, identified, integrated, and so on).

Nouns are used for the names of things and might guide us toward defining data precisely (drinks, customers, products, prices, and so on).

Adjectives are used to describe properties of nouns and might be used to classify objects in the system (e.g., creditworthy customers, sale goods, and so on).

Adverbs describe properties of verbs so they may tell us how well the function needs to be (efficiently, easily, seamlessly, and so on).

From these initial steps, we will drill down into the business and its processes in order to identify what needs doing. The goal is to develop a detailed *requirements document* that will act as part of a contract between the client and the developers. This document will describe the background to the project including any current relevant information. It will list the *functional requirements* (what the system has to do) and the *non-functional requirements* (how well it has to do it). In the latter case, this will address efficiency and speed, robustness, ease of use, and so forth.

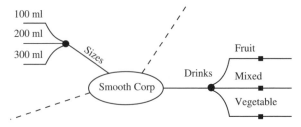

Figure 4.2 SmoothCorp mind map.

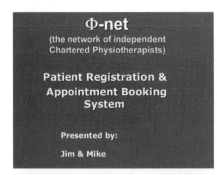

Figure 4.3 An initial presentation on the Φ-net system (also known as Fizzilink).

We have seen some examples of outline project descriptions, and *mind maps* can also help to uncover more of the issues that need to be explored (Fig. 4.2). Don't get into too much detail yet.

We will look at the initial descriptions of a real project that was done by students. This project brief was given by the clients in the form of a presentation (Fig. 4.3).

As mentioned before, these initial descriptions were for actual projects carried out by second-year computer science and software engineering students at the University of Sheffield during the second semester of 2003/2004.[2] We will follow the development of some of the Genesys and Software Hut projects and the appendices contain more detailed information about the system that was built for this client.

Having seen the presentation, the teams were able to ask some general questions of the client. They then had to prepare the groundwork for a more detailed private discussion with the client later.

4.2 THE FIRST MEETINGS WITH THE CLIENT

This might be a session involving all of the teams working on that client's problem and generally involves the client giving more information about their business and what they are trying to achieve—their objectives for the system. There will usually be an opportunity to ask general questions relating to the system, but these should not be technical computing questions (apart from general things such as the sort of network available or to be purchased for the solution). Remember that the client may know very little about computer science or programming, that's why they have come to you; you are the experts. Their expertise is in their business.

If you are not sharing your client with other teams, then the first meeting will be a more informal one. It is important to prepare for it.

Starting with the initial project description, there are a number of things you should do.

Research into your client's business:

Have they got a Web page?

Can you find any other published information about their business?

What do they sell: products, services, or what?

What sort of clients do they typically have?

Who are their competitors; what can you find out about them?

---

[2]In both cases, the students involved in the projects (6 teams of about 5 for each project) competed to build the best solution for the client. For each client, 3 teams used XP and the others used the "traditional" UML design-led approach described in most software engineering textbooks. It was an interesting experiment to see which approach did best; if there was a clear difference. As it happened, the best systems, as decided by the clients, were the XP systems. Furthermore the students who used XP found that it was much less stressful and enjoyable compared with the experience of those who used the traditional method. Some of the reasons for this have been discussed before, and we will return to a reflection of the XP process in the last chapter. Be prepared to engage with this reflection process yourself.

Preparing carefully for the first meeting will impress the client that you are professionals and will give them the confidence to proceed; don't forget that they are giving up some of their time, and this is a cost to their business.

Turn up looking smart, on time, and at the right place. Do not chew gum, turn off your mobile phones, and avoid doing anything that distracts and interferes with the meeting. You need to encourage the clients into treating you as a professional who is interested in the project and eager to deliver an excellent solution. These first impressions are important, you may think that they are trivial or superficial issues, but it is part of the business expectation that the clients will have. In later life, you will have to recognize these things, anyway, so it might as well be now!

It is important that we aim to produce a clearly structured list of requirements, in language that the client can understand, so that an overall description of the complete target system is available. This is developed in discussions with the client. The key thing is to be aware that the requirements will change and to make sure that it is used as a summary of what the current knowledge of the proposed system is. Requirements change is very hard to handle—new approaches to software engineering are being developed to address this including agile development techniques such as those discussed here, but it is a hard problem.

Clients express problems naturally in their own words, words that might be unfamiliar to us or used in different ways; don't assume that your understanding of a particular word or term is the same as theirs. We need to identify what the terminology means and to agree on it.

Write a *glossary* of business and technical terms as you go along, which should be an outcome of this dialogue.

When talking to clients, realize that there may be hidden factors at stake: political, historical, and geographical. You may need to understand these features of a business organization in order to understand the reasons for particular requirements.

The use of Appreciative Enquiry, mentioned in the previous chapter, can also be a valuable technique for developing an understanding with your business clients, especially if there are problems, uncertainties, and confusing signals coming from them.

4.3 BUSINESS ANALYSIS AND PROBLEM DISCOVERY

The initial software requirements analysis can be divided into a number of activities:

Business analysis

Problem recognition

Evaluation and synthesis

Modeling and metaphor building

Specification of user stories and scenarios

Review and discussion

In the first week or two of the project, you should be evaluating and synthesizing the problem and requirements information from the client. Always write down your thoughts, refer to these at your formal group meetings, and put a date on them. Later, you may need to revisit some issue when you have forgotten the details. Although we wish to keep the paperwork to a minimum, records of this stage should be saved, carefully.

What are the primary business objectives of the organization?

How will a proposed system support these objectives?

Is there an existing system—manual or computerized—that will be replaced?

Will the system interact with other systems—both internal and external?

What are the business processes and workflows?

How will the proposed system add value?

Systems will be involved that deal with the purchase and payment of raw materials; recording and despatching customers' orders; the factory production processes; and

A web site, which may include customer-ordering capabilities.

Many systems will have an associated database—this may be implemented as a single unified database or as separate ones depending on the business needs (Fig. 4.4).

Associated with such an *architecture* will be the flows of work and the processes that describe the dynamics of the organization. In Fig. 4.5, we can express the ways in which a user of the system goes through a number of stages to achieve an objective, in this case to purchase a product.

We can capture from the customer some of the main activities of their business or organization in a little more detail than is possible with a *use case*.

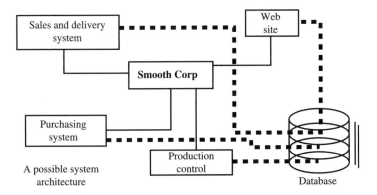

Figure 4.4   An outline architecture of a business system.

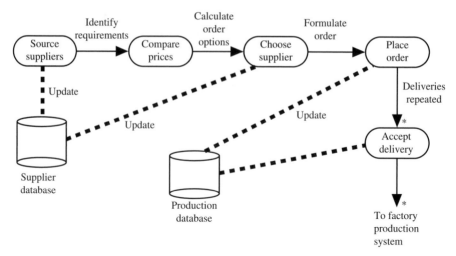

Figure 4.5 Some possible process flows.

4.4 THE INITIAL STAGES OF BUILDING A REQUIREMENTS DOCUMENT

Although we will be using stories as the basis for the software development, it is important to have a clearly structured list of requirements, both functional and non-functional, so that an overall description of the complete target system is available. However, in an agile project, the requirements are dynamic, and the document may not be complete for a long time. This means that development will be going ahead when the requirements are still incomplete. In fact, the implementation of stories will be a way of defining and refining the requirements, but this is not an excuse not to have some record of the proposed system.

This is developed in discussions with the client. At a suitable point we will develop a system metaphor and extract stories from these requirements and start developing the system.

There are a number of reasons why a requirements document may be important. Your client will often want something that can be shown to his or her superiors in order to provide some indication of what is being developed. Naturally, this document may change during the course of the project. It will be built around the stories together with the non-functional requirements and other contextual information. Some in the XP community do not like the idea of a requirements document, seeing it as an unnecessary creation that is not in sympathy with *pure XP*. We have already commented on how some businesses will require such formal statements in order to approve things like project expenditure. The key thing is to be aware that it will change and to make sure that it is used as a summary of what the current knowledge of the proposed system is. We will also consider the issue of contracts. Negotiating a contract and agreeing on a price and a delivery date are very important. We will look at this issue later in this chapter.

The process of carrying out a full *requirements analysis* in a traditional software engineering context is often done at the start of the project and only occasionally revisited in any fundamental way later. In agile approaches, we will have a more continuous dialogue with the client, and so the full requirements document will be a rather fluid document. We emphasize here the construction of an initial one. It will contain not only the functional requirements but also details of important *quality attributes* of the system.

Requirements analysis and specification is deceptively difficult as many clients don't know what they really want and they don't know what it costs or how long it will take to deliver. They often fail to recognize how hard it is to create a reliable system and how long it takes. Some might expect it to be done by next week!

Clients express problems naturally in their own words, words that might be unfamiliar to us or used in different ways; don't assume that your understanding of a particular word or term is the same as theirs. We need to identify what the terminology means and to agree on it. The construction of a *glossary* of business and technical terms should be an outcome of this dialogue.

When talking to clients, realize that there may be hidden factors at stake: political, historical, and geographical. You may need to understand these features of a business organisation in order to understand the reasons for particular requirements. Remember that there are probably more personnel involved in the business, who may have different requirements and different priorities; it is an important but delicate task to ascertain these.

In the first week or two of the project, you should be evaluating and synthesizing the problem and requirements information from the client. Always write down your thoughts, refer to these at your formal group meetings, and put a date on them. Later, you may need to revisit some issue when you have forgotten the details. Although we wish to keep the paperwork to a minimum, records of this stage should be saved, carefully.

You should already be modeling aspects of the client's business processes, in an attempt to clarify and make more specific your understanding of these processes. We will suggest a suitable way to help collect your thoughts together in the next chapter.

You should also be writing code, trying to implement a few basic stories. Before you do this, however, it is necessary to write some simple tests so that you can see how your code works. By the next week, you should be refining some of your ideas and developing code to give you and the client a better idea of what is needed.

Problem evaluation involves:

Defining all external observable relevant business objects;

Evaluating the flow and content of relevant information in the business;

Defining and elaborating all relevant software functions;

Understanding relevant business behavior (events);

Understanding user behavior (tasks);

Establishing systems interface characteristics;

Uncovering additional constraints.

All of these activities are difficult, and simple techniques that will always work are a chimera.

4.5 TECHNIQUES FOR REQUIREMENTS ELICITATION

There are a number of useful approaches that can be used to elicit user requirements and to gain user involvement. Here are four approaches that can be useful:

Interviews

Structured questionnaires

Observation: again only successful, if you can do it unobtrusively

Concurrent protocols: where a user describes his or her tasks while performing them

Interviews have to be prepared carefully. In the first meeting, when you know little about the problem, then it is important to ask the client to describe all the key aspects of the system; try to guide them away from the desire to get to intricate detail about what they want when you simply do not understand what they are talking about. As you get immersed in their business context, it is important to manage the meetings carefully. Identify what you want to know beforehand and prepare a set of questions that will help you to find out what you need. Once these questions are answered, then you can explore further areas. It will often be the case that a question will stimulate the client into telling you some other piece of information—carefully record this. It is best to go to the meeting with all the team, but make sure that there is a principal speaker and someone to record what is said. There is nothing more *off-putting* for a client than to be faced with people asking questions from all angles on all sorts of disconnected topics. Plan your meeting carefully and try to stick to it. The same advice applies to any other stakeholder you meet, such as a user of the proposed system.

If you are not able to meet the client or the user then leaving a structured written *questionnaire* is another technique. Try to group related questions together. Also try to make your questions clear, unambiguous, and relevant. Leave a contact number or e-mail in case the person filling in the form has a query. Make sure that people know where to send the finished questionnaire and try to impress upon them, with tact, of course, that you need it by a specific date if the project is not to be held up.

Sometimes it is possible to visit the client and *observe* the business in action. Here you may be able to observe users in their current work. This is helpful in providing you with a context and a better idea of what the users are like, what they expect or are comfortable with, and what sort of system you might be trying to emulate. Pay particular attention to the sort of user interfaces that seem popular. Take care not to disrupt their work too much. Some users are happy to talk their way through their tasks while you are there.

If a user is prepared to explain what they are doing as they do it and any issues they believe are important, this can be very valuable. Such concurrent protocols can, however, result in a number of conflicts and issues if different users give you different perspectives. This illustrates that there are often organizational complexities, individual preferences, and other issues to resolve.

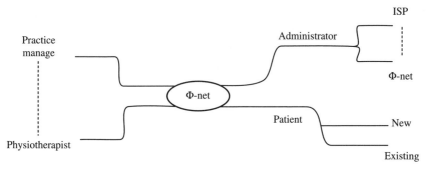

Figure 4.6   Simple mind map showing the Φ-net users.

There are other techniques that can be used in certain circumstances:

> Card sorting: useful if you want to understand the user's classification of his or her knowledge domain;
>
> Carrying out a user role yourself.

Consult a good book of requirements elicitation, for example, Hull (2002).

4.6   PUTTING YOUR KNOWLEDGE TOGETHER

Gathering all this information is one thing, but putting it all together into a coherent model of the business is quite another. There are no simple solutions to this problem. In general, common sense is the best approach; however, a simple but effective way to gather a lot of disparate information into a coherent and structured whole is to use mind maps (Fig. 4.6). See http://www.freemind.org for a useful tool.

4.7   GETTING TECHNICAL

In this phase, we need to think about the system and how it relates to its business environment, its users, and so on. We will do this in a number of stages. Some of these are outlined below. In traditional software development approaches, this phase is lengthy and tends to be inflexible. For example, we could envisage the following sequence of events, with many iterations of this basic approach, each time identifying more of the required system (Fig. 4.7).

   1. *Identify business objects: define all external observable relevant business objects.* We need to look at the sorts of things that are *coherent entities* in the part of the business we are considering. These could include products, contracts, orders, invoices, and such like. Make a proper list of them and try to distinguish between those that are involved with the external activities of the business

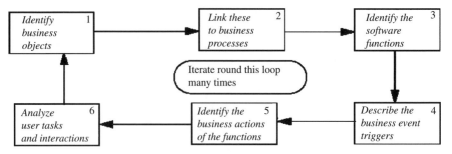

Figure 4.7   Basic stages in business analysis and system identification.

(e.g., objects that are apparent to the customers, agents, and suppliers of the business) and those involved in the monitoring of the company (such as taxation and other government authorities) and the objects that are defined for the convenience of the internal management of the company (these might be internal orders, memos and planning material, records and archives of company activity, etc.).

Many of these objects will relate to aspects of the databases that will be used to support the system activity.

2. *Link the business objects to business processes: evaluate the flow and content of relevant information in the business.* Each business process will involve a number of individual processes that take place in an organized way. What is the order in which this information is processed, what type of information is it? Try to get a general picture of what happens and when during typical scenarios of business activity. You will refer to the business objects described above; if you come across one that has not been identified previously, then it needs to be added to the list. Equally, if you found an object that doesn't seem to feature in any process that you are analyzing, eliminate it. It may be that you find some difficulty in modeling things at the right level; there is always the temptation to try to describe things in too much detail. Try to avoid this at this stage. We are looking for a rather "broad-brush" description of what is going on.

3. *Identify all relevant software functions.* Now we can start imagining what our software is going to do. It might be replacing some existing function, either a manual operation or in some obsolete software, or it might be a new feature that has not been implemented with software before. We will come back to this process in Chapter 6; at the moment, it suffices to write it down as clearly and concisely as possible.

4. *Identify the business event triggers: understand the relevant business behavior (events).* Now we have to try to figure out how these things actually relate to each other. We should try to define some common scenarios that explain the overall operation of the business processes through the medium of identifying the events that cause the scenario to operate. These could be the placing of an order by a customer; here we might need to identify what sort of customer is involved, a new or existing one, trade or retail. The business process involved for each of these may be different, and so the system will be expected to behave differently as well.

This leads to us identifying the different conditions that must apply for the different cases. Again we need to check that our business objects and processes described above are consistent with this.

5. *Identify the business actions of the functions.* What is the effect of the operation of the software function—how does it impact on the overall system? Does it lead to the storage of any information (e.g., updating a database: does it prepare the system for another specific function, etc.). It is at this stage that a clear understanding of how the various software functions fit together is needed—this can be achieved using the metaphor explained in the next chapter.

6. *Analyze user tasks and interactions: try to understand possible user behavior with task analysis.* Task analysis tends to concentrate on the way users conduct business processes now. It may include identifying user actions that do not involve interaction with a computer. Nevertheless, a task analysis model can form a useful representation for discussion with your users, helping to identify aspects of the task with which users are comfortable and familiar and that could be incorporated into the structure of interaction with the required system. Alternatively, it can help identify aspects of the task that are currently problematic and could be improved in the required system.

In an agile approach, it is best to be flexible rather than sticking rigidly to a detailed mechanistic process like this. Look for some of the objects that are clearly relevant and try to identify a coherent collection of basic ones. Many of these will relate to the type of data concerned—see how they relate to the main business processes in the organization, list the sort of functions that might feature in some basic stories, what will trigger these functions, and how are the users expected to interact. Do this with some core parts of the system, they will be extended later, when we have started making some progress and both designers and customers understand each other—and the problem scope—better.

As if requirements capture and analysis was not sufficiently complicated, we must often obtain the views of different users, who are likely to have different stakes in the outcome of the new system. Hence, you may need to identify and resolve stakeholder views. You should ask yourselves, who are your users? They are not necessarily a single, homogeneous group of people with the same tasks, the same goals, or the same view of the world—who are the clients?

In Checkland's (1990) *Soft Systems Methodology in Action*, a distinction is made between clients, who usually commission the system and stand to benefit from its outcomes, and actors.

Who are the actors? Actors are system users, who have to play a part in the system, but who may not directly benefit from it. How are you going to gain these stakeholders' involvement in and commitment to the development process? There is no simple answer—be aware that it is an issue, however. One benefit of an agile approach is that some working software is built very early; this helps to increase your credibility with the stakeholders and provides opportunities to discuss options and understand the issues better through discussion.

At the end of this process, you should have identified the dependencies that the solution needs to relate to within the business context as well as any basic assumptions that pertain. You may also have started to think about the constraints that will affect your solution, the available resources you have at your disposal, time, and technology, and so on. This needs to be clarified; it is no use trying to specify a system that you are not able to build.

4.8   DEVELOPING THE REQUIREMENTS DOCUMENTS

A collection of *requirements notes* can be produced that can help to organize one's thoughts into a more structured form. The aim is to produce a detailed list of requirements that provides a basis for early planning and approval.

The notes should lead to a clear description of the client's background and their objectives. Here are some examples from the Φ-net project.

The *functional* requirements should be stated, eventually, in a tabular form using simple English statements. These will be derived from the user stories as we will see in the next chapter. In fact, the functional requirements document is really just a summary of the story cards as they exist at the time. Where it is necessary to break a complex functional requirement down into a set of simpler ones, do so but try to preserve the connection between related requirements by grouping and numbering them together.

Looking at the Φ-net system, it is clear that one actor or user is the patient and they wish to be able register and upload their details.

Two basic requirements can be briefly stated as

Patients can create an account

Patients can edit their details

These will be *mandatory*—the system must have them. Each will be described in more detail using a story.

Another possible requirement is, *Patients can view past appointments*. This may be less critical—it is an *optional* requirement.

We thus classify each requirement as being

Mandatory: it must be present in the final solution;

Desirable: it should be present if at all possible;

Optional: only implemented if all others are done and there is still time.

Naturally the client will specify these levels, and they may change during the course of the project.

An extract from a set of requirements produced for the Φ-net system is

M: required function

D: desired function

O: optional function

Patient

ID	Description	Priority
1	Patients can create an account	M
2	Patients can edit their details	M
3	Patients can login to their account	M
4	Patients can book an appointment	M
5	Patients can view their booked appointments	D
6	Patients can view past appointments	O
7	Patients can cancel appointments (restrictions apply)	M
8	Patients can delete their account permanently	O

Clinics

ID	Description	Priority
9	Clinic staff can create an account	M
10	Clinic staff can login to their account	M
11	Clinic staff can edit their details	D
12	Clinic staff can add physiotherapists to the clinic	M
13	Clinic staff can view their physiotherapists' appointments	D
14	Clinic staff can add appointments to their physiotherapists' diaries	D
15	Clinic staff can remove a physiotherapist from the clinic	M
16	Clinic staff can cancel appointments from their physiotherapists' diaries	D
17	Clinic staff can delete their account permanently	O

Physiotherapists

ID	Description	Priority
18	Physiotherapists can create an account	M
19	Physiotherapists can login to their account	M
20	Physiotherapists can edit their details	D
21	Physiotherapists can add themselves to a clinic	M
22	Physiotherapists can view their appointments for a single clinic	M
23	Physiotherapists can view their combined diary for all clinics	D
24	Physiotherapists can add appointments to their diaries	M
25	Physiotherapists can remove themselves from a clinic	M
26	Physiotherapists can cancel appointments from their diaries	M
27	Physiotherapists can delete their account permanently	O

If some of the requirements are poorly defined or subject to change, identify them and put some measure on their risk of change, even if it is just a number 1...5 (low risk...high risk) that you allocate on the basis of your best guess given the knowledge you have available. We will find this useful later.

We will use user story cards and their implementations as the main mechanism for determining detailed functional requirements. Once we have got a basic understanding of the system needed, we can then start showing the client real examples of programs that will be the basis for further discussion at the regular (weekly, if possible) meetings. The best approach will be to build lots of little pieces of functionality every day, if possible. Keep thinking in terms of small increments, and the momentum of the project will be preserved. Large gaps between deliverables cause problems for developers, clients, and the project as a whole.

The organization of these meetings is discussed in Chapter 5.

Before that, however, we need to think about data.

If we look at the sorts of things that belong to these outline functions, we can pick out items that represent data—usually these are nouns. Here is an example.

The following will give more detail about some of the data stored by the system:

Patients:

> Each patient is uniquely identified by a username (chosen by the user). The other details stored will be
>
> First name
>
> Last name
>
> Address
>
> Postcode
>
> Date of birth
>
> Daytime, evening, and mobile telephone numbers
>
> E-mail address
>
> A password (chosen by the user)
>
> GP's name and surgery
>
> Cardholder's name
>
> Card type
>
> Card number
>
> Card expiry date
>
> Medical insurance provider (optional)
>
> Medical insurance policy number (optional)

Physiotherapists:

> Each physiotherapist is uniquely identified by a username (chosen by the user). The other details stored will be
>
> First name
>
> Last name
>
> Address (clinic)
>
> Postcode
>
> Date of birth

Telephone number

E-mail address (this could be provided by the system)

A password (chosen by the user)

CSP number

OCPPP number (optional)

Up to three areas of specialism

Clinics:

A clinic will be uniquely identified by a practice number.
The other details stored will be

Practice name

Address

Postcode

Telephone number

Fax number

E-mail address

Practice manager

A password

Appointments:

An appointment will be uniquely identified by an automatically generated appointment number.
Each appointment will also have a

Date

Start time

End time

Patient username

Physiotherapist username

Location

Diary:

A diary will be uniquely identified by a combination of practice number and physiotherapist's username.

A diary will consist of a number of appointments and unavailable time slots.

4.9 SPECIFYING AND MEASURING THE QUALITY ATTRIBUTES OF THE SYSTEM

We talk about two main types of requirements: *functional* and *non-functional*. Put simply, the functional requirement describes *what* the system has to do and the non-functional describes *how well* it is supposed to do it. This is a little simplistic but it will do for a start.

We often put most emphasis on the functional requirements and neglect the non-functional requirements or assume that they are easily dealt with. In fact, identifying the non-functional requirements can be difficult. We need to define them carefully and what is more we need to set some sort of acceptability levels for them and a means of demonstrating compliance with these levels. It is possible to refine the notion of non-functional requirements into two categories: *quality attributes*, which determine how well the system should perform; and *resource attributes*, which constrain or limit the possible solutions to your business problem. Unless these are addressed a system may not be successful, even if all the functional requirements are met.

For most software systems, some of these attributes will be **critical**; that is, unless each of those attributes achieves some required level, then the system will probably not be successful, no matter how well it may meet its functional requirements or meet the goals for its other attributes. Thus it is essential to identify all the attributes and to identify which ones are critical, and then to ensure that they are all met.

4.9.1 Identifying Attributes

The International Standards Organization provides a taxonomy of quality attributes in its draft standard[3] for software systems, ISO 9126 [ISO 9126]. As you read through the following list, based on that standard, make a note of those attributes you believe could be critical to your project. The list is not exhaustive: you may see other classifications of qualities elsewhere and you may identify critical qualities for your system that do not appear here. Some of the issues that are discussed here may not be relevant to your own project. Think about them and focus on those that seem to be the most critical. Discuss this with your client. The ISO 9126 standard is concerned with the quality of the product. There is another standard, ISO 9001, which deals with the engineering process.

There is a view, within agile circles, that non-functional issues can be left until the end as they may only require some last-minute tweaking to be satisfied. This can be misguided for several reasons.

The choice of architecture and implementation language may influence performance or security, and by ignoring these issues, there could be serious problems later.

If the team has built a similar system previously, then they will have significant knowledge about how the system performed and can generalize from that earlier experience. If this is a new type of system or the technology is new, it is risky to leave the non-functional issues to be dealt with at the end.

---

[3]Some may worry about the bureaucracy implied by the introduction of standards. However, companies purchasing and commissioning software are becoming increasingly aware of the standards issue, and some will insist that these standards are addressed.

By defining what some of these mean at an early stage, we can think about how we will demonstrate compliance with them. This is important for the client—he or she then has a clearer understanding of what they have signed up for and it will also provide the developers with mechanisms for getting feedback—to let them know how close they are to achieving the desired properties and outcomes.

New non-functional requirements may emerge as well. For example, the customer may be unhappy with some aspects of the releases the team are demonstrating—some aspect of the user interface may be difficult to use, the time for some of the processing to complete may be unacceptable, and problems like these will lead to a clearer understanding of what is needed.

4.9.1.1 Functionality

Suitability: The presence of an appropriate set of functions for specified tasks. Here we need to link what we are specifying with the business analysis. In an agile project, this will change as we progress through the project with new requirements and stories being explored throughout.

Accuracy: The presence of correct and predictable results from specified input. It goes without saying that the functions in the software should be producing the correct outputs. Test will have to be devised to show this.

Interoperability: The ability to interact with other specified systems. This should be identified and incremental releases delivered so that this interoperability can be tested at the customer's site.

Compliance: The adherence to specified standards, laws, and regulations, if appropriate.

Security: The ability to prevent unauthorized access to programs and data. Again the security requirements need to be identified if they are to be met. Think about the social aspects as well—find out how passwords and other security devices are managed and used within the organization. It's no use building in complex security protection if the operators write their passwords on Post-it notes on the monitors!

4.9.1.2 Reliability

Maturity: The frequency of faults/rate of software failure, ideally we want no faults. This is a desire that is hard to meet under all circumstances. We could set limits to the number of acceptable faults, but this is often impractical as the testing of such claims is impractical in most cases.

Fault tolerance: The continuity of software execution in the presence of faults. Again a desire, but unless one can specify the types of faults expected, it is impossible to test for them in a realistic way. Fault tolerance is usually achieved through redundancy of some aspect of the system.

Recoverability: The ease with which system performance and data can be recovered in the case of system failure. This is an important issue, and systems should be designed so that data can be recovered if there is a system breakdown before the data has been fully committed to a datastore.

Usability: The extent to which intended users of a system are able to achieve their objectives with the minimum of effort, confusion, and time. The system should incorporate an appropriate level of flexibility for users to achieve success, provide a suitable level of support, and fit in well with the operational environment in which it is to be used.

Understandability: The effort required by users to recognize application concepts and their applicability to user tasks. Users will have some kind of *conceptual model* of the system; this may well be of the form "if I see this screen and I am trying to carry out this task then the next thing I have to do is such and such." We will use a simple metaphor diagram in the next chapter to enable the designers to articulate different interface architectures and to analyze their suitability.

In order to test whether a system is understandable, it is necessary to define a number of important tasks associated with the system and to see if representatives of typical users can carry these out satisfactorily (i.e., efficiently and accurately). This can be done on paper or with a mock system and should be done early. Regular meetings with the client should focus on exploring this issue. It is often here that major problems can be identified before it is too late—or expensive—to fix.

Operability: The effort required by users to operate and control the application. We need to define some typical tasks, as we did above, and ask typical users to carry them out with the finished system. Such tests need to be defined and discussed in the requirements document—the client needs to agree that they are an appropriate way to demonstrate what they want the system to be capable of. If you apply these tests to the system and the performance of the trial users meets the level specified in the requirements document, then the client will be generally satisfied.

Learnability: The ease with which an application's functions can be learned. Repeated, similar tasks can soon be learned but there will be many features that are used rarely, and these are often a cause of delays and mistakes. User interface design provides many practical and well-researched guidelines to enable effective and learnable systems to be built.

From the ISO 9241 standard for usability in software and hardware design a number of other issues are identified such as *system efficiency (of time and resources), maintainability, portability*, and so forth.

This list of attributes is much larger than you will require. Select the most appropriate and concentrate on these.

4.9.2 Specifying the Acceptable Level of an Attribute

Having identified critical quality attributes, you need to specify what level or measure of each attribute is acceptable in your system. You should identify at least

The *worst* acceptable level

The *planned* level—be ambitious, but remain realistic!

The *best* level—just to provide a marker for what might be technically possible but infeasible for you

It might be useful to identify the current level (if there is an existing system to evaluate). These levels should be specified and measurable in quantitative terms or metrics. It is not good enough to specify that your system will be "very" efficient, "easy to use," or "extremely" adaptable. You must attempt to define *operational, measurable* criteria against which your system can be judged. This will lead on to defining a set of tests that will establish whether the attribute has been delivered to the required level. We will look at testing in a later chapter, but it will often be important to identify, at least in general terms, what the testing approach will be.

For example, if one of your usability criteria for your system is its suitability for the task:

A measure of its *effectiveness* is the *percentage of user goals achieved in a given time*;

A measure of its *efficiency* is the *time for a type of user to complete a set of tasks.*

A series of experiments (tests) could be organized in which users are asked to carry out some important tasks using the system; we would then be measuring how well these were carried out, how long it took, how many mistakes were made, and so forth. These experiments should be repeated with as many people as possible in order to get a useful result. Alternatively, a measure of *satisfaction*, for example, can be gained on a *rating* scale (e.g., a scale of 1 to 5) by using suitable questionnaires distributed to a selection of users during a trial period of evaluation. If access to real users is not possible in the timescale, you could use some of your friends, preferably those with a similar knowledge of computing, as the intended users of the system.

For each numbered attribute, we will specify a quality level and eventually a test for determining whether it is met in the final, delivered software.

4.9.3   User Characteristics and User Interface Characteristics

It is worth writing down a description of who the intended users of the systems are expected to be. Are any expected users handicapped? Accessibility is the issue of making systems available to handicapped people (e.g., blind people might be potential users), and there is legislation in some countries relating to the design of Web sites and other systems. Check these out.

Some of the basic principles behind your design of the user interface should also be documented. This does not mean that you should design some specific interface options, but some simple diagrams can help the client to visualize how the system might look.

4.10 THE FORMAL REQUIREMENTS DOCUMENT AND SYSTEM METAPHOR

XP has, in the past, worked with the set of stories and the system metaphor as the key planning documents for a project. It is worth taking a look at how these are being used in projects. There has been much confusion about the system metaphor and its role. In some industrial companies, it is no more than a glossary of terms. In others, it includes some simple architectural diagrams and general statements of intent. For a student project with a real client, it makes sense to try to use both the stories and the metaphor as a mechanism for describing the current state of the project in ways that the client can understand.

Thus we propose that these documents become the basis of a requirements document that possesses some of the attributes of the traditional formal requirements document that has been used in the industry for a long time.

The difference is that our requirements document is changing, evolving as the project develops, and so we will produce one at regular intervals. It will be a summary or list of the stories thus far identified, the non-functional requirements, and a glossary.

You must include the following information on any document you produce:

Document type (e.g., requirements document)

Author(s)

Version

Date

The main body of the requirements document should have the following components:

Introduction and background

Elementary business model

User characteristics

Functional requirements

Non-functional requirements

Dependencies and assumptions

Constraints

User interface characteristics

Plan—a schedule of work with milestones, meetings, and deliverables

Glossary of terms (with an index)

The *scope* of the project is described in the *Introduction* and needs to be clarified with the client as far as possible as soon as possible. The requirements will change as we progress; one of the key points about XP is that it attempts to address this, but if the scope changes significantly, we will be in trouble. We will therefore regard the requirements document produced during this phase as an *initial* one that will change as the project unfurls, but it is important that the client, as well as the team, have some idea where they are going.

The document should have clearly defined sections and paragraphs, referenced by number and listed on a contents page. This is vitally important for future cross-referencing between other system deliverables and the requirements specification. As Tom Gilb makes clear, thorough cross-checking is necessary for software reliability. It is also vital when we come to testing that each requirement has a suitable test or set of tests associated with it. This then demonstrates that we have met that particular requirement.

In the future, you will only be able to determine whether your designs, your test plan and test cases, and your coding are complete and correct by reference to the sections of your requirements document.

You should discuss with the client whether they could sign-off the document as a gesture of good faith. It should be made clear, however, that, in the spirit of XP, the requirements are not totally fixed. Explain to the client how XP works, so that they will expect to work with you on the stories and will help to identify the priorities while you try to estimate the resource implications. Tell them that major changes, without good business reasons, will threaten the project. Some changes will be feasible, some not, and it is important to remember that there will be a fixed time limit to the project. It's better to have a good basic and useful system than an incomplete and useless one.

Example

Software Hut Team P: Requirements Document 05/03/2004

Introduction

The system referred to in this document is a system to provide a method of linking together physiotherapists and their customers throughout the country, via the Internet [7], automating the process of appointment booking.

Problem   Many physiotherapists work on their own and have small practices that may not be able to afford to employ a receptionist, in which case a booking for the physiotherapist will have to be taken, usually over the phone, by the physiotherapist. This can cause problems, especially if the physiotherapist is currently working with another patient. If the physiotherapist does not answer the call, there is a possibility of a loss of business, and yet, if he were to answer the phone, then it may be deemed to be rude by the customer the physiotherapist is currently attending to.

Brief   The client wants a system that will allow a general member of the public to book an appointment with a physiotherapist in their area over the Internet. The system must be able to return a list of registered physiotherapist practices in the area they choose, and they must be able to choose a practice and a physiotherapist that they want and book an appointment in a free slot of the physiotherapist's diary. After the customer's choice of diary slot, they will be led to a secure payments page, at which point they will enter their credit card details and will have an appointment booked for them, (provided that the transaction completes successfully). The proposed system aims to automate the process of booking appointments with physiotherapists. This will make the entire ordeal much more efficient for both the physiotherapist and the customer. It should also allow for more business for the physiotherapists as they will no longer be losing as many appointments from missed telephone bookings.

Registration   The system will require that both the physiotherapist and the customer are registered before they may use the system. The process of registration for both parties, however, is very different. The customers will register themselves, filling out their personal details. An account for them will be created with a password. This account will be stored in a database to be recalled every time the customer logs in. The registration part of the system for them will require them to register the practice, and not each individual physiotherapist in that practice. The person who registers that practice will have administration rights for that practice, which will mean that they will be able to edit various parts of the details represented with the practice. It will be from here that the administrator will be able to add the physiotherapists of the practice. For a small practice, the administrator could be the only physiotherapist, but for a larger practice, there may be a secretary. This administrator would be able to add a profile for all the physiotherapists that work in that particular practice. These profiles will be stored in a database. An individual diary will be available for each physiotherapist in that practice. This diary may be accessed and updated by a physiotherapist when they log in.

On top of there being a profile page for individual physiotherapists, it will also be possible to have a profile page for the actual practice, giving details about it, such as address, history of the practice, when established, and so forth. This page will be updateable by the practice administrator at any time. It will be made from a predefined template, keeping a certain standard to all the pages. This template would also have the advantage of allowing people inexperienced with the Internet to create an information page easily. It would be required that each time the customer came to book an appointment, they would have to log in. This is simply done for security purposes.

Appointment Booking   There are, in general, two types of appointments that may be booked by a customer. These simply depend on whether a customer is attending the practice for the first time or whether they are returning. If this booking is the first the customer has made, then the booking will be required to last 45 minutes. If the customer has previously visited the practice, then the duration of the appointment will be a fixed length of 30 minutes. The booking process will require the customer to choose a practice in a location around them, before they can proceed to the stage of actually booking the appointment. In this system, the idea is that a customer will select their county and in doing so will have a list returned to them with a list of cities in that county that have physiotherapists registered in them. The customer will then be able to select a city of their choice and from that will receive a list of all the practices registered in that city. The customer will then be able to select a practice of their choice and from that will be led on to the appointment booking stage. The appointment booking stage will require that the customer selects a date and time for their appointment. If it is their first consultation, then the system will assign them to a physiotherapist in the practice who, on that particular day, has the least appointments thus far. There will also be an option for a newcomer to select a physiotherapist of their choice should they wish to.

For a returning patient, the appointment will automatically be booked with the physiotherapist that they saw at their last appointment, unless they choose otherwise. Once the date and time has been chosen, the customer will proceed, as described above, to the credit card page. Once an appointment has been successfully booked and added to the physiotherapist's diary, an e-mail will need to be sent to the customer, confirming the appointment date and time. It has been decided that because of the need for secure credit card processing, it would not be wise for our team to develop such a system, and so the intent is to redirect to a third-party credit card processing company. This company would be responsible for carrying out the transaction. A function that the system will have to provide for individual physiotherapists will be the ability to add appointments to their diaries. This means that if a physiotherapist was to receive a telephone booking, there would be no possibility of that booking being double-booked by another booking received from this system. In order to speed the booking process for customers, a cookie may be stored on their computer with information like their username (for logging in) and possibly the last practice they attended.

Statistics   There may be certain facts about the system that different users of the system may want to work out. An example of such a statistic is "how many practices are there registered for a particular area?" This kind of query could be used by the owners of the system, but equally, individual physiotherapist practices may want to look up information specific to their practice, for example, their sphere of influence. Such abilities for querying the database will have to be built into the system, and the types of queries available to different users will be different, according to their level of access in the system. For example, the webmaster will have a lot more privileges than will a physiotherapist administrator.

The Physiotherapist's Individual Profile Pages are the pages where a practice administrator would be able to add the profile(s) of members of the practice.

Login is an area where any registered user of the system would be able to log in, and, depending on their privileges, they would be directed to different areas of the system.

Physio Admin is the page where a designated administrator of a practice would be able to add/edit and delete information regarding physiotherapists who work at that practice.

Appointment Booking is the area of the system where a customer would be able to book their appointments with a physiotherapist, as described in more detail above.

Registration is the area of the system that would allow a customer to enter their details into the database or allow a physiotherapist administrator to register their practice.

Links will be an area where anyone who visits the Web page will be able to find other Web sites that may be of use to them. These links will be stored in a database and will be updateable by the webmaster.

In the *key*, "Mandatory" denotes an area of the system that will have to be implemented for the system to function minimally. "Desirable" areas are the parts of the system that will heavily increase the functionality of the system, and "Optional" areas are those that, if not implemented, will not heavily affect the functionality of the system but are areas that need to be considered if the system is to be updated at a future date. These areas are further explained in the *Functional Requirements* section of this document.

Elementary Data Modeling

Thus far, the all areas of the system have been mentioned, but the descriptions of how they handle data have been sparse. This next section of the document aims to describe in further detail specifically those areas of the system where data will be stored. First, we will start with users.

Customer During the registration process, the customer will have to enter details about themselves. The unique identifier for a customer will be the username they choose. The information to be stored about the customer is

Name

Full address

Telephone numbers (home, work, mobile)

E-mail address

Date of birth

GP details (name, surgery name)

Referral source

Physiotherapy Practice When a practice is registered with the service, there will be certain information that will need to be stored about the practice, separate to the information stored about the physiotherapists. The identifying key in this data will be the username of the administrator of that practice. The information required for the practice is

Practice name

Full address

Telephone/fax numbers

E-mail address

Username/name of administrator of practice

Physiotherapist An important thing to consider when talking about the data required for a physiotherapist is the fact that it must be recognized that a physiotherapist must not be tied to one single practice. They must be able to work in more than one practice. The identifier in the table of registered physiotherapists will be a unique number that all physiotherapists are assigned when they become physiotherapists. This number is their CSP number. On some of the CSP numbers, they will begin with a letter, so the registration part of the Web site will have to explicitly explain that the letter is not required. Data that needs to be stored about physiotherapists is as follows:

Name

Contact address

Contact telephone number

E-mail address

D.O.B.

CSP number

Working diary

Any specialist knowledge

Webmaster   This particular user will simply have to have a username and password stored, with the username being the identifier. From the username, the system will know when they log in what privileges they have as a user. There are many fields above for all the different users that are very similar, and so we thought it necessary to create another table, called "User," in which we would be able to store all the shared information about the users of the system. This information is listed below:

Username

Password

Full name

Full address

Usertype (defines the privileges of the user)

E-mail address

Sex

The other areas of the system that require data storage but are not directly related to any users of the system are "Appointments" and "Availability." These are defined further below.

Appointments   The point of this part of the system is to store all the appointments for all the physiotherapists registered with the system. Each time a user makes an appointment, a new row will be added to the table. The identifier for this table is a system-generated number. The information stored is as follows:

Physiotherapist identification number

Practice

Customer

Area of the body the appointment is associated with

The start date and time of the appointment

And the duration of the appointment

Availability   This table is the area that allows a physiotherapist to input into the system the times that he is working and at what practice he will be working at. The identifier for this table is a combination of the physiotherapist's identification number and the practice.

The data that this table stores is as follows:

Physiotherapist identification number

Practice

Date

Start time

End time

User Characteristics

There are four different types of user that have been identified for this system. These are:

Customer: The person who wants to book an appointment with a physiotherapist over the Internet.

Practice administrator: The person responsible for registering the practice and keeping the profiles of physiotherapists up to date. This user may also edit the diaries of the physiotherapists registered with that practice.

Physiotherapist: This user has access to his own diary, and possibly his own profile, but may not access other people's profiles or be able to delete his own.

Webmaster: This user will have access to all areas of the system, including the databases. This user will be able to find out statistical information about the system, change some features of the system, and be able to maintain other areas of the system.

For all the users, we will assume that they will be competent working with the Internet, and we will assume that, particularly for the user "Customer," they will have had some previous experience of purchasing on line. We are not assuming that the users of the systems will be experts, and so we are going to have to provide a system that is straightforward to use and consistent. We will also have to make sure that there will be suitable documentation for the system and suitable help tips on each individual page that the user sees.

Functional Requirements

Listed below are the functional requirements of the system. The rightmost cells in the tables denote the importance of each requirement for implementation. The following define those measures of importance:

M: a mandatory requirement (something the system must do)

D: a desirable requirement (something the system preferably should do)

O: an optional requirement (something the system may do)

The requirements are grouped by user type.

Customer

ID	Requirement	Level
1	Register a new user	M
2	Login to system (if user is registered)	M
3	Search for practices/physios	M
4	Book an appointment with a physio	M
5	Access Links page	D
6	Access Online Symptoms Database	D
7	Access Online Shop	O

Practice Administrator

ID	Requirement	Level
8	Add Physio Profile (physio must be registered first)	M
9	Edit Physio Profile	M
10	Delete Physio Profile	M
11	Register Practice	M
12	Edit Practice Profile	M
13	Delete Practice Profile	M
14	View Diaries	M
15	Edit Diary	M
16	View Statistics	O

Physio

ID	Requirement	Level
17	Register (create new user)	M
18	Edit Profile	M
19	Delete Profile	M
20	View Diary	M
21	Edit Diary	M

Webmaster

ID	Requirement	Level
22	Edit Links page	D
23	Edit Users	M
24	Delete Users	M
25	Add News Items	O
26	Edit News Items	O
27	Delete News Items	O
28	Edit Physio Profiles	M
29	Edit Practice Profiles	M
30	Delete Physio Profiles	M
31	Delete Practice Profiles	M
32	View Statistics	D

Hardware Requirements

Dedicated Web server running Windows Server with ASP.NET

Web server with MySQL support

SQL Database

Users of system need Internet access on computer with javascript installed

Security Issues

Only registered users may book appointments.

Only registered physiotherapists who are part of a practice may take bookings.

Users need to log in using a username and a password in order to access restricted areas of the site.

Concurrency Issues

System should allow users to access the system at the same time, independent of each other.

Two users should not be able to edit the same information at the same time (i.e., practice administrator and physiotherapist should not be able to edit a physiotherapist profile simultaneously).

Concurrency Issues

Online help system will be available.

"Tooltips" and "pop-up" help on forms/buttons, and so forth.

Non–functional Requirements

In this section, the non-functional requirements of the system are detailed. A non-functional requirement either describes how well the system should perform (a quality attribute) or a constraint or limit that the system must adhere to (a resource attribute). The non-functional requirements have been split into the categories of reliability, usability, efficiency, maintainability, and portability.

Reliability

The system should not allow invalid input from the user that would lead to it crashing.

The system should have security features installed to protect the information stored about the users, so that they cannot be accessed by any third party (i.e., hackers).

Usability[4]

User registration process should not take longer than 5 minutes.

Practice registration process should not take longer than 10 minutes.

Physiotherapist registration process should not take longer than 10 minutes.

A registered user should not have to log in anew each time he visits the Web site from the same computer, but should be requested for the password when he tries to enter a restricted area.

A registered user should be able to look up a physiotherapist and book an appointment within 5 minutes.

---

[4]These figures depend largely on both the speed of the user-end Internet connection and the Web host.

The Web site should be viewable on any computer with a screen resolution of at least 800×600.

Efficiency[5]

Any page on the Web site should load up within 30 seconds.

Maintainability   The system should be easy to maintain through the use of legible and well thought-out code and structure. Also, the webmaster has access to administration pages for the Web site.

Portability   The Web site should be viewable on any PC (running Windows or any other OS) or Macintosh that has a screen resolution of at least 800×600 and that has a connection to the Internet and a Web browser installed that is capable of reading HTML, displaying pictures, and running javascript.

Dependencies and Assumptions

For our system, it is assumed from information gathered from the client that they were thinking of hosting the Web site on their own server, which it has been assumed would be running a Windows operating system and also be running the Internet Information Services (IIS), which is dependent on the operating system, and also have a permanent Internet connection. This is because the client said they would prefer a Windows-based system if they were to host it themselves. If they don't host the Web site themselves, then it has been assumed that the Web hosting company that is going to be used will be a Windows-based server host. Also, it has been assumed that the Web servers will be capable of running ASP.NET Web pages and also running a "mySQL" database.

Also, any practice registering with the Φ-net community will need to have an Internet connection so they are able to use all the services provided by the Φ-net Web site. It has also been assumed that only patients with an Internet connection at home or that have access to one will be able to use the system.

Another assumption is that the performance of the system will very much depend on the Web host and the Internet connection or both the server and client.

Constraints

The first proposition that was proposed was the use of PHP CGI scripts along with ASP.NET and JSP, all of which do a similar thing. JSP was rejected on the principle that no one in the group had any previous knowledge of the technology. This just left the choice of implementation between PHP and ASP.NET, which two members of the group have experience of, but the choice came down to the fact that the client had requested that is was to be run on a Windows-based server. Therefore, ASP.NET was chosen due to the performance qualities of it compared with PHP scripts. To permanently store the data, both storing it in a Microsoft Access database and a mySQL database were considered. It was decided in the end to store the data using a mySQL database, due to its open source and free availability. The database would then communicate with the ASP.NET pages via ODBC.

---

[5]These figures depend largely on both the speed of the user-end Internet connection and the Web host.

User Interface Characteristics

All the users of the system will have experience with Windows applications and will have used similar Web pages before, so it was believed sensible for the system to look and feel like a normal Web-based system. By this, we mean it has Web pages, icons, menus, links, and pointers. This style reduces the time necessary to perform certain operations, and we know that the client would value this as they like patients to be able to book appointments as quickly as possible.

With this style, interactive objects such as buttons, list boxes, and radio buttons are used to enable things to be done quicker. These are used in most Web-based applications so we have no doubt that the patients and physiotherapist who will use the system will understand how these types of objects work.

In designing the user interface for our system, we shall try to follow these principles (Neilson, 1993):

- Be consistent throughout the whole interface of the system so the user feels comfortable and able to use it. Simple and natural dialogue, having no irrelevant information, using a natural and logical order.

- Provide shortcuts, so expert users can perform operations in a quicker time.

- Minimize user memory load—reduce the amount of information the user has to remember by presenting it on the screen.

- Provide feedback, ask for confirmation on irreversible actions like when making the booking for an appointment.

- Good error messages, written in plain friendly English such that it doesn't threaten the user and so the user can understand them, and provide some options to correct the situation.

- Clearly marked exits—allow the user to exit any part of the system and go back to a previous page at any time.

- Prevent errors, stop them from occurring in the first place so then there is no need for good error messages as their won't be any errors.

- Simple and natural dialogue; all relevant information should be written in natural good English and should follow a clear logical order.

- Speak the user's language; everything should be written in a way such that it is easy for the user to understand.

- Help and documentation should be well written and easy to follow and understand.

4.10.1 Commentary

In general, the description is reasonably clear.

The individual functional requirements will be expanded greatly in terms of stories that will describe the functions of the system; the current ones here are a little too brief.

Some further details could be given—here is an example from another team's requirements document for the same system:

Example

Narrative Models (Functional Requirements)

Set availability	Author: SR	Date: 05/03/04	Version: 1
Purpose	Allows the *physio* to "block-out" time in his *diary* for breaks, holidays, etc.		
Actors	*Physio*		
Objects	*Diary*		
Preconditions	*Physio* exists, *Physio* is logged in.		
Description	The *physio* can view his *diary* and set periods of "unavailability." The system should check that no appointments have been booked within this period [**! Appointment Booked**].		
Post conditions	Appointments can no longer be booked in this time period.		
Exceptions	[**! Appointment Booked**] An appointment is booked within the request unavailability period. [**? Remove Appointment**]		

A diagram describing some of the basic architecture of the system and the workflows and processes involved would have been helpful. If such information is provided, then it should be in a form that the client can understand,

The main omission is the lack of any indication of how the screens will look and how you will navigate between them.

Many clients and users think of software systems in terms of sequences of screens with their associated operations and links to other screens.

Figure 4.8 demonstrates an example from another Software Hut project that involved building a document management system.

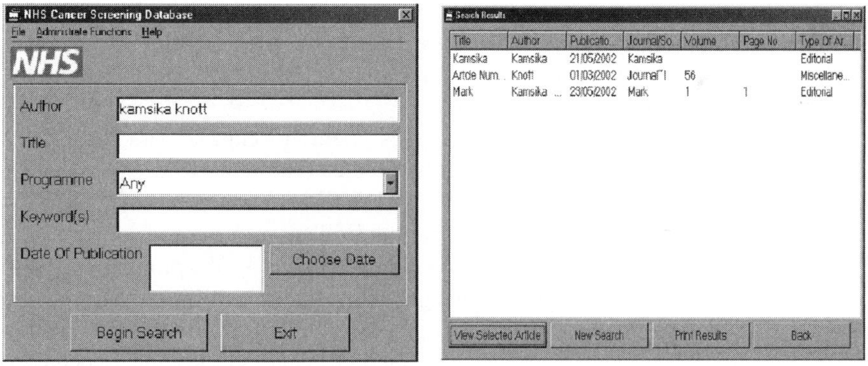

Figure 4.8   User interface screens.

We will see some examples of useful descriptive diagrams for system architectures in a later chapter.

4.11 CONTRACT NEGOTIATION

Any business activity involves parties exchanging products or services for some return, usually in terms of money. For simple transactions, there is no need for a formal contract. Software development, however, is a complex process, and a contract is vital.

The two parties to a business relationship will, at the outset, hope that trust and mutual respect will underpin the relationship, but it is always sensible to try to formalize the understandings relating to the business deal—we will build this software for you, and you will pay us for it.

The contract will be a document that defines each party's responsibilities to the other. It will describe the terms for the exchange of the assets (software for money) and describe the expectations of each party (for the client: what the software will do, how well it will do it, when it will be delivered, any after-sales service, and so on). The software developer will expect to see the agreed price and the obligations of the client in terms of providing access to appropriate aspects of the client's business—access to staff for requirements capture, examples of data, processes, and other necessary detail.

Standard formats for contracts exist and can be customized for a specific project. The contract will need to include a copy of the requirements document—although there will be an understanding in an agile development project that this will be a dynamic document and these may change.

The basis of the pricing of the contract can vary. For an agile project, the best approach is probably a payment by time (in other words, to state that each month of work on the contract will cost so much and the length of the contract is less defined—an overall desire to produce a system to suit the client's business need—might be the basis for the contract). This does bring great dangers for both sides, and if the customer–developer relationship is not a strong and positive one, there will be the risk of problems later on.

Nearly all the projects we have done have been negotiated on a fixed price and, in most cases, a fixed delivery date. This is because most of our customers are small businesses, charities, and so forth. The length of the university teaching term also tends to impose a fixed deadline as well.

This has its advantages as it encourages clients to engage with the process quicker—to think about their requirements more carefully and to deliver data and other information quicker.

For such a fixed-price contract, a fairly detailed requirements document is needed. This plays two roles. It provides a reference point for the project—although both parties will need to accept that changes will happen and those changes come with a risk to both the deadline and the cost. It also provides an audit trail for directors of finance in some companies who are uncomfortable sanctioning expenditure without some sort of statement of what will be received in return.

When an agile development company becomes more established with regular customers and a good reputation, it may be able to develop a long-term association with some customers to provide software development on a service basis—an ongoing succession of projects and maintenance that would be negotiated on the basis of payment for work done paid for at a "regular" rate (i.e., the contract would specify the cost of development support per month or similar).

The stronger the relationship becomes and the more involved in strategic planning that the software company becomes, the deeper the agile development process can become.

Note that if the project is being done as part of a university course, then the university may have some intellectual property stake, for example some universities claim these rights on all work carried out by students in their courses, so in this case some negotiation needs to take place to clarify the position.

Example Contract

Software Development Agreement

This SOFTWARE DEVELOPMENT AGREEMENT ("Agreement") is made BETWEEN ************** with offices at ******************** ******** ("Client"), and Genesys Solutions, with offices at 211 Regent Court, Sheffield ("Provider"). Client desires to obtain the services of Provider to assist in developing certain Software described on Annex A hereto, and Provider is willing to provide the development services (the "Services") subject to the terms and conditions set forth herein.

NOW, THEREFORE, in consideration of the foregoing and the mutual covenants, representations and warranties contained in this Agreement, Client and Provider agree as follows:

1. EFFECTIVE DATE
   This Agreement shall be effective as of *************** (the "Effective Date").

2. DEFINITIONS

   (a) "Software product" shall mean the computer programs in machine readable object code form and any subsequent error corrections or updates supplied to Client by Provider pursuant to this Agreement and as described in Annex A.

   (b) "Documentation" means the documents, manuals and written materials (including end user manuals) referenced, indicated or described herein or otherwise developed pursuant to this Agreement.

   (c) "Deliverable" means the software code in object and/or source format as set forth in the Annex A, provided that if not specified delivery shall be in object code format.

3. APPOINTMENT AND SERVICES

(a) Appointment and Acceptance. Client hereby retains Provider to provide the development services set forth below, and Provider hereby accepts such appointment on the terms and conditions contained herein. Provider will use all commercially reasonable efforts to develop the Software product described on Annex A hereto. Provider, at its sole cost and expense, will furnish the supplies and research, engineering and other personnel reasonably necessary to perform such Services unless otherwise offered by Client to the Provider at the expense of Client. In performing the Services hereunder, Provider hereby warrants to Client that it will perform all Services in a professional and timely manner and substantially in accordance with the standards and practices of care, skill and diligence customarily observed by similar companies under similar circumstances at the time they are rendered. Provider, however, does not guarantee specific results, and the Software will be developed only on commercially reasonable efforts basis.

(b) Compensation. As compensation for Provider's performing the Services hereunder, Client shall pay to Provider a development fee as set forth on Annex A hereto in accordance with the time frame set forth therein.

(c) Bug and Error Fixing. Provider ensures completed testing of all products before they are handed to the client, however there are some circumstances when it becomes apparent that the product does not fully meet the functional requirements as set by the client. In these circumstances Provider will advise Client and request guidance with regard to cost overrun if necessary.

4. OWNERSHIP OF INTELLECTUAL PROPERTY RIGHTS

The parties acknowledge and agree that all Work Product derived from the Services performed by Provider hereunder (the "Work Product"), including, but not limited to, the Software Product, and other product documentation prepared by Provider, if any, shall be considered to be a "work of The University of Sheffield" and that such Work Product and the intellectual property rights embodied therein are and shall become the sole exclusive property of The University of Sheffield. Client shall not, and it shall cause its affiliates not to, seek any copyright, patent, or other protection for the Work Product, and The University of Sheffield shall have the sole right to seek copyright, patent and other protection for such Work Product. At Provider's reasonable request and expense, Client shall take, and shall cause its affiliates to take, all actions requested by Provider in order to protect and perfect its rights in and to the Work Product in the United Kingdom and throughout the world.

5. CONFIDENTIALITY

The parties may wish, from time to time, in connection with work contemplated under this Agreement, whether before or after the date hereof, to disclose to each other proprietary information, data, know-how, designs, drawings, specifications, test and research results, market studies, price or cost information, supplier or customer lists, regulatory files to the extent they are not public information by law and other similar materials ("Confidential Information"). This Confidential Information will be treated as trade secrets and held in confidence. Provider and Client will use Confidential Information only in a manner consistent with this Agreement and may not disclose any Confidential Information to any third party during the term of this Agreement or for a period of one (1) year from the date of disclosure, whichever is longer. Non disclosure obligation stated in this section (5) shall not apply to information that:

(a) was disclosed pursuant to written permission by Client and Provider;

(b) is already in the recipient party's possession at the time of disclosure thereof;

(c) is a part of the public domain through no fault of the recipient party;

(d) is received from a third party having no obligations of confidentiality to the disclosing party;

(e) is independently developed by the recipient party; or

(f) is required by law or regulation to be disclosed.

6. TERM AND TERMINATION

(a) Term. The term of this Agreement as it relates to the development of the Software Product shall commence on the Effective Date ********* and, unless modified by mutual written agreement by the parties or terminated pursuant to the terms of this Section 4, will continue until completion.

(b) Termination. In the event that either party shall be in default of its materials obligations under this Agreement and shall fail to remedy such default within thirty (30) days after receipt of written notice thereof, this Agreement may be terminated 30 days from date of written notice. Termination or cancellation of this Agreement shall not affect the rights and obligations of the parties accrued prior to termination. As its sole liability upon termination under this section, Client shall pay Provider for all reasonable expenses incurred or committed to be expended as of the effective termination date, including salaries for appointees for the remainder of their appointment. Any terms of this Agreement which by their nature extend beyond termination shall survive such termination.

(c) Return of Materials Upon Termination. Upon termination of this Agreement for any reason, Provider shall furnish to Client all completed deliverables, work in process, incomplete work and other material embodying such work performed in connection with the provision of the Services under this Agreement.

(d) Survival of Certain Rights and Obligations. On termination or expiration of this Agreement, each party shall immediately return to the other party all Confidential Information of the other party in its possession. In addition, notwithstanding anything in this Agreement to the contrary, Sections 4, 5, 7 and 8 shall survive termination of this Agreement, however caused and shall continue thereafter in full force and effect.

7. INDEMNITY

(a) Provider will defend or settle at its own expense any suit or action which may be brought against Client for alleged infringement in the United Kingdom of the copyrights or trade secrets of others by reason of the Provider's design and/or development of the Software, and Provider will identify and hold harmless Client from and against all damages and costs which may be adjudged or decreed against Client on account of such infringement; provided, however, that Client shall have given prompt notice, in writing, to Provider of any claim of such alleged infringement and of the bringing, or any written threat of the bringing of any such suit or action, and Client shall have permitted Provider by its counsel to defend or settle the same; and provided, further, that Client shall not settle or compromise any such suit or action without the prior written consent of Provider. If any Software is finally adjudged to so infringe, or in Provider's opinion is likely to become the subject of such a claim, Provider shall at its option, either

(i) procure for Client the right to continue using the Software,

(ii) modify or replace the Software to make it non infringing, or

(iii) refund the fee paid, less reasonable depreciation, upon return of the Software.

Provider shall have no liability regarding any claim arising out of:

(1) use of other than a current, unaltered release of the Software, unless the infringing portion is also in the then current, unaltered release,

(2) use of the Software in combination with non-Provider software, data or equipment if the infringement was caused by such use or combination,

(3) any modification or derivation of the Software not specifically authorized in writing by Provider, or

(4) use of third party software.

THE FOREGOING STATES THE ENTIRE LIABILITY OF PROVIDER AND THE EXCLUSIVE REMEDY FOR CLIENT RELATING TO INFRINGEMENT OR CLAIMS OF INFRINGEMENT OF ANY COPYRIGHT OR OTHER PROPRIETARY RIGHT BY THE SOFTWARE.

(b) Except for the foregoing infringement claims, Client shall indentify and hold harmless Provider, its affiliated companies and the officers, agents, directors and employees of the same from any and all claims and damages, losses or expenses, including lawyers fees, caused by any negligent or intentional, knowing or reckless act of Client or any of Client's agents, employees, officers, directors, subcontractors, or suppliers.

(c) NEITHER PARTY TO THIS AGREEMENT NOR THEIR AFFILIATED COMPANIES, OFFICERS, AGENTS, DIRECTORS AND EMPLOYEES OF ANY OF THE FOREGOING, SHALL BE LIABLE TO ANY OTHER PARTY HERETO IN ANY ACTION OR CLAIM FOR CONSEQUENTIAL OR SPECIAL DAMAGES, LOSS OF PROFITS, LOSS OF OPPORTUNITY, LOSS OF PRODUCT OR LOSS OF USE, WHETHER THE ACTION IN WHICH RECOVERY OF DAMAGES IS SOUGHT IS BASED ON CONTRACT, TORT (INCLUDING SOLE, CONCURRENT OR OTHER NEGLIGENCE AND STRICT LIABILITY), STATUTE OR OTHERWISE. TO THE EXTENT PERMITTED BY LAW, ANY STATUTORY REMEDIES WHICH ARE INCONSISTENT WITH THE PROVISIONS OF THESE TERMS ARE WAIVED.

IN WITNESS WHEREOF, the parties have caused this Agreement to be executed as of the day and year first above written.

CLIENT:	*PROVIDER: Genesys Solutions*
By:_____ *Signature*	By: *Signature*
Title:_____	Title:_____
Date:	Date:

ANNEX A

Software to be developed:

1. Ruby on Rails Web site for Cystic Fibrosis patients

Compensation for delivery and timing of payments for software product:

DELIVERY: ************** (the delivery time does not include delays due to information not provided by Client in a timely manner).

PAYMENT: £******** GBP payable upon completion of all requirements described in Annex B and delivery of said software.

ANNEX B

Set out below are the requirements as captured by Genesys Solutions for the E-Commerce system.
Requirements
Functional Requirements
Key
M = Mandatory: This requirement forms part of the contract and must be delivered.
D = Desirable: This requirement should be implemented at the discretion of the Provider, time permitting.
O = Optional: This requirement will only be implemented at the discretion of the Provider.

General System Functions

Name	Description	Priority
User registration	Ability to add a user to the Web site	M
Secure user login	A user must log in to the Web site	M
Meals	Ability for a user to create a meal from a list of food items	M
User details	Ability for a user to manage their account details	M
Administration	Ability for an administrator to manage the list of food, food categories, content items, capsules, new items, user accounts, and Web links	M
Capsules game	User can play a guessing game for the number of capsules to be taken with a created meal	M
Fat content game	User can play a guessing game for the gram of fat in a food item	M
Check capsules for meal	Ability to check the correct number of capsules required for a meal	M
Menus	Ability to create a menu from a set of meals	M
Printing	Ability to print a menu	M

One comment that many make is why do we have to have all this paperwork, detailed requirements, contracts, and so forth? Although many projects are successful, the customers and the developers are in full agreement and no disputes arise, the teams are stable and the project proceeds without a hitch, this is not always the case. Sometimes projects are affected by problems, sometimes with an external cause, but problems that can be difficult to deal with.

The customer may change—perhaps they have left the client organization or have been transferred to another section. Some team members may change or leave or the development company has another urgent problem to deal with that may impact the project—this is very common and often caused by having to deal with problems from previous projects.

Sometime the client can get greedy, some clients drive a very hard bargain and start demanding far more than they are prepared to pay for; sometimes the lawyers can get involved if things turn nasty!

All of these things have happened to us. The production of signed agreements, whether they are outline requirements documents or contracts, has provided us with a pretty watertight defense position. It is always worth the trouble so that everyone involved knows what the situation is.

4.12 CASE STUDY: THE IMPACT OF ORGANIZATIONAL POLITICS—LEARNING FROM A FAILED PROJECT

We did a project with a police department to provide an information system for their *domestic violence* caseload.[6] The national police database contains information about the villains—details of the charges, court decisions, prison sentences, and so forth—but nothing about the victims. The role of the police domestic violence department is to support the victims as well as to catch the villains. The system built provided an integrated system to do this. The project was very successful and has become a core part of the police department's facilities—for example, in the case of a murder, the first thing that detectives do on returning from the crime scene is to consult DOMINIC (the system) to see if the victim might be on record. Many murders are the result of domestic incidents with the villain known to the victim. If there is a record of violence toward the victim, then the perpetrators might be worth interviewing.

The system has been running for 3 years now and has never malfunctioned in any way.

After the success of DOMINIC, we were asked to build a more ambitious system: this time there were eight different agencies involved. It had been clear for some time that the many different organizations involved in issues relating to domestic violence—police, hospitals, housing services, social services, and various victim

[6]Built by a Software Hut team.

support charities—were not talking to each other enough. There had been some high-profile tragedies where young children had been murdered by their "carers" even though many people knew that they were at risk—but not the agency with the power to do something about it.

The clients—a committee formed from these eight agencies—wanted an integrated information system so that they could each record their cases and could then share appropriate information with each other to prevent such tragedies in the future.

At the start things went well, and some basic information was collected from the clients. Finding a time when every member of the committee could meet was problematic, however. It soon became clear that the different agencies had very different outlooks and policies and it was going to be a challenge to get agreement. Some of the clients, particularly the charities, were anxious about the involvement of other authorities such as the police. They did not want other agencies to have direct access to their data.

We devised a scheme whereby there was one central, Web-based database that was very secure—all the data being encrypted on the database—and that was designed so that each agency had an independent secure zone on the server. To provide a basic alerting mechanism it was implemented so that whenever an agency (say Agency A) entered into the system details of an individual who was already present in the database of another agency (e.g., Agency B), a window would pop up to say that Agency B had records relating to this person—thus giving Agency A the option of phoning Agency B to see if there was any important information that needed sharing.

This solution—even though it offered very strong protection to the data—was not acceptable to some of the charities. Eventually the project was abandoned by the committee. Organizational politics, lack of trust, and serious social issues were the main reasons for failure.

One issue was that the different agencies had different policies relating to the privacy of data and client confidentiality. These, although significant, were not insurmountable.

The real problem was a social one. Many of the people that the agencies dealt with were very vulnerable and often frightened. Such people may not come to the charities, for example, if they believed that that this action might lead to others finding out—maybe the police or a violent family member—which could cause them serious problems. A phenomenon that several agencies found was that some of their clients would not tell them their correct name or address in case it got into the wrong hands. This, of course, causes great problems for designers of databases as the quality of the data may thus be very poor. It's a fact of life, however, that in the real world these issues happen. A national database for the probation service was abandoned for the reason that many criminals have many aliases and the system did not provide a mechanism for entering several names (including false ones) for the same person.

We tried hard to resolve these issues but ultimately we failed—even agile development cannot cope with everything!

The most important lesson is that the politics of organizations and unforeseen complexities derived from human behavior can provide almost insurmountable obstacles to a successful project. A lack of understanding of how the social environment within which the application is deployed can ruin otherwise good software.

Ethnographic studies are sometimes used to try to avoid these issues (Hughes et al., 1995; Martin & Sommerville, 2004).

4.13 REVIEW

We have concentrated on the discussions with the client and the formulation of the requirements for the project, both functional and non-functional. It is important that you maintain good communications with the client so that he or she knows what you are thinking about. Having a client on-site is a rare luxury. Later, when we get down to more detail, we will need to regularly review progress with the client, and establishing the right language and concepts to use is vital. We have considered the structure of a fairly formal requirements document, one that might form the basis of an agreement with the client about what you hope to deliver.

After the first meeting, you will have some ideas about the scope of the project. This is important, and we will refer to the scope as being an important part of the requirements.

Exercise

Read the requirements document example carefully. *Criticize* it, in particular:

Are all the terms clear?

Are the functional requirements consistent, unambiguous, and repetitive at the right level of detail?

Are the non-functional requirements clearly defined; do they have suitable acceptance levels and procedures identified?

How would you deal with any significant change in the requirements introduced by the client?

Would it be easy to maintain?

CONUNDRUM

Your team is in trouble. The client has not been in touch with her feedback on the proposed system. She doesn't have much experience in IT and only has a rather vague idea of what she wants. There are no similar systems known to you that you can show her. You need to start getting some requirements identified and some initial stories prepared.

Do you (a) wait until she has thought further about the system she wants? or (b) build a simple prototype using your imagination and background research in order to show her something that might stimulate her ideas?

REFERENCES

J. NEILSON. *Usability Engineering*. Academic Press, 1993.

T. BUZAN, B. BUZAN. *The Mind Map Book*. Pearson, 2006.

P. CHECKLAND, J. SCHOLES. *Soft Systems Methodology in Action*. John Wiley & Sons, 1990.

T. GILB. *Principles of Software Engineering Management* (S. Finzi-Wokingham, ed.). Addison-Wesley, 1988.

J. HUGHES, J. O'BRIEN, T. RODDEN, M. ROUNCEFIELD, I. SOMMERVILLE. Presenting ethnography in the requirements process. Presented at the *Second IEEE International Symposium on Requirements Engineering (RE'95)*, March 27–29, York, UK, 1995.

L. HULL, K. JACKSON, J. DICK. *Requirements Engineering*. Springer, 2002.

D. MARTIN, I. SOMMERVILLE. Patterns of cooperative interaction: Linking ethnomethodology and design. *ACM Transactions on Computer-Human Interaction*, **11**(1): 2004.

Web Sites

http://www.issco.unige.ch/projects/ewg96/node13.html.
http://www.freemind.org.

Chapter 5

Identifying Stories and Preparing to Build

SUMMARY

Creating stories and learning how to analyze and negotiate with stories.

- Identifying functional requirements.
- Checking non-functional requirements and quality attributes.
- Managing the customer.
- Techniques for estimating resources.

5.1 LOOKING AT THE USER STORIES

The business problem has been studied quite extensively, and we are now keen to make a real start. After all, we have spoken about progress being measured in functioning software, so we need to get coding!

The details that we have relating to the proposed system may seem quite daunting, and we need to take a breath and try to find something simple and useful to do.

Looking at the list of stories that have so far been identified, it may not be obvious where to start. The customer may be able to steer us toward what he or she thinks is important, but they will look at things from a business perspective, and the technical issues of building stories may not be clear to them. We, however, have to choose something that will create confidence and a sense of achievement early.

In the first case, the stories will probably comprise short sentences that describe the purpose of a small element of software, thus they could be a statement such as

"Users can login to the system" or "Users can enter the customer details and validate data on entry" or "Patients can create an account."

The key to an agile approach is to ensure that each story can be implemented in a short time period—2 weeks at the most. It has to be a coherent and clearly identifiable software function that is not too complex. The problem is that the right level of complexity in a story can sometimes be hard to define and requires a lot of experience to be able to do it without too much trouble. For those with less experience, it is important to approach the problem in a simple, structured way.

In order to think about these issues in a clearer way, it is useful to identify a sequence of actions and events that are recognizable from the perspective of a user interface. If this produces a large collection of inputs and events, then it is likely that the story is too complex. Many users and customers think about their system in this way, and it is important to try to identify how a system might work from that viewpoint. However, some stories will involve internal types of processing that has no explicit representation in the user interface.

In a large-scale industrial application, there may be many teams or departments that collaborate in the development of a large piece of software. Here the relationship might be one whereby a team acts as clients to another team and will develop stories that are of a more technical and specific nature. The principle is the same: Try to write down the story in clear language using well-defined terminology, and if your team is providing the software development effort, engage fully with the clients or customers in discussing the meaning, the relevance, the priorities, and the costs of the stories.

In your project, however, you are probably the only team involved, and your client will provide you with the key concepts for their business processes and business needs.

We'll take some simple examples of user stories from some of the systems we have built to illustrate the process.

Our starting point is the requirements document. In this we have identified a number of functional requirements, and that is what we need to look at.

Each one of these has the potential to become a story. It depends on the level at which you described the requirement. We will assume that if they are too *high level*, then you have broken them down into a series or sequence of simpler activities. For example, the decomposition of the requirement to be able to set tests in the Quizmaster system (a system that teachers can use to create on-line tests) to the subactivities of setting questions and forming a test from a collection of questions.

The initial analysis of a story is to identify the business process that it refers to. To do this consider two basic things: what is being done and to what. In other words, there is some operation described in the story that is prompted by some intervention— normally a user action, but it could be a signal from an external component or system, such as a sensor or something similar. This operation will affect some aspect of the system or its data and will usually produce some observable effect.

Now we create a card for each story; this will provide some basic information about the story and allow us to plan out our work.

The first version of a story might contain nothing more than a name and a brief description of what it does. This might be enough if the programmers are experienced and have built very similar stories before. They may well be able to create suitable test sets for the story also from their recent experience of doing something similar. But what if you have never done this before?

We will use a structured approach to describing stories that will help us to develop unit tests, the subject of Chapter 8.

Most units identified from a requirements elicitation process with a customer will have a relevance to their business needs. In other words, the customer will understand the purpose of the story. This may not always be the case, and in some projects the stories will be less visible or apparently relevant to the customer—they may be of a rather technical nature and thus less comprehensible to the customer. In such cases, it is important to try to explain why it is relevant—what business value it will provide.

From a customer's point of view, it is likely that they will interpret a story in terms of how it relates to some business function or part of a business function. In other words, the story will be involved in generating some useful result.

In order to explain this—and to exploit the most from it in terms of test set generation—it is often useful to think in the following way.

The story will be triggered by some event—a mouse click, a result, or a message from another part of the system, and so forth. This event then results in some processing, it could be a database update, a query, or the computation of a result, and so on. In order for the story to be effective, it may need to communicate with other stories or a database and it may result in changes to other parts of the system, such as a database or a screen display.

Consider the *login* story, for example. The purpose of a login system is to manage the different classes of users and to ensure that each user has secure access to the part of the system that they are registered to use. Thus the typical system will involve a user inputting their user identity (User ID) and a password. The system then needs to check that such a user exists and that the password submitted matches the password allocated to that ID. On successfully checking this, the system should then provide the appropriate start screen for that category of user. Thus we have information going into the system (ID and password), a check being made against a list of IDs and passwords, and a new screen is then presented. This screen is either the starting screen for that user or an error report if the user is not recognized—this may then provide further options to the user to correct their entry information or seek further advice.

We can thus think of many stories in the following way.

The story is triggered by some input or set of inputs; the story may then need to check some of the values of the input against some existing data—a lookup table, database and so on. The story then computes some results and outputs these somewhere—perhaps to a screen or to some other part of the system. Finally, the story might update a database or some other store.

Suppose the story is a simple *login* function (Fig. 5.1).

Figure 5.1 demonstrates a minimal type of story card; the meaning of it is fairly clear, and so it might not need elaborating. However, it is a good example to explain how a more sophisticated story might be specified.

First we look at the inputs that will trigger the story. There will, probably, be some screen that provides the login prompt that will consist of a data entry and password entry dialogue box (Fig. 5.2).

There will be a database or lookup table that contains the passwords for all the registered users.

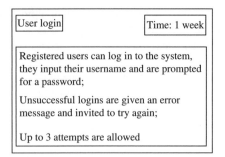

Figure 5.1 A simple login story.

The user puts in his or her username and then his or her password. There may be some data validation for the username in terms of checking for valid characters. The story will then have to check that the submitted username data exists in the list of registered users and that the password submitted corresponds with that user. If this is the case, then the login is allowed, and the user is then permitted access to the parts of the system they are qualified to use.

If the password check fails, then the error message is generated (it could be *no known user* or *incorrect password* depending on where the checking failed) allowing another try. The story needs to keep track of how many unsuccessful tries are made before disabling the system for that person.

There are therefore three things to think about: the type of input data, the internal memory (database) that is consulted, and the resultant output data. This information will be used in testing—the first being the information to trigger the test; the second defines the environment the test is run in; the third is the expected test output.

We need to think about simple tests in this systematic way if we are going to achieve the quality and delivery of products that we want.

One of the hardest things about XP is coming up with tests before we start to code. This simple approach can really help.

Not all stories will involve an internal memory check but many will, and it can take many different forms: databases, special variables in the code, and so on. We need to know these when we do the tests or it might be the case that the code works when we test it in isolation but doesn't work when part of the main system.

Username	
Password	
	OK

Figure 5.2 Login screen.

Thus we have a simple tabular description of each story. The cards define the following aspects of the story.

1 Its name.
2 What is the event that begins the story process.
3 What is the internal knowledge that is needed for the story.
4 What is the observable result.
5 How is the internal knowledge updated as a result of the story.
6 What is the current priority of the story.
7 What is the estimated cost of the story.
8 What is the likelihood of the story being changed or dropped.

All this information is needed for testing. A story card should be created for each of these with the information described. A possible template for a story card is given in Figs. 5.3 and 5.4. Some of the topics will be discussed later.

The design of story cards is a topic worth discussing. Some would just contain the most basic statement of the story and little else. Clearly we do not want to introduce too much bureaucracy, and any information included must be important and add value. We have to think about potential maintenance issues and provide just enough information to allow the programmers to understand what each story does and how it has been tested. Don't forget, when maintenance is undertaken, the original programmers may have moved on, and any information about what they thought the story should do and how they convinced themselves that it did it is invaluable.

It is also a good way to clarify what it is you are trying to do, if ever you get into a position where you don't quite understand what the issues are, write these down— using any technique you are comfortable with (free text, bulleted lists, mind maps, etc.). The process of writing it down should force you to clarify it—especially

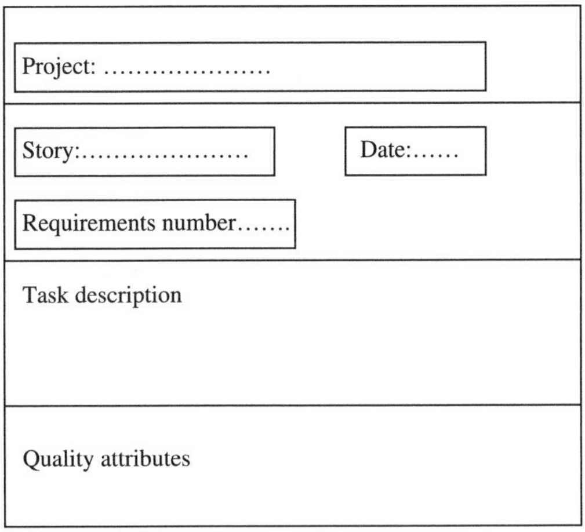

Figure 5.3   Story card template.

Initiating event/inputs	
Memory context	
Observable result/output	
Risk factor/importance	
Tests	
Associated stories	Date delivered

Figure 5.4 The reverse of the story card template.

when working in pairs or groups. The cards we use seem to fulfill this purpose without being too complex or tiresome!

We will go through each component of the card and justify its role.

The name of the project is clearly needed if the story is to be related to a specific application being developed by the company. It may be that a given story is used in several applications and while this is a sensible strategy, reusing previous components that have been successfully built, it does bring with it some dangers in that the story might have been slightly modified for a different context. We need to avoid confusion—especially during maintenance.

The name of the story is an essential component of the card!

The date is also important—a story might be revised during different sessions with a customer, and thus we need to be sure that we are using the most up-to-date version. Of course you should be using a suitable version control and management system to try to keep things in order.

Most stories will relate to a specific requirement; these were discussed in the previous chapter. The set of requirements and of stories will change over time, and it may be that we scrap some stories that are no longer needed and introduce new ones as the requirements change. An important issue—and one that has no simple resolution—is the amount of detail needed in a story. In practice, we should try to define stories so that their implementation and testing can be done within the natural timescale that we are working with—this may be a day or a week or whatever the project needs and the programming team is comfortable with.

The task description is a set of short sentences that describe in terms the customer can understand what the story does. Too much technical detail or jargon will confuse many customers.

The quality attributes may seem an unnecessary ingredient at this stage, but there should be some reference to these. A number of problems we have experienced in the past have been caused by a lack of clarity about these constraints. It is often the performance of the software that is unacceptable (a Web page that loads too slowly) or the usability of the story (e.g., a login facility that looks very different to what is expected).

On the reverse of the card are the key issues relating to the resources needed to build and test the story.

These resources include the date that the story is to be delivered—this will be based on the time that the programmers estimate will be needed to build and test the story. The overall planning of the project will be a dynamic portfolio of stories and integrations that is adjusted as the project evolves, and the stories will be situated within this framework.

The other information on the card assists in developing the tests.

When writing tests, there are a number of important issues that have to be sorted out. Remember, we have no code yet, just the descriptions of the story.

To run a test, we need to trigger the software with suitable inputs. These will be the subject of the first component of the card. It might be that a direct user input causes the story to start or perhaps a specific event or request from another part of the system accomplishes this. All of the expected inputs and events need to be identified.

The next issue is the information that the story needs when triggered. Take the *login* story, for example; this receives a username and password and has to consult a lookup table or query a database to establish if the user's details are correct. This is the memory context that we need to set up for testing. Many stories will need such an environment for testing—but not all.

Naturally we will need to know what the expected behavior of the story is to tell whether it is correct. It is important that this is written down somewhere, that way we can convince ourselves—and those that follow us—that the tests were properly written.

The next issue could be optional (some stories are more important than others). We have seen that the requirements can be clustered into mandatory, optional, and desirable so the same will be true of stories that relate to the requirements. However, there is another issue and that is the risk associated with a story. Some stories are critical—in the sense that many others depend on them, and the system as a whole is threatened by failure of these stories. We should recognize this and give these stories some extra attention.

Another type of risk is associated with the likelihood of the story being superseded by other stories as the requirements change. This allows the programmers and the customer to rationalize the order in which work is done—maybe do the stories that are fairly stable first, if that makes sense. Sometimes, however, you have to build some stories before they are stable in order to explore the overall architecture of the solutions and to allow for some interaction between different parts of the system and for testing purposes—in the same way as you might write some scripts and stubs to help test partially built systems.

Now we write some tests that will be expressed in terms of what is applied to the story, in what environment it is run, and the expected output. For example the login story (Figs. 5.5 and 5.6) will have a number of tests to explore, not only that it works in the way it should for legitimate users but also that unauthorized users are rejected and the number of rejections fits with the requirement. To do this, some temporary

Project: ...XXXXXXXXXX......

Story:...System log-in...... Date:...XXX

Requirements number...1.1....

Task description:
To permit 2 classes of users – basic users and Admin
users to log in and be authenticated

Quality attributes:
The login must run within 5 seconds
The login screen should be like the Windows XPlog-in screen

Figure 5.5 Login story card.

database or list of users and passwords is constructed to check out the story if the
main database is not yet ready. In such circumstances, it will be important that the
login function is carefully tested again when the proper database is integrated into
the system later.

Finally, we describe the stories that depend on the current story and the stories
that the current story depends on. This will help with planning out priorities
among the stories and their integration into working systems.

The XP method now tells us to write some tests for a story and then to code the
story up. Writing tests, as we will see, is a sophisticated business, and one of
the weaknesses of much of the literature is that little advice is offered about how

Initiating event/inputs: user types username

Memory context: list of usernames, passwords and
access rights

Observable result/output: correct screen accessed

Risk factor/importance: High—security, may need
more categories of user later

Tests: To be done—see Section 5.4 below

Associated stories: User
Main, Admin main

Date delivered: YYYY

Figure 5.6 The reverse of the login story card.

the tests are found; there is a lot of information about how to run tests and automate this process, but where the tests come from is something that seems to be left to experience—and this is something that you may not have!

Take one of your stories and write down some test cases. Don't forget what you are trying to do—to confirm that the code does what it is supposed to do and doesn't do anything else.

Can you think of any more examples of tests? Good testers think awkward, trying out unlikely scenarios and data in an attempt to break the code. If you are to succeed in XP, you must adopt this attitude. In traditional software engineering, programmers tend to be too gentle with their own code; it's a psychological tendency that is hard to overcome. The influence of pair programming in XP is an attempt to prevent this. It's better for the programmers to find the bugs rather than for the users to find them!

We will discuss a more systematic way to derive tests shortly.

Now we are supposed to write the code and apply all the tests, correcting the code until they all pass. Naturally, we do this in pairs.

This is the basic XP process. How long did it take? Make a note of the time you spent on writing the tests. This will give us an indication of what time it might take to write a similar story and conduct its tests. Hopefully, you will get quicker and better as you gain experience.

The story we have just discussed would need to communicate with other parts of the system and it is not worth showing this to the client yet. There will be a user interface and a database, in all likelihood, and this class needs to be able to link in with them. While some pairs in the team are writing these basic units, the others can be looking at the design of the interface and the database that will power the system. When we are clearer about these, we will be able to write some system tests, link them together, and see the results of our work; then we can show the client something that he or she would understand.

Although writing tests for simple classes such as this one is not particularly difficult, things change when objects start communicating with each other and when a more complete architecture is being put together. This is where things can go seriously wrong.

In the previous chapter, we looked at the requirements document and noted that it is not a static artifact but a dynamic entity that will change over the course of the project—as both developers and customers understand the problems better, as the business needs change, and as resources, especially time, are used. However, maintaining an accurate list of stories both those that have been implemented and those that are believed to be required is vital in order to keep a grip on the project. Some proponents of XP might criticize the more formal ways that we do things. For example, just building stories without bothering with requirements document is a popular approach. This may work in some circumstances—perhaps you have a long-term relationship with your customer and their requirements arise in a gradual and regular manner and the overall system architecture is stable. This is not the position that we have ever experienced. Usually we have a fairly fixed deadline for completion and we need to stick to that as far as possible—meeting stage deadlines and agreed installments of software—otherwise the income needed to survive may not come through. Many customers are reluctant to pay unless they think that they are getting something of value.

The next section details some simple techniques for thinking about system tests. The basic idea has been used in industrial settings and has seen massive improvements (up to 300%) in the effectiveness of the tests compared with the original test method being used.

5.2 COLLECTIONS OF STORIES

The task of taking the list of functional requirements or stories and identifying and organizing them into a coherent system can be achieved using the technique that we will describe next.

To gain a greater understanding of how all the stories fit together into a coherent system, we need to think about how they relate to each other. For example, it may be that one story can only occur after another one has occurred, or it might be that at some point in the business cycle there is a choice between several stories.

In Fig. 5.7 the initial story, story 0, is followed by either story 1 or story 2 (but not both at the same time) and then either story 1 is followed by story 2 or story 3 is followed by story 4. It might be, then, that stories 2 and 4 are succeeded by further stories or the system returns back to the initial story.

In many cases, each main story is associated with a user interface screen, there may be a whole screen to a given story, or there may be many stories that can be driven from that screen. Although it is too early to plan out the detailed graphics of the screen, it is still important to identify the key elements of the screen, the components that can be used by the user to instigate the process defined by a story, the extra information needed to be displayed for this, and the result of the operation of the story displayed suitably.

We might break down a story into tasks that, when combined, provide a natural way to implement the story. One task might be to paint a screen (e.g., a form), another might be to provide a data entry function that will connect to a task that performs some calculation with the data. This might involve communicating with a database—to check with current data, and then to communicate the result back to the screen. Once these tasks have been programmed and integrated together, we have a coherent story to show the client.

It is sometimes a good idea to show the client some of your thoughts, on paper, of how the story relates to your interface ideas before you do much coding. This can then lead to a clearer understanding of what is required.

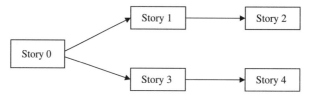

Figure 5.7 Collections of stories.

The system will respond to some *external* stimuli: these will be, for example, users interacting with a screen entering data; choosing options through mouse clicks, ticking boxes, and so on; messages from some other system; perhaps the results of a query to a database.

This data is then processed in some way; perhaps it's just a simple calculation, perhaps the system needs to contact another part of the system (e.g., a database) in order to proceed. The results of the computation may then be fed back to the user via a screen or output in some other way or to another component. It is possible that the database needs to be updated as a result of this interaction.

Thus we have four essential actors in any system: an input actor, a processing actor, a *memory* actor, and an output actor. The memory actor—this could be managing a database—will be involved in reading and writing to the notional memory and communicating with the other actors. The input actor reads the input from the screen or input device, the output actor deals with the output, while the processing actor does the actual core computation.

We conclude this section with some examples of stories.

5.2.1 Pharmacovigilance

This project involved developing an online, Web-based system for medical workers to submit details of adverse reactions to drugs by their patients. It is part of the European Union's process of monitoring the safety and effectiveness of medication (Figs. 5.8–5.11).

Project: Pharmacovigilance

Story: Add entry via XML e-mail import   Date: 5 March 2003

Requirements number: 6   Iteration: 1

Task description: Imports a report in the XML-based ISCR format. If the software is to manage the e-mail input, the user may be required to specify a source from which to obtain the e-mail. The XML data will be entered into the same form used for inputting data manually, so that the user can check its validity and add additional information.

Quality attributes: Processing of input file should be quick enough to be unnoticeable to the user.
Should be 99% successful.
Clear interface design.

Figure 5.8   Pharmacovigilance story 6 card.

Initiating event/inputs: A request is made to import the data for addition from an XML e-mail on the Add form.

Memory context: Source list and database available; Entry is added to the database

Observable result/output: The result will either be a success confirmation or an error message, specifying the error in user-friendly terms.

Risk factor/importance: 3 (high)   Change factor: 2 (medium)

Tests:
      6. Do nothing and exit [cancel]
      7. Import non-XML file [error]
      8. Import XML file that does not contain mandatory requirements [error]
      9. Import invalid XML file [error]
      10. Import empty file [error]
      11. Import appropriate XML file
      12. Failure to source e-mail from a secure repository [error]

Associated stories: Addition   Date delivered:
of data manually, main screen

Figure 5.9   Reverse of the pharmacovigilance story 6 card.

Project: Pharmacovigilance

Story: Output IHL line listing ....   Date: 4 March, 2003

Requirements number: 10   Iteration: 2

Task description: Exports a report in the IHL line listing format.

Quality attributes: Operation should be completed in an acceptable time period.
Should be 99% successful.

Figure 5.10   Pharmacovigilance story 10 card.

Initiating event/inputs: A request is made for output in this format on viewing a report	
Memory context: The report exists in the database and the current user accessing the system is an administrator	
Observable result/output: The result will either be a success confirmation or an error message, specifying the error in user-friendly terms.	
Risk factor/importance: 3 (high) Change factor: 1 (low)	
Tests: 1. Request leads to output of IHL line listing	
Associated stories: View	Date delivered:

Figure 5.11   Reverse of the pharmacovigilance story 10 card.

5.2.2 Stamps System

This project was delivered to a client who ran a retail organization that sold rare and historic postage stamps to collectors (Figs. 5.12–5.15).

Note that this story card in Fig. 5.13 is more complex than the previous ones as it also contains information about estimation of resources for the story.

This is based on a more traditional software engineering approach to estimation that relied on identifying "function points" or "object points" in the story. This is a mechanism for trying to ascertain the complexity of a story in terms of what it does—does it communicate with or query a database, is it simple piece of code or something that has some real challenges involved, and so on? There is a considerable amount of data available about industrial projects that have been classified in this way, but this data may not provide a reliable answer for our needs here. We no longer record this information on a story card since it did not seem to provide sufficient value—the estimates generated using this method were very inaccurate.

5.2.3 DELTAH (Developing European Leadership Through Action-learning in Healthcare)

This project is concerned with supporting leadership development activities for health service professionals (see http://www.deltah.org) (Figs. 5.16–5.18).

We will see how this way of looking at things is both useful for planning out a program but also for testing it. It will be the basis for our system metaphor.

Customer story card	**Project title:** Stamps

Date: 24/11/02	**Project phase/iteration:** Design

Requirements Number: 2	**Story name:** Order Maintenance

Task description (English):

This page is designed to give the user the ability to organize orders to existing customers

"Order Maintenance" contains links to the "Create New Order," "Modify/Delete Existing Order,"

"Print Order Letter," "List Unreturned Orders," and "List Returned Orders" pages.

Initiating event:

The user clicks the "Order Maintenance" link on the navigation bar.

Memory context:

The "Order Maintenance" page is only used for navigation purposes and does not alter the database

in any way.

Observable result:

The "Create New Order," "Modify/Delete Existing Order," "Print Order Letter," "List Unreturned

Orders," or "List Returned Orders" page is displayed, depending on which link the user clicked on.

Risk factor: 1 (Low risk).	**Change factor:** 9 (The system is being completely rewritten).

Related stories: "Stamp Dealer System Contents," "Order Details," "Print Order Letter," "List

Unreturned Orders," and "List Returned Orders"

Notes:

Figure 5.12   Stamps story 2 card.

Story name: Order Maintenance			

Resource estimates:

Input	☐	**Simple**	**X**
Output	☐	**Average**	☐
Enquiry	**X**	**Complex**	☐
Reference file	☐		
Database	☐		
Function/object point total:		**Man-hours total:** 2	

Functional tests:

User clicks on "Order Details" link.

User clicks on "Print Order Letter" link.

User clicks on "List Unreturned Orders" link.

User clicks on "List Returned Orders" link.

Quality attributes:

The system should work in screen resolutions of 800 × 600 or higher.

It should be quick and easy to get to any other section of the system from this screen.

All operations should take a reasonable amount of time to execute (less than 15 seconds).

The interface should be easy to use and satisfy the usability heuristics described in

(Nielsen, 1993).

Figure 5.13   Reverse of the stamps story 2 card.

Task description (English):

This page is designed to give the user information about functionality relating to units, helping to clarify the way that the system behaves.

"Unit Maintenance" contains links to the "Add New Unit," "Modify Existing Unit," "Delete Existing Unit," "Browse All Units," and "Find Unit" pages.

Initiating event:

The user clicks the "Unit Maintenance" link on the navigation bar or the "Unit Maintenance" link on the "Stamp Dealer System Contents" page itself.

Memory context:

The "Unit Maintenance" page is only used for navigation purposes and does not alter the database in any way.

Observable result:

The "Add New Unit," "Modify Existing Unit," "Delete Existing Unit," "Browse All Units," or "Find Unit" page is displayed, depending on which link the user clicked on.

Risk factor: 1 (Low risk).	**Change factor:** 9 (The system is being completely rewritten).

Related stories:

Stamp Dealer System Contents, Add New Unit, Modify Existing Unit, Delete Existing Unit, Browse All Units and Find Unit.

Notes:

Figure 5.14 Stamps story 5 card.

Story name: Unit Maintenance

Resource estimates:

Input	X	**Simple**	X
Output	☐	**Average**	☐
Enquiry	☐	**Complex**	☐
Reference file	☐		
Database	☐		

Function/object point total: **Man-hours total:** 1

Functional tests:

User clicks on the "Add New Unit" link.

User clicks on the "Modify Existing Unit" link.

User clicks on the "Delete Existing Unit" link.

User clicks on the "Browse All Units" link.

User clicks on the "Find Unit" link.

Quality attributes:

The system should work in screen resolutions of 800 × 600 or higher.

It should be quick and easy to get to any other section of the system from this screen.

All operations should take a reasonable amount of time to execute (less than 10 seconds).

The interface should be easy to use and satisfy the usability heuristics described in

(Nielsen, 1993).

Figure 5.15   Reverse of the stamps story 5 card.

Customer Story Card	Project Title: DPP
Date: 20 / 02 / 07	*Project Phase\Version*: Initial\1.0
Requirements Number: 1	*Story Name*: User can choose a language

Task Description:
The user can choose between English, Dutch, and Polish languages.

Initiating Event: The user requests the "language change" option
Memory Context: Content is available in all three languages.
Observable Result: The language of the content changes to that chosen by the user

Risk Factor: Low	*Change Factor*: High

Related Stories: None

Resource Estimates:	
X Input	O Simple
X Output	X Average
O Enquiry	O Complex
O Database	
X Other File	
	Man-hours Estimate: 2

Functional Tests:
1. Choose the current language
2. Choose the English language from either the Dutch or Polish language
3. Choose the Dutch language from either the English or Polish language
4. Choose the Polish language from either the English or Dutch language
5. Move to a different page [cancel]
6. If a page is not available in the chosen language [error]

Quality Attributes:
1. The alteration of the language should be instant
2. The language that is being chosen should be obvious

Customer Approval:	Date:

Figure 5.16 DELTAH story 1 card.

Customer Story Card	Project Title: DPP
Date: 20 / 02 / 07	*Project Phase\Version*: Initial\1.0
Requirements Number: 2	*Story Name*: User can read background project material

Task Description:
The user can find general background information about the DELTAH Project

Initiating Event: The user requests the "background information" option
Memory Context: Background information is available in the current language
Observable Result: The background information is displayed

Risk Factor: Low	*Change Factor*: Low

Related Stories: User can read promotional material, User can save promotional material

Resource Estimates:	
O Input	X Simple
X Output	O Average
O Enquiry	O Complex
O Database	
O Other File	
	Person-hours Estimate: 1

Functional Tests:
1. The material can be read
2. Move to a different page [cancel]

Quality Attributes:
1. The material is grammatically correct
2. The material is accurate
3. The material is written clearly
4. The material covers all the background information of the DELTAH project

Customer Approval:	Date:

Figure 5.17   DELTAH story 2 card.

Customer Story Card	Project Title: DPP
Date: 21 / 02 / 07	*Project Phase\Version*: Initial\1.0
Requirements Number: 3	*Story Name*: User can read promotional material
Task Description: The user can find promotional material about the DELTAH Project	
Initiating Event: The user requests the "promotional material" option	
Memory Context: Promotional material is available in the current language	
Observable Result: The promotional material is displayed	
Risk Factor: Low	*Change Factor*: Low
Related Stories: User can save promotional material	
Resource Estimates:	
O Input	X Simple
X Output	O Average
O Enquiry	O Complex
O Database	
O Other File	
	Person-hours Estimate: 1
Functional Tests: 1. The material can be read 2. Move to a different page [cancel]	
Quality Attributes: 1. The material is grammatically correct 2. The material is accurate 3. The material is written clearly 4. The material covers all the promotional material of the DELTAH project	
Customer Approval:	Date:

Figure 5.18   DELTAH story 3 card.

5.3 USER INTERFACES

Thus far, the concepts that we have discussed are oriented toward the needs of the developers; when it comes to communication with the customer, however, it is essential that we use ideas that he or she can understand. Many people look upon a software system from the perspective of how it presents itself to them. In other words, *the system is the interface!*

People are all different and differ greatly in the way they think and behave when using a software system. The designers of a user interface would seem, therefore, to have an almost impossible task when it comes to trying to satisfy every possible user of the system.

There is now a considerable amount of research and experience when it comes to this area. We will briefly review some of the commonly proposed principles that are recommended for the design of good graphical user interfaces (GUIs). Note, however, that if your client has some special factors, perhaps some of the users are handicapped in some way or have other special needs, then these will have to be investigated carefully and may result in some specialist features being incorporated in the interface.

A useful general reference on user interface design is that of Schneiderman (1998).

Most user interfaces consist of a collection of windows and screens. These have two main purposes: one is to present information to the use, the other is to permit the user to carry out some tasks. Naturally, many windows are a combination of both types.

If we are presenting information, then there are some important principles that should be followed:

(a) The information presented should not be confusing, contradictory, or misleading.

(b) The words, icons, and other visual metaphors used should be clear and understandable; the use of obscure technical jargon should be avoided.

(c) The screens should not be cluttered, full of irrelevant and distracting images and text, they should focus on the task in hand.

(d) The information should be up to date and presented in a consistent manner.

(e) If the user is expected to do something, it should be made clear what that is.

If the window is designed to allow the user to carry out some task, then other important characteristics are desirable:

(a) The action required to carry out the task should be clear; help should be given if appropriate.

(b) Similar tasks under similar conditions should require similar actions.

(c) Feedback should be given; if the operation was successful, then this should be clear to the user.

(d) It should be possible to recover if the action was not successful; make sure that error message are clear and helpful.

(e) Too many alternative ways to do the same thing can be confusing.

(f) Similar actions should be broadly consistent, so don't use radically different techniques for actions that are very similar but taking place in slightly different states.

How these windows are organized is crucial. Many simple interfaces can be modeled, as we will see, by using a state machine or an X-machine (XXM) (see Chapter 6 and Holcombe, 1998). This is well worth doing as it will relate easily to the user stories and tasks that we have been thinking about earlier. There is a balance between the desire to provide lots of information and the need to keep it clear and simple.

We also have to decide how many windows to use: too many and users find things getting tedious, too few and they may get confused. The correct level can only be found by extensive consultation and trials with prospective users or their proxies.

Because we are using XP, we can expect to show our customer examples of the sort of interfaces we are thinking of using; this is an opportunity for some useful feedback. Remember that many inexperienced custmers and users often think that the system *is* the interface.

XP stresses the need for simplicity, but do not interpret this to mean that the interfaces must be very simple; they should be good, but that may not mean the same. Interface design is a sophisticated skill; do not underestimate how hard it is. Test out your ideas as much as possible on potential users or on others with a similar background. Some student friends from other departments and schools could be helpful in this respect. The more experiments you do with people, the better will be the result. Don't forget that people may have very different opinions about the same interface. Set up questionnaires to get some evaluation from anyone who uses it, getting them to evaluate it on the basis of how easy it is to learn, how easy it was to carry out the key tasks, how well it kept them informed about what it had done and what needed to be done next, and whether it worked without crashing or failing in other ways.

Ask users to rate the key features on a 1 (poor) to 5 (excellent) scale.

Check with the non-functional requirements identified earlier.

The system doesn't stop with the interface. The system will be situated within an overall enterprise, and workflows and interactions in the company may be involved with it. Some of the tasks will be manual ones, and the introduction of a new system may influence these and perhaps change them. Customers should be aware of the implications of introducing the new system and should plan for it properly.

It is sometimes tempting, when designing an interface, to want to use whatever the latest technical feature that you have learned how to implement. This will be a bad idea in many cases. Only use appropriate technology, not technology for technology's sake. Adding complexity, whether from a programming point of view or from the users', will threaten rather than enhance the system.

Ask the customer or the users which input techniques they want to use in the different contexts. Do they prefer selecting from a drop-down menu, clicking on radio buttons, filling in forms, using hot keys, and so forth. Study the sort of systems that the users are currently using and are familiar with. Keep things similar if at all possible.

There are many different types of widgets that can be used, depending on the technology and any toolkit used: buttons of various types, sliders, drop-down lists, combo box, and so on, can all be successfully used.

Don't forget the help system; this might be a key feature for some users. It should provide some basic support to enable users to get back to a point where they can then continue. Think about the key tasks that are identified from the user stories. Perhaps use each one as the basis for a help system.

An online manual is also a good idea. This is discussed in Chapter 10.

5.4 COMMUNICATING CLEARLY WITH THE CUSTOMER AND BUILDING CONFIDENCE

At each meeting—in our case weekly meetings are the only practical face-to-face opportunities—we need to provide the customer/client with a progress report. Because some of our clients need to keep their managers informed as well, it is best to provide them with a document that summarizes the current state of the project and where it is going to. This can be achieved by producing a requirements document and updating it regularly.

After a few weeks, this can become quite a detailed description of the system being built. It is suggested that a working requirements document is kept updated as the requirements change; in particular, as the collection of stories grows and the system architecture develops, this should be recorded in a coherent way, and the requirements document is the place for this. Because a student's life is a varied one, and many other courses and activities will be taking place concurrently with this project, it is important to keep everything organized so that there is no confusion about what is being done and where one is going. This is why the requirements document is important. In many industrial companies, it will be based around a standard template.

A suggested agenda for a regular client meeting follows:

1 Progress update—what has been achieved since the last meeting.

2 Review of system requirements.

3 Demonstration of new code and interface mock-ups.

4 Changes needed to existing stories/requirements.

5 New stories/requirements.

6 Plans for the coming week.

7 Next meeting—time and place.

There will always be a number of issues that can upset the best of developer–client relationships.

Many customers expect software to be produced rather faster than is possible. It is important to know how and when to try to manage their expectations. The benefit of regular increments and deliveries is that the customer becomes more aware of progress. It is not always possible—nor even desirable in some cases— to focus on delivering working pieces of code if they are so incomplete as to prevent the customer/user from properly exercising it in a sensible context. The use of screenshots and mock-ups together with lists of stories and even XXMs will help the customer to understand where things have got to and where they are going. Some authors have tried to use UML (Unified Modeling Language) diagrams to illustrate some of the system design but to limited effect. Static diagrams such as class diagrams are unlikely to be appreciated by clients. Use-case diagrams contain so little information that they are also of marginal value. Some of the activity diagrams can be useful if they are carefully explained. We have found that XXMs are readily understood by customers and popular with developers compared with all the other approaches that we have tried (Thompson 2003, 2005). Interestingly, UML diagrams are widely disliked!

Sometimes, despite the best intentions of all concerned, relationships between clients and developers can become strained or even break down altogether.

This has happened in Genesys. Maybe it's because Genesys is a company operated by students, but some—admittedly a small minority—clients do not treat them with much respect and can act quite unprofessionally. One scenario we have experienced is the small business client who wants something for nothing. They often have a poor understanding of their own business and can change their mind in erratic ways. One customer, kept coming up with different technologies to use half-way through the project because he had found a cheaper service. This resulted in having to restart the project because of the incompatibility with what had been built with the new service technology. This didn't just happen once but at least three times! It was a major challenge to the concept of XP.

Another customer signed off a contract that had been successfully delivered and then decided he wanted a lot of changes later. He did not accept that this should be the subject of a new contract, and this led to a lot of stress among the team. Sometimes you have to be firm—the customer is not always right! Of course, if it comes to legal arguments, then that is an indication of failure—but there is always a point where you have to stand up for your side of the bargain and avoid being exploited unfairly. Under these circumstances, it is vital that you can demonstrate that you have carried out everything in a professional way, that you can produce the evidence to support your position, and that you have behaved in a reasonable way. This is the value of a good source of documentation: minutes of meetings, requirements documents and contracts, e-mails, test data, and so on. If you don't keep this information in a systematic way, then you deserve to be criticized by a smart lawyer.

5.5 DEMONSTRATING THE NON-FUNCTIONAL REQUIREMENTS

The format of the requirements document that we will be presenting to our client was discussed in the previous chapter, and examples are given in Appendix A. The important thing about this document is that it should be understandable to the client. It is built from the basic information in the stories together with some outline ideas of the how the system might look and work. Important non-functional requirements need to be specified and clear statements about how these are to be interpreted and tested included. It is no good saying that the system will be fast if we don't say what that means; for example, in a Web-based system this might include the maximum acceptable page download times under suitable conditions, and so forth.

Although we have presented the requirements document and the story cards as two separate things, they are very closely related. There will be an interplay between them. We might regard the requirements document as a *summary* of our current understanding of the overall system, whereas the stories are a more detailed description of individual aspects of its functionality with enough information to allow us to plan, test, and implement each story. The requirements document will have extra and vital information about the proposed system, context statements, assumptions, as well as global quality attributes and non-functional requirements. It is these that we turn to next.

5.5.1 Non-Functional Requirements

A non-functional requirement either describes how well the system should perform (a quality attribute) or a constraint or limit that the system must adhere to (a resource attribute). The non-functional requirements were defined in Chapter 4, and can be split into categories like *reliability*, *usability*, *efficiency*, *maintainability* and *portability*, *etc*. Here we give some example statements that might be part of the requirements document.

5.5.1.1 Reliability

For a single user, the system should crash no more than once per 10 hours.

The system should produce the correct values for any mathematical expression 100% of the time.

If the system crashes, it should behave perfectly normally when loaded up again with minimal data loss.

5.5.1.2 Usability

A user should be able to add a new customer to the system within 1 minute.

A user should be able to add a new order to the system within 1 minute.

A user should be able to edit a customer's details within 5 minutes (will vary with details type).

A user should be able to produce reports and statistics within 1 minute.

5.5.1.3 Efficiency

The system should load up within 15 seconds.

The time taken for the system to retrieve data from the server should never exceed 30 seconds.

5.5.1.4 Maintainability

The system should be designed in such a way that makes it easy to be modified in the future.

The system should be designed in such a way that makes it easy to be tested.

5.5.1.5 Portability

The client system should work on the client's current computer network, which is connected to the Internet and has Windows XP or better.

The system should be easy to install.

These statements need to be refined into a more precise statement in order to make them testable. What, for example, does *easy to install* mean? We will look at this in the next chapter.

From each story that we have discussed with the client, we extract the key functional details. These are grouped in sections with other story lines that are clearly related.

These requirements are categorized on the basis of which are *mandatory, desirable*, and *optional*. To do this, we need to have an estimate of the time we might take to complete these, and this will help us to make these decisions. The next section looks at the process of trying to estimate this.

Naturally, we must consult the client on which he or she thinks are mandatory and so forth. We have to be realistic, and you must not promise to do more than you can achieve in the time given.

5.6 ESTIMATING RESOURCES

If we have a model like the one above, we can use something like the *function point method* and *object point method*. Here we try to estimate the amount of effort required to build a story or a screen with its accompanying functionality.

To do this, we look at each story and consider the functions contained in it. We then try to categorize what sort of function this is. We can find information that estimates the amount of effort each category of function might require; this data is collected in industrial organizations, and some of it is published. We include some examples here. It is a good practice to try to measure your own efforts for these functions to see if they agree with the estimates and to inform future projects.

5.6.1 Software Cost Estimation

We need to ask some basic questions at the *start* of the project and also at suitable review points *during* the project:

How long will it take?

What resources will it need?

How expensive will it be?

The standard approach is to use the techniques of software measurement, however, there are overheads involved in doing this, and we need to consider to what extent it is worth doing this.

During the course of projects, we measure the following parameters:

Lines of code (loc) produced over the timescale

Number of observed defects over the timescale

Number of person-hours worked over the timescale

Amount of time spent on debugging over the timescale

Amount of time spent on requirements over the timescale

Amount of time spent on design/specification/analysis over the timescale

Amount of time spent on writing documentation over the timescale

Amount of time spent on testing/review over the timescale

And so forth

These are all measures of production volume, product quality, and effort. If we have some previous experience and data of this type for old and similar projects, we may be able to estimate the effort and time needed for the new project. In many cases, the type of project is of a new type, the technology being used may be unfamiliar, and the programmers may also be different to previous projects. This it is a difficult issue to decide what is best.

From the time sheets and documentation produced, we should be able to find the following for the completed project:

Lines of code (loc) per person-month (pm)

Cost per 1000 lines of code (kloc)

Errors per kloc

Defects per kloc

Pages of documentation per kloc

Cost per page of documentation

Number of requirements

Average kloc per requirement

If we have this data, then we might be able to estimate what the next project will need in terms of people and time.

But different types of project will require different amounts of effort, so we need to collect information about the type of project:

Product functionality

product quality

product complexity

product reliability requirements

And so forth

These are not always easy to measure, unlike the first set of measures.

We need to describe the software being built on the basis of the requirements in order to estimate the resources needed. There are several techniques, none of which are very precise. If the new project is very similar to the previous ones, things are much simpler. If it is a completely new type of project, perhaps involving a new technology, then it is much more difficult.

We can pick out a few simple principles from function point analysis that can be helpful as long as they do not become too time consuming. Function point analysis (FPA) was developed by Albrecht (1979) for business information systems development.

1 For each requirement/story, we decide if it is one of *input, output, inquiry, reference file, database.*

2 Assign a weight to each requirement: *simple, average, complex.*

3 Consider other influencing factors (reusability, adaptability) and weigh them according to a suitable scale.

This is, to an extent, guesswork, but if we have an idea of which requirements are hard to implement and which are easier, it will help us to plan.

Assigning these attributes needs some experience, but then what? Ideally there is a database of previous similar projects that can be analyzed and conclusions on the effort required to complete a story made.

5.6.2 Object Point Analysis

This method was introduced by Banker et al. (1992).

It is based on:

The number of separate screens: simple = 1 object point, average = 2, complex = 3.

The number of reports to be produced: simple $= 2$ object points, average $= 5$, complex $= 8$.

The number of modules that must be developed: 10 object points for each module.

A module will be any small coherent part of the system; it could be a screen or a story.

It is easier to calculate this from the high-level requirements.

The COCOMO model (Boehm, 1995) is an estimation process that is based on industrial data, see any software engineering text such as Pressman (2005) or Sommerville (2006) for more details.

5.6.3 COSMIC FFP

This is an updated version of the function point analysis. It is based around a very simple definition of a piece of software functionality: *a function process is a unique set of data movements: input, output, read and write.*

Actors trigger these movements, directly or indirectly. These movements are also identified at the lowest level in terms of the requirements, that is, we do not break them down into smaller functions. Events will trigger these functions, and we consider them to run until they complete.

Then we sum up how many of these functions there are, ignoring their type or any other factor.

Such a simple method of estimating might be very useful for XP projects; it still requires the collection of data about a team's velocity in order to be useful, though.

Further details can be found at http://www.cosmiccon.com.

Whatever technique is used, there is a number generated (function points, object points, etc.). What does this mean?

Well, it means nothing if there are no data from similar projects available. This is the key.

For each story, carry out some resource estimate, and then record this to generate some kind of useful data for the future.

As projects progress, the reliability of these estimates will be discovered, and some amendments can be made to the method.

What is important is that some method and review is attempted. We do not prescribe any particular approach as it is clear that there is so much variability in projects, teams, and technologies that it is hard to come up with a *magic* solution to the problem. The key point is to measure something on a regular basis and use that information to help with developing an understanding about how future projects might progress.

We have developed an Eclipse plug-in, PlanClipse, to support simple day-by-day planning activities and feedback. It is available from

http://www.genesys.shef.ac.uk/eclipse/planclipse/index.html

http://www.genesys.shef.ac.uk/eclipse/planclipse/2.2/org.eclipse.adpt. planner_2.2.1.jar

The basic idea is that as each story is completed—unit tests written, coding done, and tested such that all tests are passed—it is recorded in the tool together with any decisions about those stories that are still to be done. This is done using a story planning chart. If the project has a fixed delivery date, then there may be some scope for adjusting the list of mandatory stories, reducing the number if things are taking too long and increasing them if things are going well. There are usually some desirable and optional stories that can be included if an earlier delivery is not needed.

The chart in Fig. 5.19 plots weekly progress. Initially, we estimate the number of stories that will be implements—as well as we can—in the time available for the project. This is point A. As the project develops, we check the number of stories completed—so initially there was good progress and after 3 weeks things were going well. As a result, some extra stories were then planned, point B. The estimate of progress to completion indicated by the progress or pace line was drawn. The challenge is to keep above that line as far as possible. At C, the number of stories was increased because it looked as though the plan was too pessimistic.

Finally, the progress made by week 8 was reviewed and another revision of the story list at point D was made. This resulted in a reduction of the number of stories in order to allow for the time for system testing. There may be further changes as the project goes into the last few weeks, but these must be considered in terms of the risks and benefits to the project—risks of over-running and threats to the quality of the system due to inadequate systems testing versus the benefits of better alignment with the current needs of the client.

It is absolutely vital that enough time is left for thorough systems testing before delivery—*if this is not done there will be serious problems.*

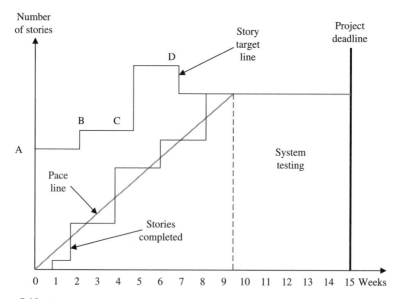

Figure 5.19   A story planning chart.

The benefit of this approach is that it is reactive, and progress can be measured easily and tactics adapted to meet the demands of the situation.

5.7 REVIEW

This chapter has looked at how the planning game and the use of story cards can help us to develop a detailed requirements document. Although the requirements are changing, it is important to bring all the changes into a single document at suitable stages through the document. We considered how the different functional requirements can be integrated into a simple (extreme) model that helps us to think through how the system will work overall. These processes will be repeated as the requirements emerge and change. Chapter 9 will examine some of the issues relating to this evolution of the system and the ways it can be articulated and managed.

Non-functional requirements were identified as a key factor in the success of a system. These need to be thought about very carefully and clear and measurable statements made about them.

Estimating the resources needed to complete a project is notoriously hard, and two techniques—function point analysis and object point analysis—were briefly described. These can only be rough and ready guides until you get more experienced. Noting down as much detail about your team's performance and the time taken to do things will provide an ongoing and useful archive for future projects.

EXERCISES

1. Read Appendix A. These requirements relate to a real project that were successfully implemented using XP.

2. Prepare your own requirements document for your client for submission also to your tutor. The contents are specified below. Use the planning game to create the individual requirements for the document.

Your requirements statement should contain the following sections and paragraphs:

Introduction: a statement of the required system's purpose and objectives.

Dependencies and assumptions: things that will be required for your system to meet its specification but which are outside your control and not your responsibility.

Constraints: things that will limit the type of solution you can deliver (e.g., particular data formats, hardware platforms, legal standards).

Functional requirements: you are advised to prioritize your requirements into those that are

Mandatory

Aesirable

Optional

Non-functional requirements: with accurate definitions and an indication of how they are to be measured and the level required.

User characteristics: who will the users be?

User interface characteristics: some indication of how the interface needs to be structured and its properties.

Plan of action: defining milestones (key points in the project):

Deliverables: an indication of when increments will be ready

Times when these events will occur.

Glossary of terms.

Any other information such as important references or data sources, and so forth.

Below is a simple tabular template that could be used for some of the functional and non-functional requirements. It includes a column for trying to set priorities for the individual requirements and to identify the risk of change in the requirement, a difficult thing to estimate but worthwhile for planning purposes.

Number	Description	Mandatory/optional/ desirable	Priority (1–9)	Risk (1–9)	Function point
1.					

CONUNDRUM

The company wanted an *intranet* that provided support for many of their business activities and also their personnel management. The site would contain information about the various company activities, a diary system, and templates for administrative tasks such as the submission of illness and absence forms. The users would be able to log on remotely to carry out tasks as well as from within the company offices. The customer was able to maintain a very close relationship with the development team and had a clear idea of what the company needed. There were three teams using XP working on this project, each competing with all the others. Initially, all the teams thought that the project would take 10 weeks. It didn't quite work out like that. When the first team delivered their first increment, they discovered something important that had not emerged from the planning game. The company had a service agreement with a third-party network solutions company that provided the computer system and the Internet connection for the customer. This led to a serious problem for some of the teams and resulted in some failing to meet the 10-week deadline despite the careful planning.

What might have been the problem?

REFERENCES

A.J. ALBRECHT. Measuring application development productivity. *SHARE/GUIDE/IBM Application Development Symposium*, Monterey, CA, 1979.

R. BANKER, R. KAUFFMAN. An empirical test of object-based output measurement metrics in a computer-aided software engineering (CASE) environment. *Joural of Management Information Systems*, **8**:127–150, 1992.

B. BOEHM. *Cost Models for Future Life Cycle Processes: COCOMO 2*. Balzer Science, 1995.

M. HOLCOMBE, F. IPATE. *Correct Systems: Building a Business Process Solution*. Springer, 1998. Available at: http://www.dcs.shef.ac.uk/~wmlh/.

R.S. PRESSMAN. *Software Engineering: A Practitioner's Approach*. McGraw-Hill, 2005.

B. SCHNEIDERMAN. *Designing the User Interface: Strategies for Effective Human-Computer Interaction*. Addison-Wesley, 1998.

I. SOMMERVILLE. *Software Engineering*, 8th ed. Addison-Wesley, 2006.

C. THOMSON, M. HOLCOMBE. Applying XP ideas formally: The story card and extreme X-machines. In *Proceedings of the 1st South-East European Workshop on Formal Methods*. Thessaloniki, Greece, South-East European Research Centre, 2003, pp. 57–71.

C. THOMSON, M. HOLCOMBE. Using a formal method to model software design in XP projects. In *Proceedings of the 2nd South-East European Workshop on Formal Methods*. Ohrid, FYR of Macedonia, AMCT, Vol. 1 (3), SEERC, Thesalonilli, Greece, 2005.

Chapter 6

Bringing the System Together as a Coherent Concept

SUMMARY

Finding the right initial architecture for the application

- Three-tier architectures
- Deriving architecture information from the model
- Extreme modeling and the system metaphor

6.1 WHAT IS THE PROBLEM?

The requirements have been expressed in the details of the stories and the non-functional requirements, but currently the overall picture of the system may be unclear. Some stories can be implemented more quickly than can others. In terms of trying to deliver working pieces of software on a rapid timescale of a few days, these stories will be relatively straightforward. Many authors recommend that systems should be built using very small units that do not have a complex internal structure and that can be tested thoroughly. This works up to a point but it may result in the developers being unclear about how the final system will look. There is also the risk that the final system is not very well organized from these components, and it may possess a very complex and poorly understood communication structure between the classes, thus making the complete system very difficult to test at the systems level.

XP suggests that gradually building the system through gradual integration of units will be a way of addressing this problem. This does suppose, however, that we know how the units behave as components of a more complete subsystem. This is a major weakness if we do not fully understand what this subsystem is supposed to do in terms of its position within the complete system.

We need to find a way of thinking about how the overall system is meant to be organized and how it will operate, as well as how any significant subsystems work. Some call this a system metaphor or an architecture.

For more complex stories, thinking about them as a subsystem of interacting units will help to prevent problems in testing later.

In this chapter, we look into the way that simple notations such as state machines and XXMs might be used to explore the behavior of a story that was more complex than a simple one. We will build on that here. First, however, we need to think more about the relationship between the stories and the complete system.

Clearly, a starting point is the stories and requirements that are being developed with the customer. One issue that dominates the process is the different levels of abstraction that may be involved.

This conceptual gap (Fig. 6.1) has a major impact on the testing process, and it is important that we make sure that it does not hide vital aspects of the system. An effective system metaphor is needed to make the link across this gap and ensure that the testing process is also effective.

If the metaphor can be turned into an accurate model of the intended system that links the overall "big picture" of the system to the lower-level "story" view, then we will have a mechanism to maintain the integrity of the system as it evolves to suit the emerging needs of the customer. A problem with an ever-changing set of stories and requirements is that the understanding of the overall system may get lost. Naturally, there will be an ongoing cost in terms of maintaining the model and its relationship with the stories as things change.

If the system metaphor model is kept fresh, then it can be used to design system tests. This adds value to the process of building a metaphor as it will play an important role in testing as well as conceptualizing the target system.

A number of candidates for a system metaphor have been considered by many authors, but none seem to have considered how it might impact system testing. In many cases, the metaphor is an analogy, such as a spreadsheet, a production line,

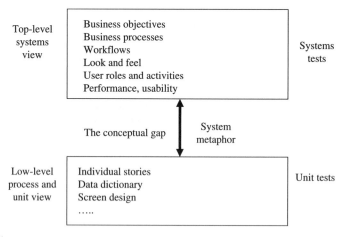

Figure 6.1   The conceptual gap.

and similar such examples drawn sometimes from familiar types of software or from everyday experience.

Whereas these are valuable for a general understanding, they rarely seem to relate strongly to the individual stories, and thus the conceptual gap becomes an issue. The techniques used here, the extreme X-machine, has turned out to be very useful for both programmers and users.

Essentially we need to provide some framework within which we can discuss the software being developed in order to relate what we are building to what problem we are trying to solve. This can be achieved in many ways. It depends on what the application is.

A metaphor may consist of some of the following elements:

An exemplar system with a similar purpose: this might be a well-known package or some existing bespoke software used in the client's organization. We will call this a metaphor *exemplar*.

A general architecture of the solution expressed in terms of components or layers of software organized to communicate in particular ways; for example, a *client–server architecture*. This will be an example of a metaphor *architecture*.

A high-level model that describes in some suitable language the essential features of some aspect of the software; it might be the structure of the user interface, communication protocols, database structure, and so on. We will call this a metaphor *model*.

It could be a class diagram or some similar organization of the software components into a structured and hierarchical representation.

The metaphor also needs to consider the system boundary, where the software system meets the rest of the business, the business personnel, not just the system users, the customers, and all the stakeholders. There are dangers at these interfaces if critical aspects are ignored. We need to think about some of the issues carefully.

What if there is no clear metaphor? Then we need to try to discover the metaphor by creating some software and seeing how it might help in clarifying what is needed.

Suppose your customer has no real idea of what he or she wants—they know they want something but what? From your knowledge of software systems, you may be able to identify something simple that could be built without a lot of effort and that could demonstrate something to the customer that might trigger some greater understanding of what is possible and what might actually work for them.

Sometimes it pays to offer them two possible alternative ideas, and they might then choose one they prefer (as opposed offering just one that they don't think is right). People can ofter choose one from two rather than identify what is not there in a single candidate.

This effort is not wasted; it might result in your code being thrown away, but better that than persevering with something that isn't going to work for your customer.

6.2 A SIMPLE COMMON METAPHOR

If we think about the system that we have been considering in the previous chapters, a simple customer and orders database, then it is Possible to identify some basic components. We can envision it in the form of a classic *three-layer structure* (Fig. 6.2).

The user interface is represented by the machine state space and the business logic by the definitions of the transition functions. The interaction with the database is carried out through the business logic layer responding to and supplying output to the interface. For an e-commerce system, the user interface is probably accessed through a Web browser, and the client–server communication is made through the Internet.

If we look back at the way that we developed the requirements, we note that the role of the story cards was central. If we then consider these the way in which the requirements were described in terms of the inputs, the internal memory, and the outputs, then we can capitalize on this information in developing the system metaphor and the class architecture.

Consider, for example, a story such as "*UploadCustomer*"; then we note that there is a series of interface events that are involved at the user interface. Thus information is communicated between the user interface and the business logic server. This carries out a number of checks on the data supplied, for example, checking that the rules defined for the data are satisfied, making sure that text is supplied when text is needed, perhaps checking zip or postal codes are correctly formed, and so on.

On confirmation of the details presented at the interface, the data is committed to the database using a suitable object database connection technology if you are using a relational database (Access, MySQL, etc.) or another suitable technology if you are using XML as a database.

In a similar way, querying will involve building up a query through the user interface; this will be validated at the server and the database queried, the results being presented through the user interface in a format defined at the server.

Thus how do we design the interface, the server, and the database?

The conventional principle is to separate out the different areas of concern into layers and to ensure that the separation is clean and efficient. The Sun java J2EE model is a typical example of this idea (Figure 6.3).

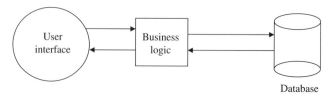

Figure 6.2 A classic three-layer architecture.

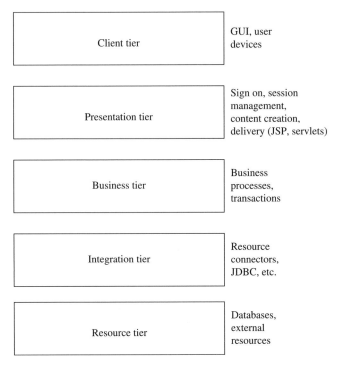

Figure 6.3   An e-commerce architecture.

Patterns such as the above are created to permit a clear separation between the different technologies needed to develop such a system, and each technology has its own standards and construction methods.

Such systems should be easier to maintain as there is a clear separation of concerns, roles, behavior and code, although there is a shortage of empirical evidence that this is so.

In commercial systems, the lower tiers of the system will service many different types of upper tiers. These upper tiers are also more likely to change with new applications. The lower levels are more stable, but when they do have to be reengineered, it is expensive.

But how do we do this when we are basing our approach around small increments. This raises a nuber of questions:

Does this mean that the smallest increment has to involve all of the layers?

Should we build the database first or the GUI and regard these as increments?

What happens when there is a major requirements change and we have to make revisions to the database structure, for example?

The idea of a separation of concerns is great if it is introduced at the appropriate time as it allows for detailed work on a part of the system without affecting other areas.

However, it is possible to get too obsessed with this idea too early; for example, before we fully understand the real needs of the customer. We need to make some judgments here, and good judgments usually need experience or some guiding principles.

What is driving the incremental approach in XP and the desire to produce the best solution in a changing world is the principle of the last responsible moment, which means that we should not fix on a definite solution or rigid architecture before we are ready.

This then poses the question of how do we interface an agile approach to an architectural framework such as the three-layer model?

There are a number of development environments that can support some of these standard architectures, particularly in the realms of Web-based database systems.

Ruby on Rails is one such language that can be used to generate such systems rapidly—it is based on the Ruby language (an object-oriented language developed from Smalltalk and Python) and provides support for the development of the underlying database as you go along. This may make building small increments easier. Further details are at http://www.rubyonrails.org/.

Another similar environment is Symfony, which is PHP based and is claimed to be very compatible with XP. In both these approaches, the development of the GUI is the main driving force, and the database is dealt with as you go. Further details on Symfony may be found at http://www.symfony-project.org/.

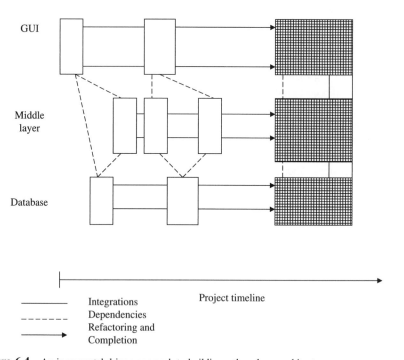

Figure 6.4   An incremental driven approach to building a three-layer architecture.

If you are dealing with the three-layer architecture and trying to build small increments, then the way to do this will depend on the circumstances. However, you might find that the increments may involve just parts of the GUI or parts of the database or some more complete *slice* through the architecture.

Figure 6.4 provides a hypothetical view of a small project that starts with some GUI increments, then a partial database is built that is then connected to the GUI through a middle layer, which then needs further increments; the GUI is developed further, and this leads to more database work, more in the middle layer, and then the integration. Testing will take place as we go along so that the connections through the layer should be working when the final build is made.

6.3 ARCHITECTURES AND PATTERNS

Whatever system is finally built, it will have an architecture: it will be composed of a number of components, and the architecture describes how these are put together. Some standard architectures are used for standard types of problems: they all have their strengths and weaknesses. Decisions have to be made about the architecture—sometimes at a time when the full implications of the system being built are still unclear. Once an architecture has been chosen, it is difficult and expensive to change. This is needs to be considered carefully.

Essentially, an architecture is the outline of a design solution to a problem. In an agile project there is a dilemma—how do we fix an architecture when we may not fully understand the problem?

There is some benefit in exploring the problem through a conceptual model with the customer before the architecture is finalized.

The XXM approach described later in this chapter can be really useful in this situation as many people can see the way that the system might behave and how it might relate to their business needs.

Once we understand what it is that we are trying to build—and this develops gradually over the course of the project—we can start thinking about the architecture.

There will be many possible choices to make, and the way this decision is made has to be a team decision with everyone committed to it. Unfortunately, this is an area where opinions can be strong—all the more surprising as for many there is very little evidence to support them. It is better to choose an approach that has been shown to work than to pick something that has been the subject of hype or is "hot of the press"! Don't forget that simplicity is one of the key values in agile development—don't use an architecture that is more complex or difficult than the problem needs. Certainly don't take the view, "I want to use this architecture," before you have really understood the problem.

A recent Genesys project underlines some of the dangers in adopting a potential solution before all of the issues are understood. Our customer wanted an e-commerce retail system that was integrated with a stock control system. A popular ASP.NET shop framework, supported by Microsoft and PayPal, was adopted fairly early on, and the project proceeded reasonably smoothly—and rapidly.

It became apparent, after several weeks of work, that it was not an ideal solution. The underlying architecture was not either very well articulated or flexible, and too much of the key data was hard coded into the framework and just did not allow for the flexibility the team needed in order to meet the customer's requirements. It seemed to have been designed to impress rather than to deliver! If the customer could have taken the framework and customized it to his needs, then it would have been a quick and effective solution. However, it was completely unsuitable as a basis for anything other than the standard solution that it was produced for.

The project started again with a more suitable architecture. Progress was fairly rapid after this as many of the issues relating to the customer's requirements had already been considered so the team was able to deliver a good solution on time despite the problems.

An important trend in object-oriented programming is the design pattern. There are now many types of these, and they are intended to provide a reliable framework for many common tasks in programming. The same advice is relevant here—don't decide that you must use a particular pattern before you understand the problem well.

6.4   FINITE STATE MACHINES

We take a small diversion at this point and start to think about how stories might appear in action. Software is dynamic; in other words, it responds to events and inputs, and this behavior is dependent on the internal status of the program—the state it's in.

Extreme programming encourages all the participants to continually explore the assumptions about the needs of the customer; to encourage everyone in learning more about the processes involved in an attempt to provide the greatest possible value for both customer and developers. The analysis and design effort is spread right across the project and not just concentrated at the beginning.

However, its success is dependent on identifying really rigorous system test sets as these are what constrains the software solution to a high-quality and suitable solution.

Testing is a dynamic activity; you supply some test inputs and see what happens. Thus a dynamic model of software is needed in order to predict what are the best tests that will provide convincing evidence that the software—the story, the system, or part of the system—works in the sense that the requirements are met.

It is impossible to define stringent test sets without knowing some details of what the system has to do. This is the basic dilemma that we face and one that has not been fully resolved within the XP movement.

What is needed is a notation that is simple to use and understand, adaptable to changes in requirements, and which can add value to the project in as many ways as possible.

Ideally, it should be possible for customers to understand what the diagram tells them. This is quite a challenge, and few of the current notations seem to be suitable.

Unified Modeling Language (UML) is widely taught in universities and is used in many design-led projects. However, it is a very complex and sprawling set of different types of model that can cause as much confusion as enlightenment.

Let's try to identify something that is lightweight, easy to use, flexible, understandable to both developers and clients, which can contribute to a clearer view of the way that the application works, and, as an important bonus, provides the framework for systems testing.

It is also based on some ideas that are taught in most computing courses, although usually presented in a theoretical way and which may not have been obviously useful for practical software projects.

The notion of a finite state machine is core to the understanding of how computers work, both in terms of hardware (sequential processors) and for some software applications (simple control systems) and, in a more general form, compilers (lexical analyzers). Many universities teach courses on finite state machines although very little use of them is made afterwards in software engineering. A variant, statecharts, is featured in UML but is generally restricted in its use.

A *finite state machine* (also called an *automaton*) consists of a finite set of states together with transitions between states that are triggered by streams of inputs.

In Fig. 6.5, we have a machine with five states $\{1, 2, 3, 4, 5\}$. There are two *input* symbols $\{a, b\}$ and three *output* symbols $\{x, y, z\}$.

This machine starts in state 1 (the *initial* state). The machine will read whatever is the first input symbol and move to another state while outputing an output symbol. An input of a will move the machine to state 2 and generate an output of x; but an input of b will move the machine to state 3 and generate an output of y.

Streams of inputs will produce streams of outputs, thus the sequence a a b a b (read from the left) will cause the output sequence x z y y y and end with the machine in state 5.

Other sequences will have different effects.

For a simple log-in function, we might have a little diagram something like Fig. 6.6.

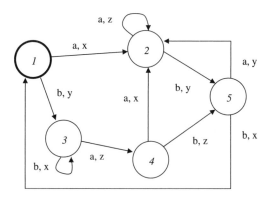

Figure 6.5   A simple finite state machine.

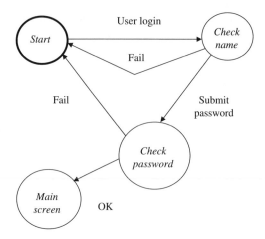

Figure 6.6 A simple state machine of a log-in process.

This is quite a descriptive diagram as it shows the sequences of possible actions that the system undergoes—initially the user starts at the *Start* state and logs in. This takes them to the *Check name* state, and if the username is not recognized, the system returns through the fail transition to the *Start* state. If the name is registered, the user is then prompted for a password, which is then checked. Again the log-in will fail if this is not correct. Otherwise the user is into the main part of the system.

The problem is that it is not a proper finite state machine for a number of reasons:

1 The user inputs are sequences of symbols rather than a single symbol.

2 The output is not specified in the diagram.

3 The *Check name* and *Check password* states hide a lot of invisible behavior; in particular, the machine needs to look up information in some database or similar memory component.

Thus finite state machines are not powerful enough for our purposes. There are other, more powerful machines that can be used, for example, pushdown machines are popular in theoretical computer science courses. They contain a simple stack like memory that can be used to do more sophisticated things such as to recognize certain types of formal languages (context-free languages).

Furthermore, finite state machines tend to be too low level for practical use, but a generalization of these has been developed based on ideas of a famous mathematician of the 1970s (Samuel Eilenberg).

This will be discussed in the next section.

Our approach is to apply this extremely powerful modeling paradigm that seems to be fairly easy to use and has *proven* excellence in the construction of functional test sets.

6.5 EXTREME MODELING (XM)

It makes a lot of sense to have a simple and lightweight method of describing the system or parts of a system in terms of what it does and the order in which it does it. If we have such a picture, we will be able to use it to define test sets that do more than just test one simple function.

The extreme X-machine (XXM) is a suitable candidate. These were introduced by Thomson (2003, 2005), and we have been using these for a number of years with great success. They are popular with programmers, and customers can also make sense of them.

The simple machine of the type in Fig. 6.6 is called an X-machine by Eilenberg (1974) and is discussed at length in Holcombe (1998). It can be used to describe many things, but it is not always convenient.

One problem is that each state transition (indicated by an arrow) needs to be triggered by an external input or event. Sometimes, especially in object-oriented programs, we would like to allow the system to call some other function or method without an explicit external input.

Thus we might have the diagram shown in Fig. 6.7.

Here the input from a potential user is supplied in one go, by completing a simple form, and the *Validate user* state then generates a result that triggers one of the three transitions *Fail*, *User access*, or *Admin access* internally.

The operations that are labeling the transitions (arrows) represent functions of various levels of complexity. The real power of these machine diagrams is that they can be hierarchical. In other words, the functions labeling the transitions can themselves be broken down into a series of operations at a lower level described by a subsidiary machine.

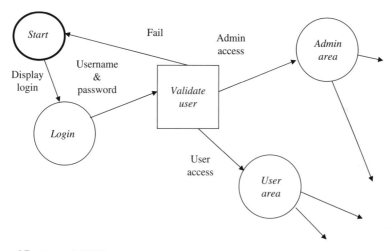

Figure 6.7   A simple XXM.

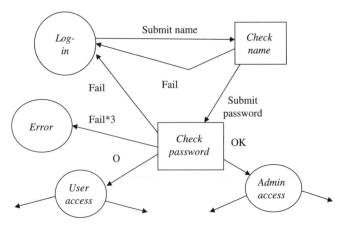

Figure 6.8 A detailed XXM model of the transition *Username & password* in Fig. 6.7.

Thus the *Username & password* function could be defined in another diagram (Fig. 6.8).

In this system, consider what happens in the *Check password* state. There are three possible transitions from this state:

The password is okay and the user has Admin privileges.

The password is okay and the user has User privileges.

The password fails, and if this happens three times, the error state is reached, and a message is displayed on the screen stating this.

There are no other possibilities and so the system will be fully defined at this point.

In some cases, you may find a state where there could be cases that have not been specified—in these cases it is important to decide what the system should do—it might ignore an input and remain in the same state, for example, or raise an error and transfer to an error state from which some suitable recovery is defined.

Now consider the benefits for testing. As soon as you have defined an XXM, it is possible to define some testing sequences. An obvious strategy is to design test sets that will trigger each transition either singly or in sequences derived from the diagram.

For Fig. 6.8, the following operational sequences can be defined, immediately.

1 Display *Login* (essentially running the program from the beginning)

2 *Username & password*

3 *Admin access*

4 *User access*

We are using the labels of the transitions to denote these sequences. We need to consider the Fail transitions, also. Thus a set of test sets can be constructed to do this.

Table 6.1   Basic Data for Some Tests

Name	Password	Administration rights
User1	Pass1	Admin
User2	Pass2	Admin
User3	Pass3	no
User4	Pass4	no

Suppose we define a set of users with passwords—some with admin access (Table 6.1).

We need also to define some other strings to represent invalid users to the system.

Now we can set up a simple set of tests to see whether the entire machine is implemented correctly in the implementation of the story. Thus a test such as <User1> ; <Pass1> should result in getting to the Admin section initial screen. However <User1> ; <Pass2> should produce a failure, which returns the system to the Start screen. Thus the strategy is to make sure that every path through the machine (a path is a sequence of transitions taken one after the other) is explored and tested.

The model thus far discussed puts the main focus on the *control* of the software—what can be done and when. Software, however, consists of two principle elements: control and data. They are intimately linked together—one without the other tends to provide an incomplete view of things. In languages such as UML, there are diagrams and notations that can describe the control (e.g., statecharts), and there are diagrams that describe data (often from an implementation point of view such as class diagrams together with local methods).

In the approach taken here, we have a tighter link between the two aspects. The XXM diagrams show the flow of control in the system; the states divide up the system in such a way that the operations are managed in a suitable way. But what do these operations do? They process data, and it is here that we can introduce the type of data that is important to the application.

The example discussed above involves data in some kind of database. Thus the operations in the system manipulate this database—uploading information, querying information, and deleting information. Each of the operations can be defined in terms of what it does to the database state.

In another example, consider a word processor. Here the operations will manipulate text, inserting sections of text into an existing document, formatting parts of the document, saving and opening text files, and so on. The data can be described in very general terms as a set of sequences of characters or symbols, including spaces. In a rather simplistic way, we could describe the state of a document as consisting of three sequences:

<sequence1> , <sequence2> , <sequence3>

Each if these sequences could be empty.
The sequences

$$<\text{A cat sat}> , \ <> , \ <\text{on the mat}>$$

represent a document with the text "A cat sat on the mat" and the cursor positioned immediately after the word *sat.*

The sequences

$$<\text{A cat sat}> , \ <\text{quietly}> , \ <\text{on the mat}>$$

represent a document "A cat sat quietly on the mat" with the word *quietly* highlighted at the cursor.

The sequences

$$<> , \ <> , \ <>$$

represent a blank (new) document.

Thus we try to identify the operations that are important, the data that they operate on, and the state space that provides the organization of these operations into a system.

In many cases, these operations relate to stories, and the identification of the data that they operate on will be an important activity.

As we gradually build up the system in increments, we will find that the data being operated on will gradually expand or become refined (in a database application the database structure may change), new tables added when new stories need them; in the word processing example, the structure of a document will become more complex (e.g., if we are inserting pictures into the text, this will need an extended vocabulary including file references for the pictures that are inserted in the appropriate place in the text).

6.6 MULTIPLE STORIES AND XXMs

What if we have a number of connected stories such as in Fig. 5.7? Here is an example: Φ-*net* (see Chapter 4).

Figure 6.9 is a top-level view of the system illustrating how different sections relate to each other. The diagram is not complete as the subsidiary pages have no arrows leaving them—the convention here is that they will return to the main page, but final decisions have not yet been made, and the diagram may be expanded at a later time.

Now we are beginning to see how the system might fit together; how it might look to the user and behave. It is worth showing the client some mock-ups of the interface at this stage and work through the scenarios derived from the requirements analysis that you have been doing. We can get some feedback to enable us to check if we are going in the right direction. The client can also reexamine his or her ideas and perhaps see new opportunities or problems with their original thoughts.

Main XXM for Fizzilink APRABS Version 2.1

Links (NHS Direct etc...)(D)

Online Shop (O)

Login (M)

Main Homepage (M)

Physio Direct (Advice section (O))

Registration (M)

Physio Admin (M)

Appointment Booking (M)

Customer's Individual Page (M)

Register Customer (M)

Register Physio practice (M)

Physio Admin Page (M)

Webmaster's Admin Page (M)

Register Physio (M)

Key:
- *(M) – Mandatory*
- *(D) – Desirable*
- *(O) – Optional*
- ⟶ *– Will be implemented*
- ⟶ *– Will be considered*

Diagram 1 Main Extreme Machine

Figure 6.9   Main XXM for Φ-net system.

The next, more detailed example that we will consider is the DELTAH project (Fig. 6.10) that involved a set of Web pages organized as follows: The user interface contains nine main Web pages called FrontPage, Home, Deltah, About, News, Downloads, Questionnaire, Links, and Contact Us. Each of these Web pages may

Figure 6.10   The DELTAH home page.

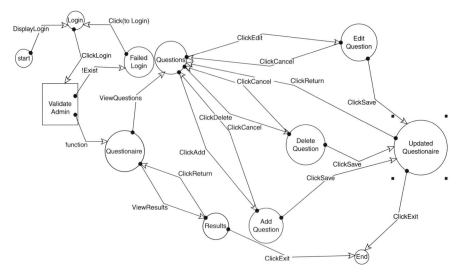

Figure 6.11   XXM for Questionnaire section.

also include one or more subpages as well. The user can open each Web page simply by clicking on its name.

The next task is to think about the order in which these screens will be deployed and the tasks that can be done on each screen. The sequence of Web pages are described using the set of XXMs shown in Figs. 6.11–6.15.

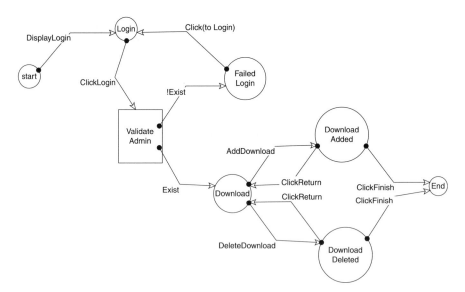

Figure 6.12   XXM for MailingList section.

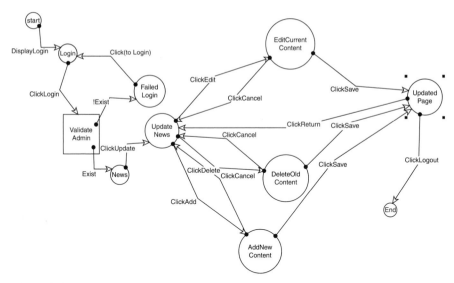

Figure 6.13   XXM for News section.

From the diagrams, one can see how the basic functions are organized. These machines differ from the standard finite state machine and from the statecharts sometimes used in UML in the sense that there is a memory in the machine, and the transitions involve functions that manipulate the memory as and when an input

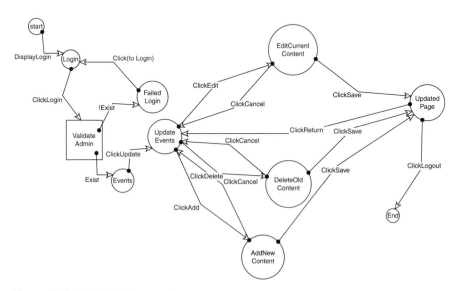

Figure 6.14   XXM for Events section.

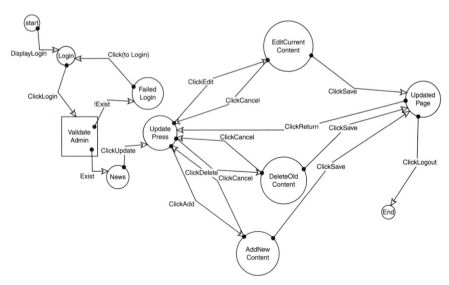

Figure 6.15   XXM for Press section.

is received. This provides an integrated modeling approach that combines in one diagram both processing and data.

This is explained by referring to the requirements table and the story cards where the memory connection is described.

For example, in the first diagram (Fig. 6.11), the memory in this case is likely to be the database that contains the questions in the questionnaires together with the answers, and so on, etc. of customers and orders.

The function ClickLogin simply navigates between two screens and has no memory implications, but the function ClickEdit will involve some interaction with the database; it will download questions to be edited—generating a message if none are on the database. There may be some dialogue with the user to identify the precise questions that need editing. This would be described in a subsidiary diagram, using the hierarchical properties of XXMs.

The function ClickSave in Fig. 6.16 actually changes the database by updating the records with the new or altered questions.

The memory structure now needs to be discussed. Essentially, we need to think about this in terms of what basic types of memory structure are relevant at the different levels. At the top level, for example, we could represent it as a small vector or array of compound types of the form:

$$\text{Questionaires} := \text{set of questions}$$

where

$$\text{questions} := \text{question\_number}; \text{question\_text}; \text{question\_answer}$$

and the data is text.

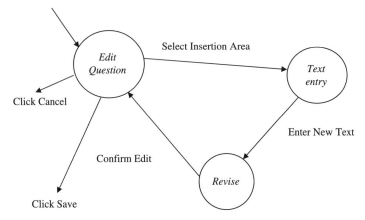

Figure 6.16   Expansion of EditQuestion state in Fig. 6.11.

The diagram can be used to define when and under what conditions different processes and stories are available. It will also help us to test the system thoroughly.

6.7   BUILDING THE ARCHITECTURE TO SUIT THE APPLICATION: A DYNAMIC SYSTEM METAPHOR

Thinking back to the X-machine model, it now becomes clear that this structure is entirely in keeping with what is going on in the Business Logic tier of the simpler architecture in Sections 6.3 and 6.4 What we can do is separate out the different parts of the Business Logic layer in terms of what communication it is expected to carry out. The X-machine will define the overall structure of the controller, which would represent a number of *if-then-else* statements; the model will reflect the current state of the system separated out from the underlying database.

We can develop an XXM model of a system, such as Fig. 6.17 and the next stage is to try and map that onto the architecture.

The Ignore transition is designed to deal with situations where the mouse is clicked in an area outside of the buttons Customer or Order.

From this state, we have one of three mutually exclusive situations:

Mouse is clicked over the Customer button

Mouse is clicked over the Order button

Mouse is clicked over the rest of the screen or any keyboard key is pressed

This ensures that there is some defined behavior for the system under all possible conditions that can hold in this *Start* state.

We should include Ignore functions like this in many other states so that there is a full specification of what the system should do under all conditions, but the diagram will get cluttered.

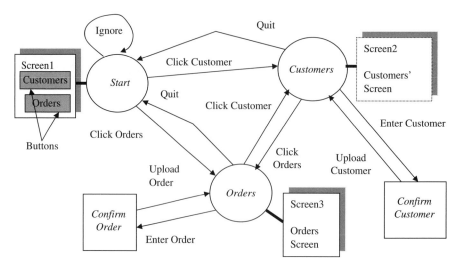

Figure 6.17 An XXM diagram.

Another aspect to consider is the identification of potential *error states*—states where the system can no longer continue without endangering the integrity of the system somehow. We need to identify these error states and decide how to handle them.

The process of adding all these Ignore or Error transitions is to produce a *complete* machine.

What is important is that we should think about every state and examine what will happen under all possible conditions. There are two questions to ask:

1 Is there always a transition that will be valid?

2 Is there only one valid transition?

If there is more than one valid transition under some conditions, the system will be *nondeterministic*, which means that its behavior will not be predictable—usually a bad idea!

Returning to the system under discussion, we need to consider some of the operations and, in particular, the data they are processing in more detail.

The first stage is to consider the data requirements and construct the underlying database. To do this, we examine what the information is being stored and what it is used for. Some of this will be described at a high level and will need decomposing into more detail; for example, there are customers and these have been defined in terms of their names, addresses, phone numbers, and so forth. This is clearly a suitable structure of a database table with an appropriate customer key (Table 6.2).

The machine can be refined to include more detail, and an example of this is Fig. 6.18. (Note that we have indicated some of the Ignore functions to remind ourselves of the need to complete the machine.)

Table 6.2 A Simple Customers' Table

Customer_ID	Customer_name	Address_line1	Address_line2	Address_line3	ZIP/postcode	Phone	E-mail
ABC123	WidgetCity	345 Biz Park	Some Road	Big City	BC1 4 AS	564 583	Widg.com
ABC124	ThingArama	Corp HouStart state.se	Little Street	Townsville	TV2 7BB	530 986	ThingArama.co.uk

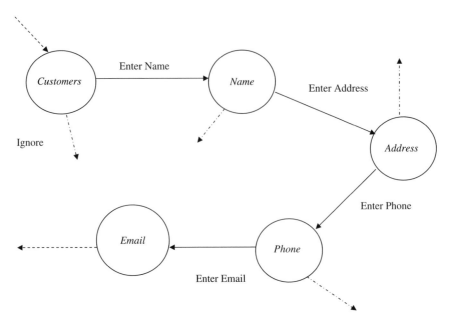

Figure 6.18   Unpacking an X-machine function.

Another table is defined for the orders component, and so on.

One problem with databases is that they are often hard to maintain in the sense that, if our customer comes along with some fundamental new requirements and these involve substantial changes to the tables and their relationships, then we could be in trouble requiring a major reengineering of the database. There is no easy solution to this; relational tables are highly optimized for performance and integrity, and the price that is paid for this is in their inherent inflexibility in the light of changing requirements.

Increasingly, databases are being developed using the language XML (Bray, 2000), which is much more flexible. There is technology available to connect application programs to these XML databases. The main APIs (Application Programming Interfaces) for providing an interface for XML documents in Java are JAXP, the Document Object Model (DOM), the Simple API for XML (SAX), and JDOM. All these APIs offer advantages and disadvantage with no single API standing out as the standard, although JDOM is becoming popular in Java-based applications due to its efficiency and ease of use (JDOM, 2001). Other technology includes the Extensible Stylesheet Language (XSL) (Adler, 2001).

Now we consider the way that the problem can be interpreted using the XXM of Fig. 6.5.

Suppose that the ClickCustomer function is triggered. This then requests the system to present the Customer Screen, which it does through the Viewer component.

The User then submits data through the Customer screen, the data is then analyzed to see if it passes the integrity tests on the data—is it of the correct format for the field involved—and if there are problems, the response is to send an error to the screen.

If the data passes the integrity check, the system then queries the database to see if the record already exists, and if it does it will generate another error (different screen).

If it is a genuine new customer, the system will update the database with this information.

The GUI will comprise different screens for display to the user: some will be the screens listed on the XXM diagram, and others will be error screens associated with business logic clauses that fail—the type of data submitted is invalid, the data conflicts with that on the database, and so forth.

To explain these different actions, we can envision them in the following sequence diagrams.

The simplest case is a direct interaction between the User Interface and the Business Logic layer that does not require the involvement of the database. The functions to control the slider bar, to resize the screen, and to migrate between screens using mouse clicks and mouse movements are of this nature. Thus transitions in an XXM are triggered by *events* such as button clicks or the results of queries, and the results of these transitions are *actions*, which include changing the screen, committing data to a database, sending data to some other actor or component in the system, and so on.

We can see how this general model works in a few examples.

A simple class will handle the sort of function shown in Fig. 6.19. It will listen for the specified *event* and change the interface accordingly.

A more complex situation will arise if the interface view has to reflect some other factor, for example to present specific information and functions that depend on the current state of the database and system generally. Thus the system may cause the GUI to disable or "gray out" a button or data field because it is not valid to have access to the function beneath it under the specific circumstances pertaining at the time.

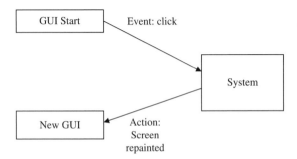

Figure 6.19   A simple interface action.

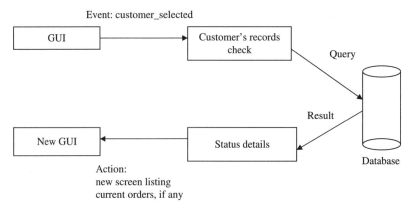

Figure 6.20   A conditional user interface action involving a database query.

An example of a general process for doing this is to select the specific customer and check whether there are any current orders and to present links to these orders on a new screen (Fig. 6.20).

Similarly for a function that submits data, carries out a check with the database, and then allows a commit action with reflection of success onto the screen.

Another example might be the validation of the format of the data supplied by the user. The business logic needs to check that the input data is in a valid format, for example a string of characters of length less than 30, a correct date format, and so forth. If necessary, the model will query the database to see if there is already data there in this field; depending on the outcome of this query, the logic will either commit the data or report an error to the user interface. After successful database update, a confirmatory message may be sent to the user.

The analysis of these events and actions will provide us with some guidance on how the program should be structured and what classes will need to be developed.

If there is a number of places where there has to be a check that the entry data submitted satisfies some predefined format, for example a text string of length less than 30, then it makes sense to write a class with a method that does just this. This class is then available to the other parts of the program that require this check to be made. This is better than embedding this check separately in all the methods that need it.

The overall machine perspective is useful for the development of a simple system metaphor. In the next chapter, we will look at the way in which we might derive the class structure from it.

Because projects vary enormously, it is hard to provide examples of useful metaphors that will be applicable to them all. In the next section, we look at an area that provides an increasing number of projects, that of the e-commerce application.

6.8 ANOTHER LOOK AT ESTIMATION

The simple models that we have built using the X-machine approach can provide some clues to the resources needed to carry out the project.

If you have been building these models and seeing what the stories that they involve take to construct, then there is a way of identifying a general estimate for the project.

Suppose that we have an overall architecture that indicates how the system might appear when it meets most of the requirements that the customer identifies. We know that the system architecture may change with time and these machines will need to be updated—this is discussed in Chapter 9.

The diagram might have a top level description as in Fig. 6.21.

Each of the circles describes a state or a mode (aspect) of the system, and the arrows describe a mechanisms for moving between these modes. These may be defined in a variety of different ways. These operations may involve quite complex activity that needs to be unpacked into a lower-level machine in the ways that we saw above.

The idea is to continue unpacking the machines until we get to a level of abstraction that corresponds with a story or set of stories that can be completed in a short iteration.

In Fig. 6.20 we see that there are seven of these high level operations. Suppose that these are then decomposed into further lower-level operations until we get to the level where we can start building stories.

In Fig. 6.22, we have decomposed some of the operations in the top level into lower-level machines—and then some of these have been decomposed further. In the top level, we have some simple transitions (operations) as well as some more complex ones. The complex ones are then decomposed at the lower level and so on.

At the bottom level, each of the arrows represents an operation that can be coded up as a small iteration, and we can use this as a means of making an estimate of the effort needed.

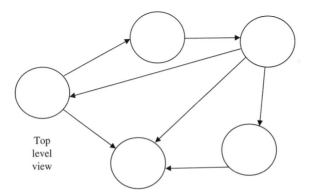

Figure 6.21   A system architecture.

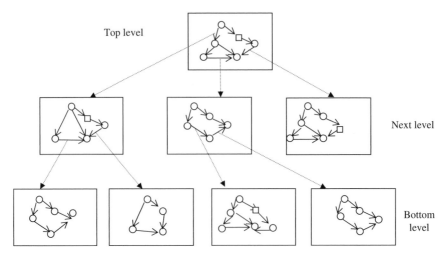

Figure 6.22   A hierarchy of machines.

We can then collect together how many stories might be involved to give us a rough idea of what effort is needed. These diagrams, however, provide a richer structure map of the system and can help to identify critical areas and their complexity.

In this hypothetical example, we might count up the basic stories and states (screens) from all of these levels—so many at the top level, so many at the next level, so many at the bottom level.

It may be that all of these are roughly equivalent in terms of how complicated they are to implement, but we may have a more subtle view, knowing that some will take longer than others from our previous experience. It may be possible to categorize these operations or stories and screens into different types and make estimates on the effort needed to implement and test these from this information—recalling previous similar examples.

In some of our analysis, we have looked at the structure of the individual operations—some involve database communication, others involve the construction of a complex interface with a lot of data validation, and all of this information is useful in estimating the development time.

If we return to our simple XXM (Fig. 6.23), then we can put some numbers on the tasks involved in building this part of the system.

For the outline structure, which involves setting up a framework for the machine, we can estimate, say, 2 days. For each screen, perhaps another 3 days each. For the EnterCustomer function—which includes data validation—we allow 5 days. The UploadCustomer involves database queries so that might take another 5 days—to include the extension of the database if needed. In this way, we can put some better estimate together for this part of the system. As always, it is based on our prior experience, and we should look through our archives for similar activities to see how we did with them.

We must not forget the impact of system testing in our resource model. The sizes of the test sets can be estimated from the diagrams, and this can be an indication of

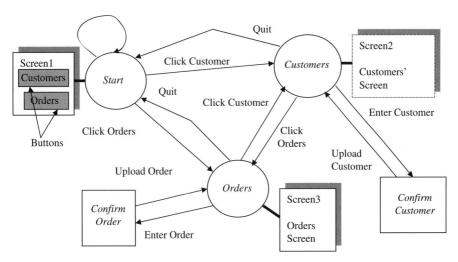

Figure 6.23   A simple lower-level XXM.

Table 6.3   Estimates of Effort Required for the System
Described in Fig. 6.22

Activity	Estimate of time (days)
Framework	2
Screen 1	3
Screen 2	3
Screen 3	3
EnterCustomer	5
UploadCustomer	5
Integration testing	10
Debugging	20
Total	51

test time—but then there is debugging time which is always a factor. Maybe we should add a factor of 2 to cover this! Experience will tell you if this is reasonable (Table 6.3).

6.9   REVIEW

The concept of the system metaphor is a rather inprecise one, and this is both good and bad. It allows teams to develop their own approach relevant to their application domain, but it then raises the issue of whether this is very helpful for maintenance when a different team may be involved. What is important is that the approach taken and the representations used are clearly explained and documented.

We have described a number of approaches to structuring the architecture of the system that makes change more manageable. The thing to avoid is an unstructured system where changes made in one area can have unpredictable consequences elsewhere. Various *layered* approaches are common these days, and the separation of the data, the business logic, and the presentation layers seems to make sense.

The user interface is a key component; spend as much time as you can on getting this right. It is not just the design of any screens bit but also how they interconnect with each other and their place in the system overall. The XXM idea seems to be quite useful for both designers and customers—it is fairly lightweight and flexible. It has value for a number of issues, testing being a major one.

EXERCISE

1. Look at several different Web sites and try to establish if their user interfaces meet the criteria spelled out in Section 6.6.

CONUNDRUM

A local retailer specializing in luxury goods commissioned an e-commerce system. This was completed and installed satisfactorily. The shop gave the job of printing out the Internet orders and processing them through the orders system to one of the sales assistants to do at the end of their shift. This worked well at the beginning as the numbers of orders were small and only grew gradually.

After a few months of steady growth, the sales figures of orders placed through the Web suddenly collapsed to nothing. Initially, it was thought to be a software fault but no problems were found when we investigated.

What could have gone wrong?

REFERENCES

S. Adler, A. Berglund, J. Caruso, S. Deach, T. Graham, P. Grosso, E. Gutentag, A. Milowski, S. Parnell, J. Richman, S. Zilles. *Extensible Stylesheet Language (XSL) Version 1.0*. Available at: http://www.w3.org/TR/xsl/.

S. Eilenberg. *Automata, Languages and Machines*, Vol. A. Academic Press, 1978.

M. Holcombe. *Correct Systems. Building a Business Process Solution.* Springer.

B. Schneiderman. *Designing the User Interface.* Addison-Wesley, 1998.

C. Thomson, M. Holcombe. Applying XP ideas formally: The story card and extreme X-machines. In *Proceedings of the 1st South-East European Workshop on Formal Methods*. Thessaloniki, Greece, South-East European Research Centre, 2003, pp. 57–71.

C. Thomson, M. Holcombe. Using a formal method to model software design in XP projects. In *Proceedings of the 2nd South-East European Workshop on Formal Methods*. Ohrid, FYR of Macedonia, AMCT, South-East European Research Centre, Vol. 1 (3), 2005.

Chapter 7

Designing the System Tests

SUMMARY

What are tests?

- Developing a model to aid test generation

- Building the functional test sets for the stories

- Documenting the tests and the test results

- Design for test

- Non-functional testing and testing the quality attributes

7.1 PREPARING TO BUILD FUNCTIONAL TEST SETS

Testing is incredibly important. If we skimp on testing, we will suffer big problems. The problem is often that the oncoming delivery deadline does not include enough time for testing. However, it is better to be a couple of weeks late than to deliver poor-quality software that may come back to haunt you!

We are very aware of this at Genesys as it could be that the original development team has left and we have to do some maintenance without as much understanding of the system as we would like. To avoid this, we must test very thoroughly, system testing being particularly critical.

This chapter looks at systematic ways to design system tests.

7.1.1 Tests and Testing

First, what is a *test*?

A test is an application of some user or system input in a particular state of the system to establish if the system response is what is expected or is faulty in some sense—it might produce an incorrect response or output, no output, or the system might crash. A test must comprise both the *test input* and the *context* that the system must satisfy together with the *expected* output.

Going back to our interface models (Fig. 6.17, Chapter 6), we might consider the first screen and apply a test by clicking on the *customers* button. The expected result is a new screen, the customer's screen. That is all. We would not want the database to be deleted also.

When in the customer's screen, we might wish to test the data entry of the customer name and address. We have to specify the state that the test starts from and the data that we will insert. Now the data entry requirement will be based around some part of the software architecture—some classes or functions that accept user input and do things with it. The extent of the system testing that needs to be done is related to the level and extensiveness of the testing that has been carried out at the unit testing stage. Unit testing will be discussed in the next chapter; this is the testing of the classes and components. These will be put together to form coherent subsystems that will provide some functionality that we can relate to some of our stories. The stories are integrated together to form some useful business functions, and it is the business functions that we must deliver correctly.

For example, if there is data being input into the system, then there may be data integrity checks being carried out; these have to be tested to see if they work. If there are table lookups, for example the system might check that a specific postal/zip code exists by consulting an official list of these, or it might need to check that the format of the input is correct (letters where letters are expected and numbers also), then all this must be tested. If no control characters are expected, then the system must be tested to ensure that if they are, then no harm is done, and so forth. The system might need to check whether the customer is already registered on the database, and this will involve a query of the current database state.

The decision as to where the testing should be done—unit level or system level—and when is not always clear. Obviously, the more complete the testing at unit level, the better, but it is not possible to do all the things that are needed because interclass communication and communication with databases and tables may not be possible at that point in the project.

We will have to include in our system testing test cases that will expose faults in the data entry checking. We would do this by having test cases with *draft* input, for example. This might be invalid symbols or no symbols—perhaps just return—and so on.

We should also test the system under different conditions relating to the database, if any. For example, at the beginning the database is empty; we would test the system under these conditions, also when the database has some data in it and when it has a lot in it.

Where data entry has been carried out and hopefully stored in the database, we need to establish that the data has been stored correctly. This needs either setting up queries as part of the test or writing a suitable script to pull the data out to check that it is okay.

Thus test cases must reflect all of these things—what we put in and what we expect to see, and what we actually see.

The tests that we are talking about here are tests that relate to coherent pieces of a functioning system, and for them to be carried out we will need some code to test. In an XP project, we will have implemented and tested some stories and integrated them into such a subsystem. We can then apply the tests developed according to the methods in this chapter. The stories will be built from units of code, and how these units are tested will be the subject of this chapter.

7.1.2 Testing from a Model

One of the biggest challenges in testing is the constructions of tests themselves. The purpose of testing is to provide confidence that the software produced meets the requirements of the customer. For some customers, this can be met by an extensive period of evaluation in the customer's organization with the software being used in its intended operational environment by its intended users. This is rarely possible to any great extent and, anyway, it is not a good idea to leave things that late. Agile development should embrace the ability to be able to deliver the software with a high certainty that it will work as intended. Delivering working increments for the customer and users to evaluate is a big part of the approach. However, the relationship with customers and users can be damaged if these increments keep failing to meet the requirements. Furthermore, some customers just do not get round to trying out the increments when they are delivered, and thus the development team is getting no direct feedback from the customer about the quality of the system as it is being developed.

Having the customer design the system tests is often proposed. Our experience is that this rarely works well unless the customers really know what testing is about. Customers know—or should know—the fundamental business processes involved and can therefore describe these in such a way as to provide a useful basis for constructing test sets. Testing is a very difficult activity—some (e.g., Myers, 1978) claim that it is harder than any other aspect of the development process—anyone can write a set of tests, but designing efficient and effective tests that can give you a very high level of confidence about the behavior of the software is a major challenge. Why would customers know how to do this? Very few programmers do unless they have a lot of experience, often honed by big mistakes they have made in their past!

Where do we begin? Many test tools and methods assume the existence of some code to form the basis of the tests. This is something we do not have. So what do we have?

The machine-based model we started to develop in the past chapter will be very useful when it comes to finding good system test sets.

If we can build a machine diagram like Fig. 7.1 and relate all the main requirements to it, we can then create some very powerful test cases.

We developed our model for two main reasons. First, it was to try to understand, from the point of view of the behavior of the system, how it all fit together and mapped onto the requirements. Second, we will use it to generate test sets that will be fundamental to how we will establish that the system works.

Our model was based on identifying a set of states and the operations (functions) that operated between the states.

Recall the diagram from Chapter 6 (see Fig. 7.1). We will consider how to create test sets that will systematically exercise the system.

An obvious starting point is to try to check out the paths through this system (machine); this means looking for the conditions and activities that will force the system through paths made up of sequences or arrows. This we will do, and then we will consider how such *path sets* could be turned into test sets.

Suppose that we start with the system in the start state. Recall that our system also contains an internal memory component that needs to be considered. Let's assume

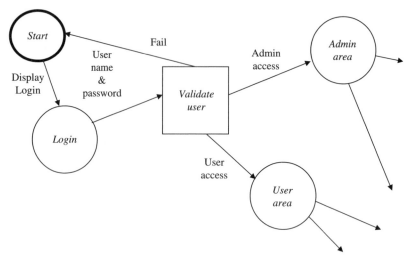

Figure 7.1   An XXM model from Chapter 6 (see Fig. 6.7).

that we are starting the system with some initial memory value, perhaps the set of records in the database is empty—we are awaiting the insertion of the details about our first customer. We will call this the *initial memory value*.

The first thing we have to do is to make the *Username & password* function operate as one might expect; this is achieved by inputing a username and password and clicking a submit button in the initial menu page. If this part of the system has been built properly, we should expect to move to a new state, either the screen for adminstrators, for users, or receive an error message due to the failure of the details submitted.

At a minimum, we need three types of test input: one that triggers the path to the Admin area; one that triggers a path to the User's area; and one that is rejected by the system.

In fact, this is really just testing the login story, but it illustrates that many stories can be expressed using these types of diagrams.

For the next stage, we need to look at Fig. 7.2. This is another system with a feature providing several options once the login has been achieved.

The general strategy is to design a series of tests that force the system to move through every possible path. There are some more sophisticated strategies that will be discussed later.

We need to exercise the functions that lead from the *Questionnaire* state next. This will be achieved by either viewing results of questionnaires or designing a new one. The state *Questions* is reached through the function ViewQuestions, and then the path might be

$$\text{ViewQuestions} \rightarrow \text{ClickEdit} \rightarrow \text{ClickSave} \rightarrow \text{ClickReturn}$$

which will involve inputing the information needed for each function (not just clicking on a button—in these GUIs the submission of information is through a

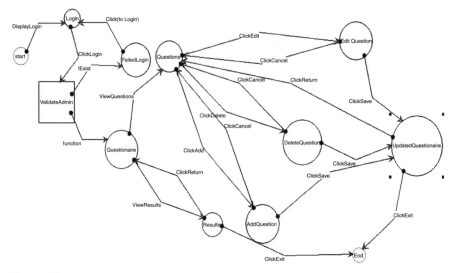

Figure 7.2   A more complex system (see Fig. 6.11).

form that is filled in and then the confirm button is clicked). The result should be a return to the *Questions* state.

This is just one test that needs to be applied. We should go through all the machine's paths to see that the software behaves as required.

A simple notation to describe these sequences of operations is to use the sequence operator ";" that well-known to those who have studied functional programming or formal methods. Thus:

ViewQuestions ; ClickEdit ; ClickSave ; ClickReturn

using semicolons instead of arrows.

We continue in this way forming sequences of legitimate operators to represent possible paths through the system. Each sequence will define a test that has to be carried out in a systematic way and the results observed and compared with what the model and requirements state.

If we find a problem, then it has to be investigated and fixed.

Another set of tests would be carried out by following the paths

ViewQuestions ; ClickDelete ; ClickCancel

ViewQuestions ; ClickDelete ; ClickSave ; ClickExit

ViewQuestions ; ClickAdd ; ClickSave ; ClickReturn

ViewQuestions ; ClickAdd ; ClickCancel

ViewQuestions ; ClickAdd ; ClickSave ; ClickExit

and so on.

This approach to finding test sets, or paths through the model, is one of the simplest and is called the *transition tour*.

In a transition tour, we choose a number of paths beginning at *start* and try to visit as many states as we can.

Some further examples are

ViewResults ; ClickExit

ViewResults ; ClickReturn ; ViewQuestions ; ClickAdd ; ClickSave ; ClickExit

and so forth.

The second test will exercise the interrelationship between the two parts of the system, which are likely to be the subjects of different stories. In other words, we are testing the integration of the two stories—viewing questionnaires and making questionnaires

To turn these sequences of transitions into a set of test inputs, we need to choose the various inputs that cause these sequences of transitions to operate. It's easy here, we look at the screens and identify either suitable buttons to press or we insert data in appropriate places to make it all happen.

It isn't always the case, and the choice of what data to input needs careful consideration. We will look at this later.

Such test sets will provide a good basis for testing the functionality of the overall system but they can be improved. There are a number of faults, for example, that such a test strategy may not reveal, including extra states, some faulty transitions, and so on.

These tests will tell us if the system is doing the things that we know we want it to do. However, they will not tell us if the system is doing anything else, possibly something undesirable. The key to good testing is to know enough about what it is you want and to test that this is what you get and *you don't get anything else* (Fig. 7.3). Thus we need to try to see if any *illegal* operations are possible. We need to do this throughout. The simple strategy is to take a path through the system to some state and then to introduce tests that test whether any functions that are not defined at the state are actually present. Thus we send the system to the target state and then try to apply all the functions that are *not* supposed to be

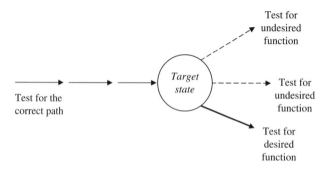

Figure 7.3 Testing for what we want and for what we don't want.

defined there. This should cause an *error* and we want to see that happen. Otherwise, there is something going on in that state when this *supposedly absent* function is called. This aspect will be considered in Section 7.6.

7.1.3 Developing the Model

A good way to think about these machines is to draw the state diagram and remember that the transitions that act between each state represent system functions that are triggered (usually) by an external event (user actions) and that carry out processing over some database or a global or local memory store. In many cases, the functions can be described very simply. One could use the formal notation Z^1 or VDM^2 for this, but I prefer a simple functional notation. This memory will be derived from the requirements in a natural way, so we refer to the requirements table where the memory connection is described.

Consider a simple *Sales* system typical of the sort of thing used by many companies (Fig. 7.4). It allows the addition of new customer details and of editing them; it also allows for the recording of orders by these customers.

In the XXM diagram of Fig. 7.4, the GUI screens are highlighted with shadowing to distinguish them from the decision states.

In this example, the memory is likely to be the database that contains the records of customers and orders. We need to think about the data in the system when testing it. We will only be able to show that the functions work if we test them with both the

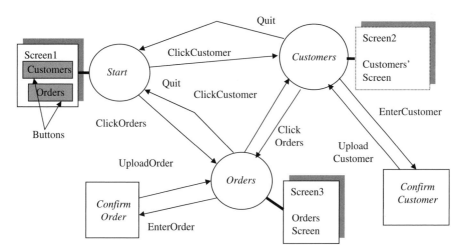

Figure 7.4   A simple XXM model of a sales system showing screens (see Fig. 6.17).[3]

---

[1]Z is a mathematical notation for specifying simple systems (Spivey, 1992).

[2]VDM is a similar notation (Jones, 1986).

[3]The ignore and error transitions have been ignored for the sake of simplicity.

type of data they expect and examples of the data they should not accept—checking
that the system will respond in a safe and timely manner.

The function ClickCustomer simply navigates between two screens and has no
memory implications, but the function EnterCustomer will involve some interaction
with the database—it might search to see if the supposed new customer is in fact new
before proceeding, generating a message if the customer is already on the database.
The function will involve moving between the different slots in the form filling in
the required details. It shouldn't matter which order we do this in, so the testing of
the EnterCustomer function will involve typing in suitable data values into these
slots in various orders.

The function UploadCustomer from the decision state *Confirm Customer*
actually changes the database by updating the records with the information relating
to the new customer, and the UploadOrder function from the *Confirm Order* state
updates the order.

In planning any of these tests, we need to think about the data we will supply to
the system as each function is triggered. Selecting suitable data is just as important as
identifying the sequence of functions.

The data structure now needs to be discussed in detail. Essentially, we need to
think about this in terms of what basic types of data are relevant at the different
levels. At the top level, for example, we could represent it as a small vector or
array of compound types of the form

customer_details

order_details

filling in the actual details later. It may be, for example, that these will represent part
of a structured database with a set of special fields that relate to the design of the
screens associated with these operations. Thus customer_details would involve
name, address, and so on, which would be represented as some lower-level compound data structure, perhaps, and there would be basic functions that insert values
into the database table after testing for validity, and so forth.

Now we can describe some of the functions from the diagram. First note that the
memory or database that the functions are interacting with is just a set of records with
two main fields, the first might be structured into

$$customer\_details : name, \ address, \ postcode, \ phone, \ fax, \ email$$

and the second into

$$order\_details : customer\_ref, \ order\_ref, \ order\_parts, \ delivery, \ invoice\_ref$$

Then the set of all *current* customer details is given by

Customer_details

so *Customer_details* might be {customer1, customer2, customer3} after three customers have been put in,

where customer1 = [name1, address1, postcode1, phone1, fax1, email1] and so on.

The notation using the braces, {,}, is a way of describing all the members of a collection of data elements that we want to refer to as a whole.

The set of all possible sets of customer details that there ever could be can be defined as CUSTOMER_RECORDS.

Thus *Customer_details* ∈ CUSTOMER_RECORDS.

For those who have not attended a discrete mathematics course, this is simply read as

Customer_details is a typical member of the collection of all CUSTOMER_RECORDS

and the current order details is {order1} after one order has been put in (Fig. 7.5), for example,

$$Order\_details = \{order1\}$$

where order = [customer_ref3, order_ref5, order_parts6, delivery, invoice_ref8].

Thus *Order_details* ∈ ORDER_RECORDS.

When a new customer is entered, the function UploadCustomer is triggered, the function should take the current state of the database, *Customer_details*, and add a new line to the database with the new customer's details. Thus the set *Customer_details* will change.

Recall that a typical element of the cutomer part of the database is

([name, address, postcode, phone, fax, email]

The function definition for UploadCustomer would now look like:

UploadCustomer ([name, address, postcode, phone, fax, email], *(Customer_details)*

$$= (Customer\_details) \oplus \{([name, address, postcode, phone, fax, email])\}$$

if [name, address, postcode, phone, fax, email] ∉ *Customer_details*

else error message: "customer already present"

name1, address1, postcode1, phone1, fax1, email1 name2, address2, postcode2, phone2, fax2, email2 name3, address3, postcode3, phone3, fax3, email3	customer_ref3, order_ref5, order_parts6, delivery, invoice_ref8
Customer_details	**Order_details**

Figure 7.5 A schematic of the state of the database after three customers have been entered and one order has been placed.

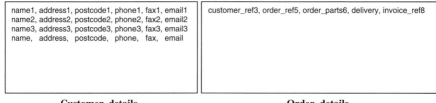

Customer_details   **Order_details**

Figure 7.6   The database after one new customer's details have been uploaded.

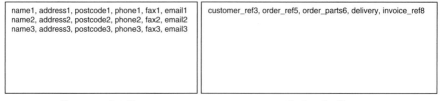

Customer_details   **Order_details**

Figure 7.7   The database after the attempt to upload an existing customer's details has been made.

Here ∉ means "is not a member of" and means that we add a new line to the current table containing what is in the newly supplied data: the six elements name, address, postcode, phone, fax, e-mail (Fig. 7.6).

The precondition is that these details are not already in the database. The *Order_details* part will not be changed by this operation. There should be an error message displayed.

The function's effect is thus either as shown in Fig. 7.6 or no change if the customer is already on the database (Fig. 7.7).

This is now the state of the memory after the UploadCustomer function has been applied with the new customer data: name, address, postcode, phone, fax, e-mail.

The symbol ⊕ simply states that we have added a new row to the database table containing only the new information that was not already there.

All the other functions in the diagram can be defined in a similar way.

If the function has been attempted with the wrong type of data for some or all of the fields needed for the UploadCustomer function, then the system should also keep the current state of the database the same. This is where we build in data validation—an essential and useful feature of most systems.

We can extend the function definition to emphasize this. First we have to define the types of the individual fields.

Thus

NAME is the set of acceptable names of customers (probably a string of characters)

ADDRESS is the set of acceptable addresses (it may have some more detailed structure involving City, State, Country, etc.—it will be a set of strings)

POSTCODE is the set of zip or postal codes (a string)

PHONE is the set of phone numbers (a string of digits, usually)

FAX is the set of FAX numbers with a similar format as PHONE

E-MAIL is the set of e-mail addresses (a string with @ and characters and full stops)

Thus we need a test to check that the following are true when the UploadCustomer is triggered:

name ∈ NAME;

address ∈ ADDRESS

postcode ∈ POSTCODE

phone ∈ PHONE

fax ∈ FAX

e-mail ∈ E-MAIL

If any of these fail, then an error message must be produced without changing the database.

Now we should consider the types of test that follow a similar overall strategy but using data of the wrong types or of values that are out of range in some way. This we will consider in the next section.

All types of systems can be described in this way—we need to identify the functions involved, the data and memory or database they use, and the states that sort out which function is valid and when.

We are going to use this type of state diagram to define how we can build a set of functional system tests that will link to the requirements and be extremely effective.

Most testing is *ad hoc* in the sense that the creation of the tests is left to the tester's common sense. This may not be a very effective way of finding faults—and this is what testing is all about.

7.2 TESTING WITH THE DATA IN MIND

Having studied the types of data that we expect to be processing, we will need to select examples of data to feed into the system tests.

Let's consider the data needed to test the UploadCustomer function.

There are six fields to be completed. Each field has a type, and the test data needs to be of two sorts—data that is of the correct type and data that is not. Within these two general categories, there will be a number of cases to consider that will be used to explore, as far as is possible, the set of possible inputs that could be expected. Don't forget, we want to see that expected data is treated correctly but also that the system does not break if data is supplied that is unusual or inappropriate.

Under the NAME field, we will have decided some format for the names that the system will deal with. Perhaps this will be a string of letters and numbers including some punctuation such as ".", "-", " ' ", and so forth. It may ignore "spaces" also.

We may have also decided that this string should not exceed 20 characters and punctuation.

Then we could consider the following examples of data input:

(a) Empty string

(b) One-character string

(c) Strings of 5, 10, 15 characters

(d) String of 20 characters

(e) String of 21 characters

(f) Strings containing one character that is "illegal"

(g) Strings contining a mixture of "illegal" and legal characters of different lengths

We do the same for the other fields ADDRESS, POSTCODE, PHONE, FAX, E-MAIL.

The data supplied during the testing of the function should then incorporate combinations of data that have been produced that explores all the possible mixtures of legal and illegal values relevant to the system.

This can be a little tiresome, but it could be automated.

7.3 THE FULL FUNCTIONAL SYSTEM TESTING STRATEGY

Each requirement in the requirements document should be traced to a test or tests. Because our requirements have been numbered and defined on story cards, it is important that each test should have a number that identifies which requirement it is testing for. Many of these requirements are represented by stories and will define unit tests. These are discussed in Chapter 8.

In order to understand the "big picture," the stories have been integrated. The requirements have been integrated into a dynamic machine-based model that defines the operational relationships between them. This model will now provide us with the system-level test sets. It is important to identify these at this stage. The testing of the individual requirements or the units/classes that implement them is covered in a later chapter.

We identify paths from the start state and derive a test for each path. However, we do more than that. Notice that the paths through the machine involve driving the system between the states by carrying out the various functions that are available at each state.

As we have seen, we start at the state *start* with the initial state of the internal memory, probably in some basic initialized state, and the aim is to visit every state in turn. When we have reached a state, we need to confirm that it is the correct state, and this is done by following more paths from that state until we get outputs that tell us, unambiguously, what the state was.

Looking at Fig. 7.4, we develop a test set. We consider the outline path obtained by operating the following functions these paths are based on listing the sequences of transitions (arrows) in the diagram:

ClickCustomer ; EnterCustomer ; UploadCustomer ; ClickOrders ; EnterOrder ;

UploadOrder ; ClickCustomer ; EnterCustomer ; UploadCustomer ; Quit

At each point in this sequence, we will be submitting data values or mouse clicks and we will have to choose these to enable the test to be carried out. We expect certain things to happen, and these have to be recorded, and the test will be evaluated in respect of detecting what actually happened and seeing if this matches the expected behavior. Did the buttons work, do the correct screens get displayed, was the correct data put into the database, were the correct error messages displayed (if appropriate) and the correct screen displayed subsequently, and so on?

This test tests what should be there. However it often happens, particularly with object-oriented programs, that the system can do unexpected things that were not planned for. We need also to test that *the functions that are not supposed to be there are not there!* We will look at how to do this in Section 7.5.

When preparing to choose test sets, there are thus two aspects to consider: the operations that are being tested and the data that they are processing. Selecting both carefully is important. We will need to test every data-processing operation and all possible combinations, and this will be discussed in the next section. Chapter 8 will discuss tresting at the unit level.

Another, rather draconian, general test is to reboot at an arbitrary point in the program. This is important as some users may panic and do this; we need to ensure that minimum data is lost in this situation.

7.4 THE THINKING BEHIND THE SYSTEM TEST PROCESS

We assemble the full test set in stages.

First, we return to the X-machine diagram, Fig. 7.8. We will look at a part of the diagram to explain the process.

What is our basic strategy for testing? If you look at the diagram, which represents what we want our software to behave like, then there are a number of ways in which we could have faults. We could find that a transition does not operate from the desired start or source state to the desired target state, for example, perhaps the event ClickCustomer leads us to the orders state or to some other state. The output we were expecting was the *Customers* state with its screen. Perhaps the function EnterCustomer fails to correctly accept the customer details— maybe they are just lost when we enter them. Perhaps there is no confirm state, and the transitions that are supposed to go there go somewhere else. Perhaps there are states that we did not intend to exist within our software; some extra states that cause the system to behave wrongly. In the diagram there is a *False_state* state that

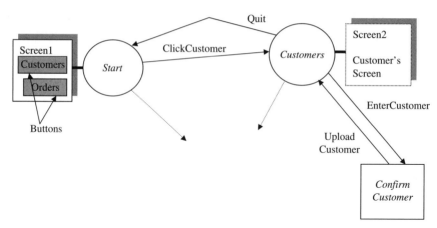

Figure 7.8 Customer section.

should not exist; it is unclear how we get into this state, but the EnterCustomer function can only operate to this state and not to the correct state, *Confirm Customer*.

To summarize, the software can differ from the machine model in a number of ways:

1 There are *too few* states.

2 There are *too many* states.

3 There are transitions going *from* an incorrect state.

4 There are transitions going *to* the wrong state.

5 There are transitions that carry out the *wrong function*.

Faults of type 1 (Fig. 7.9): In this example, the Orders state is missing. The transition to the *Orders* state, ClickOrders, exists in two places, the first takes

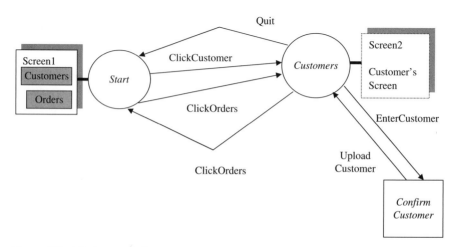

Figure 7.9 Missing state fault.

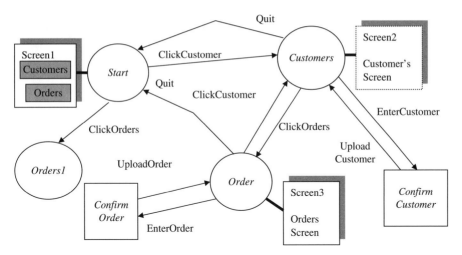

Figure 7.10   Too many states.

the system from the *Start* state to the *Customers* state and thus the wrong screen; the second from the *Customers* state back to the start.

Any test of the form ClickOrders or ClickOrders ; ClickOrders will detect the fault by virtue of an unexpected screen display.

Faults of type 2 (Fig. 7.10): A test that uses ClickOrders from the *Start* state will detect this fault, but not the same test from the *Customers* state.

Faults of type 3 (Fig. 7.11): In this example, the "faulty" transition is the Quit transition from *Customers* to *Start*, which goes from *Start* instead. Again a single test such as Quit will detect this.

Faults of type 4 (Fig. 7.12): A test ClickCustomer ; EnterCustomer will detect this.

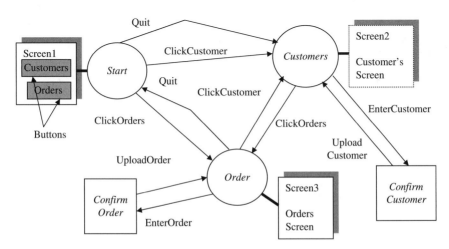

Figure 7.11   Transition *from* an incorrect state.

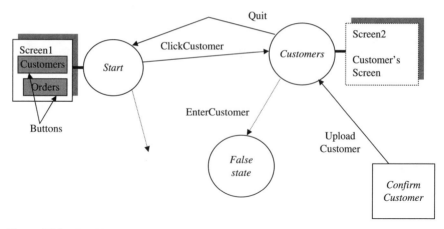

Figure 7.12   Transition going *to* the wrong state.

Faults of type 5 (Fig. 7.13): Here we need to consider the data as well.

The UploadCustomer operation is supposed to insert the details from the EnterCustomer operation into the database. To test this, we need to output the result of this operation somehow. This might be done as part of the user interface, but, more generally, we will need to run a report on the database to see if the operation was successful. This leads to a set of tests that vary according to the data being input. Thus, it might work for some cases but not for others.

Our systematic way of building tests will expose all these faults.

We are going to build a number of sets of function sequences as we did above but in a more complete manner.

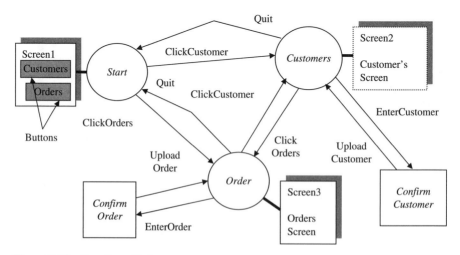

Figure 7.13   Transition with the wrong operation.

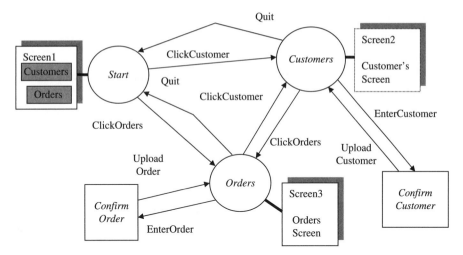

Figure 7.14   The desired model.

The first set is called the *transition cover*. What this consists of is a set of sequences that systematically work though the state space of the machine from the initial state. We start with the shortest sequences and extend them by trying out all the functions from the state we get to in turn. Then we take each of these sequences, and for those that should lead to another state, we then extend them by all the defined functions. We will look at the outputs from the software when we apply these sequences to see what happens; does it produce the right results?

Let's look at part of the machine in order to understand the process (Fig. 7.14).

We start at the state *Start*. The first test is the ClickCustomer event, which should take us to the *Customers* state. Now, how do we know that we have reached the *Customers* state rather than some other state? We will have to test for this separately. We should have already tested the function beforehand; this would be part of out unit testing process, which will be described later. If the function on the transition is more complicated than this, it might require a more complex use of this testing technique [this is not discussed here; see Holcombe (1998) for further details]. Having observed the results of this simple test, we now introduce some more. These consist of applying *all* of the possible transition functions after we have reached the *Customers* state; for example,

ClickCustomer

ClickCustomer : Quit

ClickCustomer ; EnterCustomer

ClickCustomer ; ClickOrders

ClickCustomer : Quit ; ClickOrders

ClickCustomer ; EnterCustomer ; UploadCustomer

ClickCustomer ; ClickOrders ; EnterOrder

ClickCustomer ; ClickOrders ; Quit

and so forth.

These are the sort of tests that should succeed if the implementation is correct. There are other sequences we should apply, also. These are expected to fail

Quit

ClickCustomer ; UploadOrder

ClickCustomer ; EnterCustomer ; Quit

and so forth.

These should generate failures during the testing. We need to check these out because it is important that the software does not do anything unexpected; checking that it does what it is supposed to do is only half the story. We also need to show that it doesn't do what it shouldn't do!

An issue that arises is that it is not immediately clear how you can apply a test sequence such as ClickCustomer ; UploadOrder as there is no trigger for the second function from the *Customers* state. In order to do this, we need to introduce some special triggers that access this function from the *Customers* state but that are only used in testing. This is an example of something that is discussed in Section 7.5.

Now we consider the position from the *Customers* state. We know how to get to this state, and we have to check that only the expected transitions operate from it and these have the right behavior. Thus we will try sequences such as

ClickCustomer ; EnterCustomer ; UploadCustomer

ClickCustomer ; EnterCustomer ; EnterOrder

ClickCustomer ; EnterCustomer ; UploadOrder

ClickCustomer ; EnterCustomer ; Quit

and so forth.

Some of these should succeed, but some should fail. We are trying to apply any operation from any state to prove to us that there are no hidden problems. The system may do things that we are unaware of; if the test ClickCustomer ; EnterCustomer ; Quit does not fail, then we may have some problems with the way that the database is being used.

We would only expect the first test to work, the others should fail.

7.4.1 An Algorithm for Determining the Transition Cover

Much of the process for generating and applying test sets to real cases can be automated. We consider the case of constructing the transition cover.

We first build a *testing tree* with states as node labels and inputs as arc labels.

From each node, there are arcs leaving for each possible input value. The root is labeled with the start state. This is level 0.

We now examine the nodes at level m from left to right:

If the label at the node is a repeat of an earlier node, then terminate the branch;

If the node is labeled "undefined," then terminate that branch.

If the label at the node is a state such that an input s is not defined, then an arc is drawn, labeled by s, to a node labeled "undefined."

If an input s leads to a state q′, then insert an arc, labeled by s, to a node labeled q′.

Beginning at *Start*, we see that there is an arrow with label ClickCustomer leading to *Customers* and so we draw a branch of the tree as shown (Fig. 7.15a). There is no arrow leaving *Start* with the label Quit, so this means that we draw an arrow from *Start* labeled with Quit to a node labeled "undefined" (Fig. 7.15b). There is a label ClickOrder that leads to Orders, and so this is drawn in the tree (Fig. 7.15c). The test sequences we need can be read off as labels of the various paths through the tree.

This process continues. It will detect many of the faults in the software, but there are still things we need to do. We need to check that the state that we have reached at

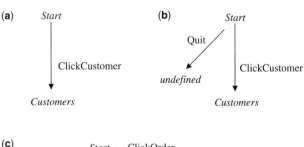

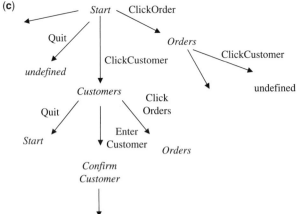

Figure 7.15 (a) Part of a testing tree. (b) A further branch of the tree. (c) Some further development of the testing tree.

the end of the test sequence that we have applied is the correct state. Unfortunately, we cannot just look to see what state we are in; the software is like a black box, we can only see what goes into it and what comes out. We need to add some more operations at the end of our test sequences in order to ascertain the state we have reached and thus know whether the software is behaving correctly or not.

The next set we need to work out is called the *characterization* set. This will consist of a set of sequences that will enable us to distinguish between any two states in the intended system.

To work out this set, we need to look at the machine diagram (Fig. 7.16).

Consider the states *Start* and *Customers*'; the functions ClickCustomer, EnterCustomer produce different observable outputs from the two states. In the first case, the first function should lead to a customers' screen and the same function should have no effect on the customers' screen. Using the second function in the two states will result in the confirm screen in the case of the state *Customers*' and nothing in the case of *Start*.

We choose for our characterization set a collection of functions (transitions) that can distinguish between the states.

Having reached a particular state, we then apply values from the characterization set; the results will confirm what the state was that we reached.

We now need to estimate how many more states there are in the implementation than in the specification. Let us assume that there are k more states.

The shorthand A is used for the collection of all possible transitions in the machine model. Let W be a characterization set; it consists of a number of short sequences of transitions.

Now choose any transition from the machine and apply that followed by one of the transitions from the characterization set W. This will provide a sequence of two

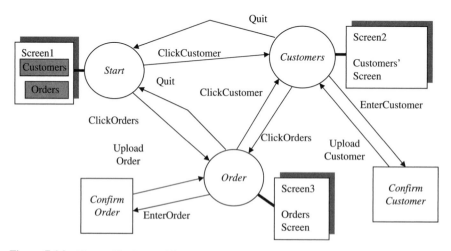

Figure 7.16   The specification model.

transitions, one from A and one from W. We do this for all possible combinations of transitions from A and transitions from W.

Thus we have moved in the machine from the start state to another state using the first transition and followed it up with an element from the characterization set. This will tell us what state we have reached—if the software is faulty, we may have taken the transition but gone to the wrong state.

This is the key idea. Try all transitions from all states and then try to see where we have got to. The assumption about the number of possible extra states in the implementation is used in the following way. Suppose that this number of possible extra states is k. We then apply all possible sequences of transitions of length k each followed by transitions from the characterization set. This is part of our full test set and can be described in the following mathematical formula:

$$Z = A^k W \cup A^{k-1} W \cup \ldots \cup A^1 W \cup W.$$

That is, we form the set of sequences obtained by using all input sequences of length k followed by sequences from W, then add to this collection the sequences formed using input sequences of length $k - 1$ followed by sequences from W, and continue building up a set of sequences in this way. The symbol $\cup$ is just mathematics for "together with" when applied to sets of things.

The set Z is simply built up from test sequences that are made up of trying every test input in ones, then in sequences of twos, then in sequences of threes, and so on until we have sequences of length k. For each of these sequences, we then apply all the sequences in W so as to find out what state we must have ended up in.

The *final test set* is TZ where T is a transition cover. This set consists of any sequence from the set of tests in T followed by any sequence from the set of tests in Z. We do this for all possible combinations.

Clearly, this will lead to a lot of tests, and automation is required to manage the size of the test set. There are some test tools that support this approach to test set generation (see http://www.dcs.shef.ac.uk/~nw/statechum.html).

This particular approach to testing provides us with an extremely powerful set of tests, tests that will find almost every fault that could exist in the software. The exercise to this chapter takes a more detailed look at a specific example.

Computational theory can show that such a test set will find all likely faults, subject to some conditions that we look at below.

7.5 DESIGN FOR TEST

Sometimes, it is hard to test a program because it has not been designed to make testing easy. This will usually result in a poor-quality program because testing is very expensive—as you will find—and many software developers will stop testing, not when the system is suitable for release or delivery, but when they run out of money in the test budget. Often, they take a risk that the cost of fixing the client's bugs later, or of supplying patches, is cheaper than continuing testing in-house. The client ends up doing some of the testing and they may not appreciate it!

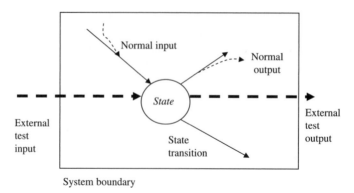

System boundary

Figure 7.17   Illustrating how to achieve design for test compliance.

In order to make the testing easier, we introduce two strategies that will help. These are called *design for test* principles.

7.5.1   Design for Test Principle 1: Controllability

This amounts to designing the X-machine of the system so that you can access any state with any value in the memory. It can be achieved by using a special test input to do this.

This issue mainly arises when there are functions that exist in several states of the machine. We wish to send data (inputs) directly to them without going through intermediate states that may change the internal memory in ways that will not allow the functions to be fully tested, for example preventing the preconditions to be satisfied or violated in some way (see Fig. 7.17).

We write special code to access this function under the conditions that we need, setting, for example, internal variables to suitable values. In practice, this type of stringent testing is only used on critical parts of the system.

7.5.2   Design for Test Principle 2: Observability

This problem arises when we have carried out a test but we are not sure which function has operated and what it has done. The outputs might have been masked by other activity. The solution here is to define a special output value that is used to determine if the test has run properly. We therefore write some extra code that will print out, for example, some critical variable values, messages that will tell us what has happened, and so on. This is a common practice in programming where you often interrogate a variable to see what its value is, and so forth, during debugging.

In both of these cases, we have code in the implementation that is used only for testing and is not part of the original requirements. We can either leave it there or remove it—comment it out, for example—but whatever we do, it needs to be done with care or else it might break the system!

Returning to our main example, we now have a mechanism for testing for the nonexistence of unneeded behavior. For example, the sequence ClickCustomer ; UploadOrder cannot be triggered without some test input that causes the UploadOrder operation to be stimulated. This is done by the special test input that has been incorporated precisely for this purpose.

Then we repeat the path to that state and check what happens if we try to apply every basic function from that state, some will have succeeded but some should fail. Have the correct ones passed and failed? This is then repeated for every state.

As an example, once we have reached state *Customers*, it should not be possible to use any of the order functions that are available for the *Orders* part of the system. We could do this by trying to see if we can make these functions work as part of a test. Thus we ought to test that the data we entered for the customer does not also get put into some other part of the database dealing with orders.

Thus we can assemble a set of test cases based on paths of various lengths through the machine diagram and tests of the nonavailability of functions in certain states. Here are some more examples:

ClickCustomer

{should pass}

ClickCustomer ; EnterOrder

{should fail}

Clearly, this will lead to a lot of tests, and automation is required to manage the size of the test set. In industry, sometimes very expensive test tools and environments are available to generate tests, to apply tests, and to analyze test results. Some of these can be found on the Internet, and we have used some test tools that support this approach to test set generation. None, however, are perfect; all have an overhead in terms of learning the tool, preparing the test cases, and so on. It would be nice if the return on investment for these tools in improved testing was always there—sadly it often isn't.

7.6 TEST DOCUMENTATION

It is vital that all the tests are properly documented so that testing can be carried out systematically and effectively. We also need to keep a record of the results so that the quality assurance can be convincing. Maintenance will also require information about the testing results.

For each requirement, which should be properly numbered in the requirements document, we will generate a set of tests. The details should be kept in a suitably designed spreadsheet.

Table 7.1 shows an example.

Table 7.1 Systems/Acceptance Test Definitions

Requirement	Test reference	Test purpose	Test input	Constraints/ prerequisites	Expected output	Final state	Comments
1.1.1	1.1.1	Test front page	Load program	Browser open	Page loads	Start	
1.1.2	1.1.2.1	Load customers page	Click(customers)	Start page open	Customers page displayed	Customers	
	1.1.2.2	Load customers page	Type random keyboard characters	Start page open	No change in display	Start	Invalid input
	1.1.2.3	Load customers page	Reboot	Start page open	Close down, database unaffected		Invalid input
1.1.3	1.1.3.1	Enter customer details	Standard data entry1*	Customers page open	Data displayed	Confirm	
	1.1.3.2	Enter customer details	Standard data entry2*	Customers page open	data displayed	Confirm	
	1.1.3.3	Enter customer details	Standard data entry3*	Customers page open	Data displayed	Confirm	
	1.1.3.4	Enter customer details	Empty data entry	Customers page open	Error message	Customers	Invalid input

*The definitions of standard data entry1, standard data entry2, and standard data entry3 need to be made somewhere in an appendix to this plate.

Table 7.2 Test Data File

Test ref.	Function sequence/ path	Test sequence	Expected output	Final state
. . . . .				
2.3.2.1	click(customer) ; enter(customer) ; enter(order)	\<click(customer)\> ; \<enter("standard_data_entry1")\> ; \<enter("order_details") \>	No change to database	Confirm customer
. . . . .				

Table 7.3 Test Results Table (System Version 1.0)

Test ref.	Date/ personnel	Result pass/ fail	Fault	Action	Comments
1.1.2.1	12/3/02 Pete	P	—	—	—
1.1.2.2	12/3/02 Pete	F	System crash	Debug	Jane alerted (13/3/02)
1.1.2.3	12/3/02 Pete	P	—	—	System closes, no losses

The next stage is to try to automate the testing as far as possible. We need to create a file of test inputs, one set of inputs for each test. These could be kept in a spreadsheet, the test data file (Table 7.2) and a script written to extract these inputs and put them into a standard text file, one line per test. Another script would extract each input sequence and apply it to the code. This is sometimes easier to do in some cases than in others. With GUI front ends, it is sometimes difficult to access the key parameters/events from inside like this, and anyway one would want to test the overall program as well. Test software is available, at a price, to automate a lot of the interface interactions, but for university projects it may be necessary to rely on manual techniques.

The test results file (Table 7.3) is a vital resource that will have to kept up to date during testing. It describes what has been done, what has been fixed, and what remains to be done.

7.7 NON-FUNCTIONAL TESTING

Although the principal purpose of the system test is to confirm that the functional requirements have been met, it is also necessary to consider the non-functional requirements and quality attributes. We will establish compliance with these also through suitable types of testing. This is done prior to final delivery of any version. We can regard the testing of the non-functional requirements together with the testing of the functional requirements as playing the role of the acceptance tests for the software. This needs the active involvement and the agreement of the customer.

Let us look at some of the non-functional requirements mentioned in the previous chapter.

7.7.1   Reliability

For a single user, the system should crash no more than once per 10 hours.

For the first requirement, there is very little alternative to just running the system and logging any problems where functionality is lost. Other approaches would be to examine the technology in use, age and type of workstations and servers, and type of software technology used, in particular how stable it is and what is currently known about its reliability. Demonstrating compliance with this requirement will be difficult within the constraints of this type of project.

The system should produce the correct values for any mathematical expression 100% of the time.

Showing that the calculations, if any, are always correct is pretty well impossible; one can log errors if they arise during final testing, but there is very little more that can be done in a practical way.

If the system crashes, it should behave perfectly normally when loaded up again with minimal data loss.

It is easy enough to crash the system, carrying out a reboot for example, and this can be the basis for this type of test. What is meant by *minimal information loss* needs to be thought about. A bare minimum would be no loss of any data that has been committed to the database. If some temporary recovery files can be developed, this would be better but probably beyond the scope of the project.

7.7.2   Usability

A user should be able to add a new customer to the system within 1 minute.

A user should be able to add a new order to the system within 1 minute.

A user should be able to edit a customer's details within 5 minutes (will vary with details type).

We need to define a user. It might be best to consider the sorts of qualifications and experience that a typical user might possess; for example, left school at 16, successfully completed an initial secretarial and office course, 3 years experience with MS Office, and so on. The test would then be to find a number of people, perhaps some of your friends and relations, and to get them to try these tasks on the systems a few times. What we are looking for is the number of mistakes in carrying out the task, the time it takes, and any apparent confusion observed during the session. This could indicate that there are problems with your user interface.

A user should be able to produce reports and statistics within 1 minute.

For this requirement, we need to specify what sort of reports and statistics are meant. Then we can ask a user to see if they can do the task.

7.7.3 Efficiency

The system should load up within 15 seconds.

The time taken for the system to retrieve data from the server should never exceed more than 30 seconds.

These requirements can be checked directly by measuring the time for these activities to complete. They should be tested on a number of occasions and under a number of conditions: database containing a few entries to one with many entries to approximate the intended operational context of the software. To do this, it is best if the data that is loaded into the database is similar in nature to the client's intended data. If this is not available, then you should write a script to generate suitable data.

7.7.4 Portability

The client system should work on the client's current computer network that is connected to the Internet and is running at least Windows 95.

This may not be so easy to test as it seems, it depends on whether you have access to a system similar to that of your client. It is very easy to find that the software works perfectly on one system but not on an apparently similar one. This is particularly true of PCs and Windows, of MS Office–based products using for example Visual Basic and for Java programs. It is important that all the ancillary files and directories are available and in the right place on the client's system.

The system should be easy to install.

The definition of this needs some elaboration. The install process must be defined. It might mean inserting a CD and following simple on-screen instructions. If this is the case, then it has to be carried out on a number of occasions by a number of people to see that it does work.

A final area where we need to test is the User Manual. We will describe this in more detail later but mention it here to emphasize that it will need careful thought, and someone needs to review it, preferably not someone who wrote it. In the spirit of XP, it could be the client, but any drafts should be checked by the team beforehand.

7.8 TESTING INTERNET APPLICATIONS AND WEB SITES

There are many issues relating to testing these types of applications.

Users of the Web site could be using one of many different types of platform (e.g., PC, Mac, Unix), as well as different browsers (e.g., Netscape, Internet Explorer, etc.). It is best if the system interface can be tested under all these combinations of platform and browser. It is surprising how different some Web pages can look under different circumstances.

Where the users are can also be a factor; not just their geographic location but also how they connect to the Internet.

The number of potential users is also an important issue. Your client may have an internet service provider offering a service; is this sufficient for their needs when the system is up and running?

Among the load measures that affect the operation of the site are

Static: hits per day, page views per day, unique visitors per day

Dynamic: transactions per second, megabytes per second, number of concurrent users, number of session initiations per hour

Load profiles need to be estimated based on the profiles of the potential users as well as dealing just with the volume of users. Some transactions occur more frequently than others and a test script should acknowledge this. Browsing is more frequent than buying. Thinking time is also a factor. Users arrive and leave at random. The rates are not related, the time it takes a site to respond can affect subsequent behavior with customers abandoning slow sites in favor of faster ones. Downloading large graphics files over a slow connection can be a disaster. Graphics files should be optimized to suit the conditions. Huge swings in usage are often found. For e-commerce, browsing peaks in early evening; purchase commitment and validation peaks at lunchtime. Time zones also affect things.

There are a number of client network connection options—multiple connections open (Netscape), buffer size options, and so forth, all affect performance. The use of HTTP v1.1 over HTTP v1 is also significant. Client preferences can affect behavior, and the configuration of the browser comes into play here; for example, is javascript on/off, graphics on/off, cookies on/off, cache sizes, encryption and so on.

The ISP companies are organized in tiers: tier 1 ISP (e.g., AT&T), tier 2 ISP (e.g., AOL), tier 3 ISP (e.g., local ISPs), each further from the backbone. How many tier 1, 2, 3 users are among the user profile? Your client may have to investigate this with his or her business and marketing advisers.

Background noise can also affect performance: client virus detectors, intruder detectors, e-mail, and so forth, all take up processing resource and may slow some sites down on some machines. Geographic location response times vary around the world.

All of these variables leave us with a real problem of modeling the load and testing for it.

Figure 7.18 provides a simple picture of how the response time is affected by the load on the servers. In order to test a system, we could try to identify the worst set of parameter values to define a user profile and the best case. These give extreme performances values as in Fig. 7.19

We might decide where in this region we wish to establish our typical user mix and test this for compliance with our desired performance requirements.

This is rather a specialist area and may be beyond the scope of the project. However, it is useful to be aware of some of the issues.

Building an e-commerce site introduces a number of risks for businesses. It allows for possible connections to internal company systems, accounting, customers,

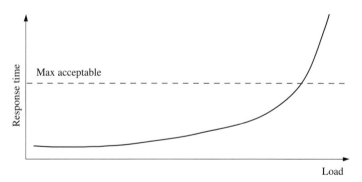

Figure 7.18   A typical response/load graph.

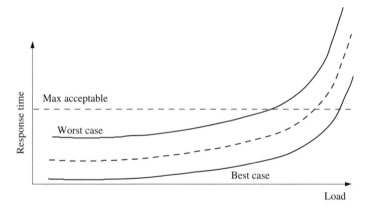

Figure 7.19   Typical response load/graphs with best-case and worst-case profiles.

orders, and other confidential and critical content. This can be attacked, stolen, and so forth. If Web users can access part of the company network, then it is important that suitable security checks are in place. Internal hackers/trojan horses are the single biggest threat. All businesses should be aware of this, and you may like to bring this to the attention of your clients if you think that it could be an issue for them. They will need to seek professional advice.

7.9 REVIEW

There are many aspects to testing; we have only just scratched the surface. Later we will look at unit testing and testing for non-functional requirements. For further information about the type of testing described here, consult the book by Holcombe and Ipate (1998).

A final series of tests that could be carried out on a completed system is done by repeatedly trying out arbitrary input values and arbitrary mouse clicks at all stages of the operation of the system. It is a type of random testing that seeks to break the system by creating unusual combinations of events. It can be quite effective.

Testing non-functional requirements is also vital. If the system is too slow or too hard to use, it will be a failure, and that is not what we want.

Some projects will involve the building of a Web site, perhaps with a database back end. Whereas we can test an in-house system reasonably well, it is much harder to test if it is to be available on the Internet. The testing of such Web sites is a specialist activity and requires a lot of understanding of the technology and of the key issues at both the client end and at the server. For critical e-commerce business, there are many security threats also. You have to know what you are doing.

EXERCISE

This exercise works through a simple test generation example in the form of a learning exercise.
You may wish to refresh your knowledge of the mathematical notation by referring to a book on discrete mathematics or formal languages and machines.
Consider a simple machine with four states. There are two functions: a and b (Fig. 7.20).
Putting in a stream of functions, say ababab, the result is a transversal of the diagram to state *1*.
If there is a state where a given function fails to operate, then the machine will halt (e.g., abb starting from start halts in state *1* after the second function is applied as function b is not defined in this state).

Constructing a Test Set

The test generation process proceeds by examining the state diagram, minimizing it (a standard procedure), and then constructing a set of sequences of functions. This set of sequences is constructed from certain preliminary sets.
We require some basic definitions; these apply to any finite state machine.
Distinguishability: Let L be a set of function sequences and q, q' two states, then L is said to *distinguish* between q and q' if there is a sequence k in the set L such that the output obtained when k is applied to the machine in state q is different to the output obtained when k is applied when it is in state q'.

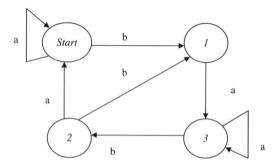

Figure 7.20   A simple finite state machine.

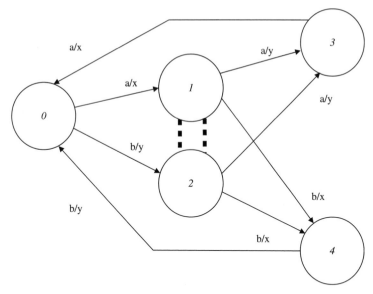

Figure 7.21   A machine that is not minimal.

Minimality: A machine is *minimal* if it doesn't contain redundant states. There are algorithms that produce a minimal machine from any given machine—the minimal machine has the same behavior in terms of input–output as does the original.

Example (Fig. 7.21): In this machine, states *1* and *2* can be merged to form a machine with fewer states and the same input–output behavior.

Let us consider, from now on, a minimal finite state machine.

A set of input sequences, *W*, is called a *characterization set* if it can distinguish between any two pairs of states in the machine

Example: In the first machine, $W = \{a, b\}$ is a characterization set (the machine is minimal).

A *state cover* is a set of input sequences *L* such that we can find an element from *L* to get into any desired state from the initial state start.

$L = \{1, b, ba, bab\}$ is a state cover for the first machine; 1 represents the null input.

A *transition cover* for a minimal machine is a set of input sequences, *T*, which is a state cover *and* is closed under right composition with the set of inputs *Input*, so we can get to any state from start by using a suitable sequence *t* from *T*, and for any function *a* in *Input* the sequence *ta* is also in *T*.

Here $T = \{1, a, b, ba, bb, baa, bab, baba, babb\}$ is a transition cover for the example.

Generating a Test Set

We first need to estimate how many more states there are in the implementation than in the specification. Let us assume that there are *k* more states. Let *W* be a characterization set:

We construct the set $Z = A^k W \cup A^{k-1} W \cup \ldots \cup A^1 W \cup W$, that is, we form the set of sequences obtained by using all input sequences of length *k* followed by sequences from *W*, then add to this collection the sequences formed using input sequences of length $k - 1$ followed by sequences from *W*, and continue building up a set of sequences in this way.

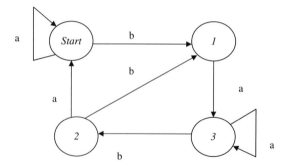

Figure 7.22   A state machine.

The final *test set* is *TZ*, where *T* is a transition cover.
Example (Fig. 7.22): The diagram of Fig. 7.23 represents an implementation of Fig. 7.22 with
one extra state, a missing transition, and a faulty transition label (a′ instead of a).
The value of *k* is assumed to be 1 for this example, the set $Z = AW \cup W = \{aa, ab, ba, bb\}$,
and the test set *TZ* is thus

$$TZ = \{1, a, b, ba, bb, baa, bab, baba, babb\} \cdot \{aa, ab, ba, bb\}$$

This means the following tests:

    aa, ab, ba, bb

    aaa, aab, aba, abb

    baa, bab, bba, bbb

    baaa, baab, baba, babb

    babbaa, babbab, babbba, babbbb

The extra transition is exposed by the input *bb*, which produces a different output in the
implementation than in the specification where no effect should be observed for the
second *b*; the missing transition is exposed by *babb* and the faulty transition by *baa*.
The transition cover ensures that all the states and transitions of the specification are present in
the implementation, and the set *Z* ensures that the implementation is in the same state as the
specification after each transition is used. The parameter *k* ensures that all the extra states in
the implementation are visited.

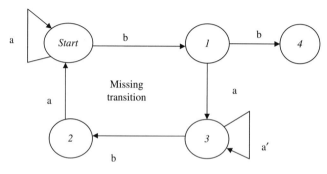

Figure 7.23   The machine of Figure 7.22 with some faults.

CONUNDRUM

Two leading supermarket chains introduced their first Internet ordering system at around the same time. Their e-commerce sites, although superficially looking similar, fared rather differently. One saw a much greater growth in business than did the other. Yet the technology used and the warehousing and delivery systems were very comparable. Customers just didn't like using one of the sites.

What could have been the differences between the two user interfaces that made this happen? (It was nothing to do with the look and feel of the Web pages or the way that the orders were managed or the price of the goods.)

REFERENCES

M. HOLCOMBE, F. IPATE. *Correct Systems—Building a Business Process Solution.* Springer-Verlag, 1988. Available at: http://www.dcs.shef.ac.uk/~wmlh/correct.

C.B. JONES. *Systematic Software Development Using VDM.* Prentice Hall, 1986.

G. MYERS. *The Art of Software Testing.* John & Wiley Sons, 1978.

J.M. SPIVEY. *The Z Notation: A Reference Manual*, 2nd ed. Prentice Hall, 1992.

Chapter **8**

Units and Their Tests

SUMMARY

From stories to tasks to classes and methods

- Finding the unit tests
- Running the tests
- Documenting the test results

8.1 BASIC CONSIDERATIONS

The nature of the system architecture and implementation languages are dependent on the application, the resources available, and the knowledge of the team. Having said that, however, such a project as this is an excellent vehicle for developing one's programming knowledge and understanding, even in a new language. In fact, once one has some programming experience in any language, it is usually possible to develop skills in another rapidly.

If there is a need to learn a new language, then it is vital to go about it in a sensible way. One approach is to gather elementary information, introductory texts, teaching aids from the Web, and so on. Some members of the team should take the responsibility for organizing the collection and organization of this information, and someone could then plan some presentations, demonstrations, and discussion sessions with the rest of the team. It is surprising how quickly progress can be made, especially if you have a real and specific target system to develop. You may not be able to get detailed technical support from your tutors and professors, but that is not critical. Any computing degree should have as one of its objectives the development of the skill to learn new things—technologies, languages, processes—and this type of practical project based activity is where this can be done most effectively. At the end of the project, you will be technical experts in areas that your teachers may not know very much about!

As part of some languages, there are development environments, libraries, and other supporting material. It is important that these are exploited where this is feasible. It is also important to look around for examples of similar applications and to

Running an Agile Software Development Project. By Mike Holcombe
Copyright © 2008 John Wiley & Sons, Inc.

examine how these are organized. It may be that you can use this information with your own project.

8.2 IDENTIFYING THE UNITS

Each project will be different, there will be different stories, different programming languages used, different operating environments, and so on. Furthermore, the programming courses that have been taken may have approached the issue of breaking down a high-level story requirement into "bite-sized" pieces of code in different ways. It is therefore impossible to provide a definitive method that will enable the programmers to create a framework of units, classes within which the programming can be set.

One approach is to take a story and to try to identify a series of chunks of functionality or *tasks* that need to be defined and that could form the basis of some suitable units.

Consider the following story (Figs. 8.1 and 8.2). It is concerned with a system, Quizmaster, which allows the user to set up *quizzes* on a variety of different *topics*; these quizzes can then be provided online to people taking the quizzes.

The story begins with the task of requesting an option by clicking on a screen button.

The list of papers should be displayed and one chosen.

The next task is to display a suitable window with simple edit facilities to allow the user to input some simple text, namely the topic name for a paper.

The information supplied needs to be validated. In this case, is the same topic already declared on this paper? This will involve a query to the database. The functional tests defined on the card provide guidance as to the checking required. Be prepared, however, to identify other things that may need to be considered,

Project: Quizmaster......

Story: Adding topics to a paper   Date:...XXX.

Requirements number...1.1....

Task description:
Users (quiz setters) can define a specific
topic to be used in a given paper for a quiz

Quality attributes:
There should be a confirmation of the success
The confirmation should be instantaneous
Success should be achieved in 99% of attempts for
typical users

Figure 8.1 Add topic story card.

Initiating event/inputs: a request to add task is made thrusuitable	
Memory context: list of papers and topics is available and can be updated	
Observable result/output: confirmation of success, database updated	
Risk factor/importance: High – security, may need more categories of user later	
Tests: 1, Define a topic for an existing paper 2, Define a topic for a nonexisting paper [error] 3, Define an illegal topic type [error] 4, Do nothing and exit the function [cancel] 5, Define a topic for a paper for which this topic already exists [error]	
Associated stories: Delete topic	Date delivered: YYYY

Figure 8.2   The reverse of the add topic story card.

there is no guarantee that all the special and awkward cases have been identified at this stage. Always try to think *"What if."*

If the validation fails, then a warning message should be given and a repeat try of the previous task enabled.

Finally, confirmation should be given to the user that the operations were successful.

These tasks can then be the basis for a series of units that will provide the functionality required. If an object-oriented language such as Java is being used, then it should be possible to define a simple set of class diagrams that will contain the main class outlines, variables, attributes, and outline methods.

We will need to build a database model that will have a class to handle data access functions.

Recalling what we said about keeping the user interface, the business rules and the database as separate layers, we should organize our classes to respect that principle (Fig. 8.3).

There will be a screen class to provide the initial user interface for the start of the story, which we will call the *homescreen*. The button will be provided with an adaptor/listener method to enable the story to be started.

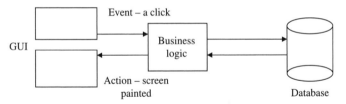

Figure 8.3   A classic three-layer architecture (see Fig. 6.2).

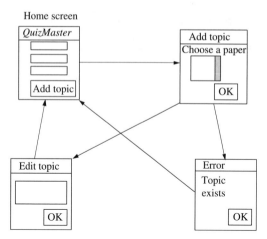

Figure 8.4   Some screens and their relationships.

Class *homescreen* will handle this. The button click will cause an event that calls the *addtopic*, a class that provides the basic interface for this story.

Thus a new object will be created giving a screen with edit facilities. This will include a button for data submission together with checking and recovery methods. To capture and report data entry errors, an *error* class is included (Fig 8.4).

The *topicscreen* class will need information from the database, so a *table* class is used. The *row* class will write to the database.

The results will be displayed in a list box using a suitable component by the *addtopic* class.

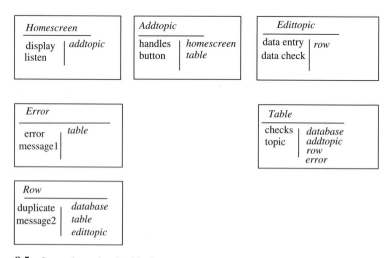

Figure 8.5   Some classes involved in the story.

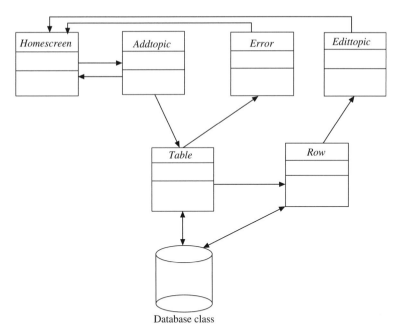

Figure 8.6 Task sequences, classes, and their interactions.

Figure 8.5 illustrates a possible collection of classes for this story, displayed as Class–Responsibility–Collaborator (CRC) cards (Cunningham,), and Fig. 8.6 shows how the three layers are organized.

8.3 UNIT TESTING

For each class we are building, thought should be given to how the class is to be tested. As we have seen, the extreme programming (XP) approach suggests that test sets should be created before any coding starts. This is not as simple as it seems because at the start of the coding of a unit, it may not be entirely clear how it will be written, and some important tests may not be easily defined. Furthermore, many of the popular types of testing such as the white box testing techniques are based on the structure of the code. But we have no code as yet, so this won't work. The lack of discussion of this point is one of the weaknesses of some treatments of XP.

What is important here is that a basic framework for testing the unit is defined, and this will be developed into a more detailed set of tests in tandem with the coding. At the end of the initial exploratory coding stage, a complete set of tests should then be available so that thorough testing of the class is possible.

Given the outline description or structure of a class, we have to identify two important things: (a) What are the ways in which the method will be accessed and what, if any, are the preconditions on the data that is supplied to it? (b) What are the ranges of values that need to be provided for the methods?

Once we have identified these, the expected outputs have to be considered and, in particular, action taken to ensure that the output information of interest can be read or displayed in an appropriate form.

We will be writing some test scripts that will be used in conjunction with the class code to establish whether it is behaving in a desired manner. These scripts, themselves forming classes or modules in the language concerned, will provide the basis for automating many of the tests, but it is unlikely that all the tests can be done automatically.

The test scripts will have to provide the information needed to prepare the class for testing, and this will involve identifying the entry points to the method and supplying suitable data to make the test work.

In any method that we want to test, there will be some data input values needed from a defined data structure or type. It is important to ensure that the data selected for this purpose is sufficiently varied to expose the method to all possible types of failure as well as success. We are trying to do two things during testing: gain some confidence that the method works and at the same time try to break it. Only then can we be sure that the class is trustworthy enough to be considered for integration into our existing working system.

Most values of data will be defined in the context of limits or boundaries that describe their validity so that, for example, we may have taken the decision earlier that a particular data value that is a string must be between 1 and 30 characters long and that falling outside that range will cause an error and some suitable recovery—perhaps inviting a user to try again if it is a data input through some user interface. Numerical values might also be restricted, and it is useful to be proactive in this respect and not rely on the system to deal with *out of range* values.

When choosing numeric data values for use in unit testing, it is useful to consider the following simple categories of data values, where we are assuming that there are upper and lower boundaries on the values:

A value below the lower boundary

A value equal to or at the lower boundary

A midrange value

A value equal to or at the higher boundary

A value above the higher boundary

A value in an incorrect format

A null value or no input

If we are dealing with the type of a string of literals that must be of length between 1 and 30, then we could generate the following distinct tests:

<return>

a

abcdef

abcdefghijklmnopqrstuvwxyz1234

fkdiorufberk5486jfkjfkdlk

309475bfbldflkjslkj

abcdefghijklmnopqrstuvwxyz12346

4onkfkdpkfmlk8e3;im65687^^7E@@cmei;pd

%'¬&*

null_input

Table 8.1 Test Planning Table

Test number	Input name (string)	Boolean flag	Expected result	Comments
1	*<return>*	*True*	Error "no proper input"	To GUI
2	*<return>*	*False*	Error "no proper input"	To GUI
3	*a*	*True*	Screen message "already present"	To GUI
4	*a*	*False*	"Submit to database" message	Needs to connect with database
5	*abcdef*	*True*	Screen message "already present"	To GUI
6	*abcdef*	*False*	"Submit to database" message	Needs to connect with database
7	*abcdefghijklmnopqrstuv wxyz1234*	*True*	Screen message "already present"	To GUI
8	*abcdefghijklmnopqrstuv wxyz1234*	*False*	"Submit to database" message	Needs to connect with database
9	*abcdefghijklmnopqrstuv wxyz12346*	*True*	Error "input too long"	To GUI
N	*abcdefghijklmnopqrstuv wxyz12346*	*False*	Error "input too long"	To GUI
$n + 1$	*%̀¬*&*	*True*	Error "invalid input type"	To GUI
$n + 2$	*%̀¬*&*	*False*	Error "invalid input type"	To GUI
$n + 3$	*null_input*	*True*	Error "null input"	To GUI/system
$n + 4$	*null_input*	*False*	Error "null input"	To GUI/system

. . .

If the algorithm used in the method needs to deal with some valid range data differently, then tests with all the types of data that will exercise all the paths through the program graph of the method should be used.

If the input data to the method consists of several different types of values for different parameters in the method, then all combinations must be considered. It is possible that some combinations should not be valid during the operation of the method in the software overall. It is a false economy, at this stage, to ignore these. Such combinations can cause problems when the code is integrated if there are undetected errors that cannot be found easily during integration. It will help debugging if care is taken at the unit testing stage to create tests that will report the results in a suitable way.

Suppose that a method is required to take as an input a string of literals of length between 1 and 30 together with a Boolean flag that describes how the data is to be treated, true being the prompt for a message to be sent to the interface that the data is already present (perhaps a customer's details are already in the database) and the false flag determines that the details should be checked for valid format and submitted to the database for insertion.

The method should then be tested using pairs of input parameters in the form of Table 8.1.

The comments column is there to provide some reminders of the possible interactions that the class might need to undertake or that need to be considered by the programmers during and after the testing of this class.

The important thing about designing a test is to *think awkward*—try to invent combinations of inputs and values that are unusual as well as the obvious ones. One common adage is "if it can go wrong, it will go wrong"—there is no such thing as a perfect system, the best we can do is to minimize the impact of any failure or error in our code.

8.4 MORE COMPLEX UNITS

Not all the classes developed will fit into the simple pattern of a few independent methods that can be tested independently. More complex structures are likely, and we need to identify how these might be dealt with. Luckily, we can capitalize on our earlier modeling and test generation ideas.

Each class has its own life cycle; its operations have specified active sequences (during correct use) that must be obeyed by any user or client class. On the other hand, a class cannot control the access sequences of its clients. The operations are driven by events; it is never known when an operation will be called. In such cases, to ensure the system's correctness, the programmer must use suitable error handling to deal with incorrect or unexpected use.

The active sequences of the operations could be represented in an X-machine: the input alphabet of this X-machine includes all input parameters of *construct* and *operation* methods, the output alphabet includes all output values of the operation methods, the transitions represent class operation methods, the memory being the data values, and the output of *access* methods.

Using an X-machine to represent the class activity can help to generate the test set more easily and completely and potentially automatically.

8.4.1   Case Example: The *AddElement* Function in JHotDraw

This example is taken, with permission, from a more detailed paper by Walkinshaw and Bogdanov (2007).

HotDraw is an application written by Ward Cunningham and Kent Beck in the Smalltalk programming language. It has also been implemented in Java by Erich Gamma (JHotDraw, 2007) and called JHotDraw and is an open source program.

JHotDraw allows the user to construct simple graphical images using a number of standard shapes (rectangles, circles, freehand etc.). It also allows you to add text and arrows to the pictures being created (Fig. 8.7). A story card for JHotDraw is in Fig. 8.8.

The top level X-machine can be described in Fig. 8.9.

As far as identifying inputs is concerned, most of the functions in the diagram are too abstract to be activated by a single input. Functions such as add_element are triggered by a combination of inputs (select a tool then click and drag mouse on canvas). If we want to document the detailed behavior of this function, and especially if we want to test it, it needs to be modeled at a lower level of abstraction. To illustrate how this can be done, we refine the AddElement processing function as a separate X-machine with the following processing functions:

The AddElement function can be described also as an X-machine (Fig. 8.10).

Ultimately, especially if we aim to use the machines as a basis for test case generation, we need to make sure that each transition in each machine is labeled

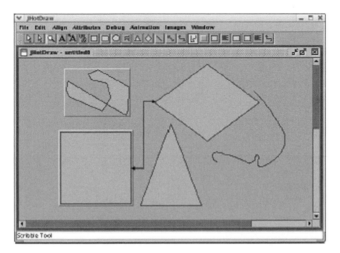

Figure 8.7   A screenshot of JHotDraw in use.

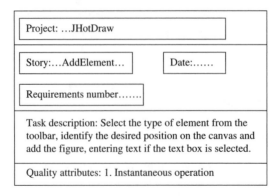

Project: …JHotDraw	
Story:…AddElement…	Date:……
Requirements number…….	
Task description: Select the type of element from the toolbar, identify the desired position on the canvas and add the figure, entering text if the text box is selected.	
Quality attributes: 1. Instantaneous operation	

Initiating event/inputs Select text or figure button	
Memory context: Current state of picture	
Observable result/output: Figure with new element added	
Risk factor/importance: High	
Tests: Add each graphical element within the canvas Add elements outside canvas Add element overlapping canvas edge Add text – add no text, etc.	
Associated stories: Clear Canvas	Date delivered: -

Figure 8.8   A possible story card for AddElement.

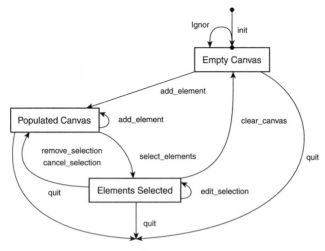

Figure 8.9   X-machine model of JHotDraw.[1]

[1]One Ignore function is added to the diagram to remind us to think about completeness.

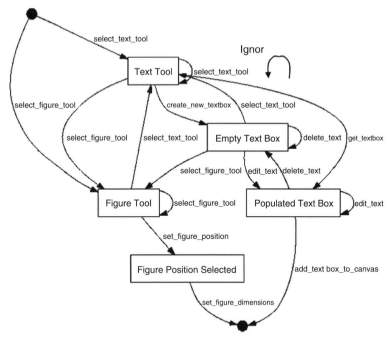

Figure 8.10   JHotDraw AddElement model.

with an input symbol. Depending on the system function, an input may either correspond with an actual program input (e.g., the click of a button in the user interface) or a method invocation at a lower level. Here we demonstrate the process of identifying inputs for the add_element function in Fig. 8.10 (Table 8.2).

Select_mode is the default control state allowing users to select elements to be placed on the canvas. Most of the other details are fairly self-explanatory.

The next stage is to construct a lower-level X-machine that describes the behavior of the select_text_tool as an example.

Table 8.2   Function Details for AddElement

Function	Input trigger	Memory	Output
Select_text_tool	Text_button	—	Text_mode
Select_figure_tool	Figure_button	—	Figure_mode
Get_textbox	Click(over text box)	Mouse_position (x,y)	textbox
Create_new_textbox	Click(over canvas)	Mouse_position (x,y)	textbox
Edit_text	Text_entry	Textbox	textbox
Delete_text	Text_entry	Textbox	Select_mode
Set_figure_position	Mouse_down	Mouse_position(x,y)	(x,y)
Set_figure_dimensions	Mouse_up	Origin (x,y), Mouse_position (x,y)	(x,y)
Add_textbox_to_canvas	Textbox		Select_mode

This section is not concerned with identifying individual objects as part of the software development process. Object modeling is more a matter of software architecture than of functional specification, so for the sake of simplicity, this section assumes that there exists an *a priori* object model and is merely concerned with (a) picking the objects that are relevant to a high-level element of functionality (a system function) and (b) creating a machine that models the object's contribution to that element of functionality.

Here we illustrate how to model the individual objects for the select_text_tool processing function from the add_element machine in Fig. 8.10.

Because JavaDraw is a Java application, its implementation is largely based on the Java AWT (Abstract Windowing Toolkit) library interfaces. It is no longer sufficient to simply break down the system into arbitrary functions because they have to conform to an existing set of interfaces. At this level, the design becomes specific to the underlying language and component interfaces; a similar specification for a different language and different libraries (e.g., C# and its GUI libraries) could differ significantly.

There are a number of traditional state machine object representations (e.g., UML statecharts), but these make the simplistic assumption that an object reacts solely to method calls, thus a state transition is usually labeled with the method that triggers it. In practice, however, object interactions are more complex; behavior can also be affected by values that are returned by method calls, exceptions can be thrown that deviate from expected behavior, and call-backs can occur, all of which are difficult to intuitively denote with traditional state machine notations.

To account for this fine-grained object communication behavior, we model objects using Bogdanov's specialized X-machine model (Bogdanov, 2005) called the "object machine." His model extends the range of inputs that can affect the behavior of an object to include values returned from collaborating objects, exceptions, and call-backs, as well as conventional method calls. In terms of the source code, every possible input (incoming communication) and output (outgoing communication) corresponds with a particular type of statement, as is shown in Table 8.3.

Table 8.3   Object Machine Inputs and Outputs with Their Corresponding Statements

	Statements
Inputs	
Incoming method call	First statement of a method
Return of control from called method	Call site
Caught exception	First statement of a catch clause
Outputs	
Outgoing method call	Call site
Return of control to a calling method	Return statement
Thrown exception	Throw statement

Perhaps the key benefit of adopting this specialized model is the fact that it can be used as a basis for generating unit tests that rigorously test objects at a fine granular level.

From the user's perspective, the select_text_tool function executes when they select the text tool in the control panel (i.e., click the Graphics button). This deactivates the current tool (if there is any existing active tool) and activates the new tool, which involves setting the cursor to the text pointer. The sequence diagram in Fig. 8.10 details the object interactions that constitute the select_text_tool function. Again, the reader is not expected to refer to the JHotDraw implementation itself, but it merely serves to provide a point of reference for the rest of this subsection.

To summarize, the most important interactions are the following:

- Call 1.1 establishes what tool has been selected by the user (i.e., the text tool).
- Call 1.3.1 finds out if there is a currently active tool (if this is the case, call 1.3.2.2 deactivates the currently active tool)
- Call 1.3.4.2 activates the text tool.
- Calls 1.4.* ensure that the text tool button is selected.

Sequence diagrams (or collaboration diagrams) such as the one shown above are useful for constructing object machines, because they indicate which object interactions are especially relevant to the feature that is being modeled. In the case of JavaDraw, the implementation already exists, so the sequence diagram for select_text_tool was simply reverse engineered from the implementation (using the Borland Together reverse engineering capabilities; see http://www.borland.com/together/).

Instead of testing every class with respect to all of its methods, we can focus on a selection of classes and only test those methods that play a part in the sequence diagram(s). If no definitive interaction diagrams exist, it is probably safer if the object machine is constructed conservatively, without omitting methods.

The rest of this section illustrates the process of constructing an object machine with respect to the DrawApplication class, the key object in the select_text_tool function. Although we focus on a single class here, the process would be repeated for the other objects that participate in the function select_text_tool.

The process of constructing object machines consists of two steps: (1) Identifying the inputs and outputs of each object as specified in Table 8.3 and (2) determining the order in which these can occur.

The sequence of inputs and outputs can be largely determined from the sequence diagram, although certain semantic ambiguities can only be resolved by inspection of the source code or domain knowledge that isn't encoded in the diagram (Whittle, 2000). Figure 8.11 illustrates the DrawApplication object machine, along with a table of its inputs and outputs. For an insight into the significance of individual method calls, the reader can refer to the sequence diagram. The DrawApplication machine was constructed as decribed in the following text.

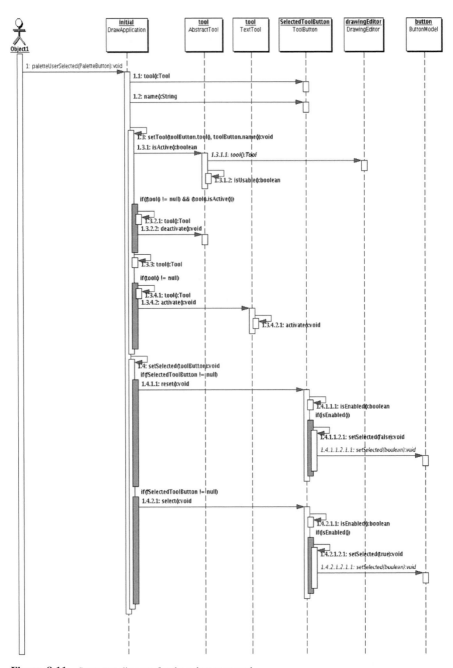

Figure 8.11   Sequence diagram for the select_text_tool.

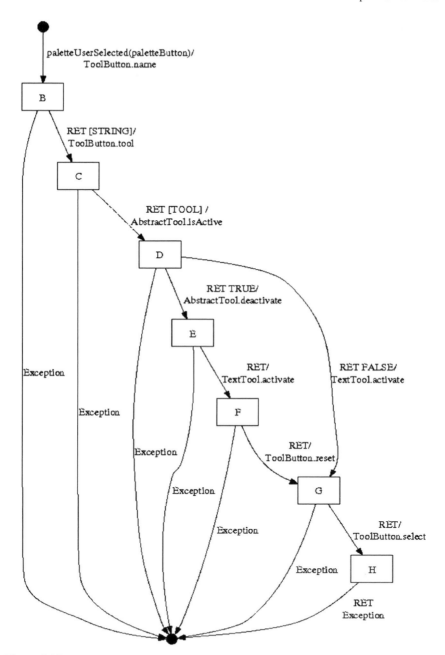

Figure 8.12   X-Machine for the DrawApplication object.

The states and transitions of the machine are assembled from the sequence diagram and bearing the following algorithmic details in mind.

The DrawApplication.paletteUserSelected method is called with the paletteButton parameter. The first outgoing method call is to paletteButton.name(), to determine the name of the tool that has been selected ("text tool" in our case).

Once the object representing the text tool is returned from paletteButton (RET[TOOL]), the DrawApplication object determines whether there is a currently active tool (fTool).

If a current tool (fTool) is active, it must be deactivated, and its toolbar button must be reset (toggled to the "off" mode).

If there is no currently active tool (fTool is not active), the tool that is represented by paletteButton (text tool) can be activated, and its respective toolbar button can be toggled to the "on" mode.

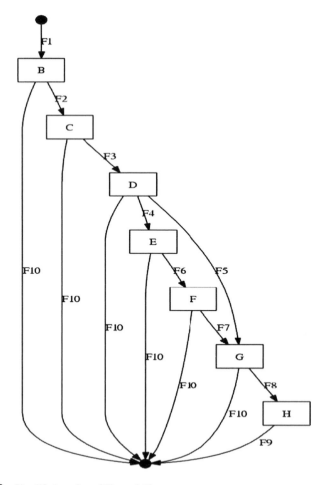

Figure 8.13   Simplified version of Figure 8.12.

The assumption is made that any communication with a collaborator object can raise an exception. Because the DrawApplication class doesn't cope with exceptions, these lead to the terminal state.

The behavior of the DrawApplication object (specifically with respect to the select_text_tool function) depends to an extent upon whether or not there is a tool that is already active. Thus, the memory of this machine must contain the currently active tool. In practice, the fTool variable is stored as a data member of the DrawApplication class. Although there are obviously a number of other data members, this is particularly important because it determines the behavior of the object specifically with respect to the select_text_tool function.

Now we are in a position to apply the X-machine test method. The details are not given here, but a full set of tests for this example can be found at http://www.dcs. shef.ac.uk/~nw/Files/testSets.html, and a tool, *statechum*, which allows you to create X-machine models and generate the test sets, can be downloaded from http://www.dcs.shef.ac.uk/~nw/statechum.html.

A small sample of tests from this are given below; these refer to functions in the simplified version of Fig. 8.12 such as RET[Tool] being replaced by F3, and so forth, in Fig. 8.13, and so on.

Some test sets are shown in Table 8.4.

Table 8.4   Sample Tests for the JHotDraw Function DrawApplication

DrawApplication Object Machine
Transition Cover:
F1, F2, F3, F4, F10, F3,
F1, F2, F3, F4, F10, F5,
F1, F2, F3, F4, F10, F10,
F1, F2, F3, F4, F10, F8,
F1, F2, F3, F4, F10, F1,
F1, F2, F3, F4, F10, F6,
F1, F2, F3, F4, F10, F4,
F1, F2, F3, F4, F10, F9,
F1, F2, F3, F4, F10, F2,
F1, F2, F3, F4, F10, F7,
F1, F2, F3,
F1, F2, F5,
F1, F2, F10,
F1, F2, F8,
F1, F2, F1,
F1, F2, F6,
F1, F2, F4,
F1, F2, F9,
F1, F2, F2,
F1, F2, F7,
F1, F2, F3, F5, F10, F3,

The test sets of Table 8.4 have to be interpreted and run within a suitable environment. Further examples can be found in Yuan et al. (2003).

8.5 AUTOMATING UNIT TESTS

If a fundamental part of XP is to test continuously and to test everything, then it is important that we make sure that testing is easy—or at least that the application of well thought out test sets is easy.

There are a number of ways that this can be achieved through automating parts of the process.

The first thing to say, however, is that there is no easy solution to the problem of automating testing. Even when the test cases have been defined and the tests created, there is still a lot to be done. There are many tools that are available, some commercial and very expensive, others are public domain applications that are widely used. We will mention some of the latter, but it will depend on the type of project being undertaken as to how useful these are.

Many projects will have a graphical user interface, and the way in which information, results, and so forth, are displayed on the screen will be important. It is difficult to completely automate the testing of this type of application. There will need to be some human intervention even if it is just to evaluate the appearance of the screen output according to some predefined requirement.

Nevertheless, at the class level, there are sensible things that can be done.

One approach, and a popular one among the XP community, is to use a tool such as JUnit (Beck, 1999) (see http://www.XProgramming.com). This allows you to create a test class around the class under test and to submit tests to the code in a simple and effective way. It is highly recommended that you look at this tool.

Similar tools are freely available for other programming languages, for example VBUnit and PHPUnit and the Web site mentioned previously is useful for other languages.

It is not always appropriate to use such a tool in some projects, and in this case it is possible to write one's own scripts to automate the testing of methods.

In any case, it is important to organize one's test data in a sensible way; for example, creating a number of text files with the data in some suitable predefined format. A comma-separated value (csv) file is one sensible approach.

The test script program will then take the test file and parse it suitably, then insert the appropriate values into the method and execute it. The results will either be collected together in a suitable output file for analysis or the results passed onto some other code for display through a suitable interface component.

Depending on the application context, this output file is either examined manually to see if it "looks right" or some automated checks on the output data are performed using suitably written scripts, involving evaluating, for example, whether the result is equal to a predetermined output value or not. In the latter case, all of this can be done within the context of a single test program for the unit.

8.5.1 Writing Unit Tests in JUnit[2]

JUnit is one of a family of unit testing frameworks available (see http://www.Junit. org). Most of the unit testing frameworks available for other languages have been written to emulate the JUnit style, although language constraints often prohibit a direct correspondence. They are often referred to as XUnit—where X represents the particular programming language.

The easiest way to structure unit tests using JUnit is as follows: A unit test in JUnit can be taken to mean a test of a class. If there is a class called *Vector* in the package *mypackage.util*, there should be a class that tests it called *TestVector* in the package *mypackagetest.util*. For ease of reference, the directory structure of this test package should match that of the main package.

The template structure for a test class is as follows:

```
package mypackagetest;

import junit.framework.*;//the junit testing framework
import mypackage.*;

public class VectorTest extends TestCase //Must extend TestCase
{
private Vector empty, full; //Just some vectors we can test on
public VectorTest(String name) {//Standard constructor, cut & paste
super(name);
}

public static Test suite() {//This is used later in collecting tests

return new TestSuite(VectorTest.class);//standard structure
}

/**
* In here we can set up the variables we will be using in our tests.
* This method is run immediately before every individual test
method.
*/

public void setUp() {
full = new Vector(2);
full.add("element1");
full.add("element2");
empty = new Vector();
}

//--- Now some actual tests ---
public testAdd() {
assert(empty.add("1").size() != 0);
//...
}
```

[2]Notes on JUnit prepared by Dave Carrington of Genesys Solutions from material available on www.XProgramming.com.

```
public testRemove() { //if Remove removes the last element
assert(full.remove().size() == 1);
assert(empty.size() == 0); //setup() is called before each test
method
assert(empty.remove().size() == 0);
//...
}
}
```

Each test method is essentially just a list of assert statements, which will raise an exception if passed *false* as an argument. JUnit automatically collates all methods whose name starts with "test" to add to the set of tests, so if we were to add a method named *testInsert()* to the above code, JUnit would automatically detect it. (Note: Other unit testing frameworks require you to explicitly name all individual test methods.)

Once we've got some of these test classes, we'll want to be able to run them. To do this, we must first create a test collection class in the following format:

```
package mypackagetest;

import junit.framework.*;

public class AllTests {
public static Test suite() {
TestSuite suite = new TestSuite("All of the mypackage tests");

suite.addTest(VectorTest.suite());
suite.addTest(StringTest.suite());
suite.addTest(WhateverTest.suite());

    return suite;
}
}]]>
```

The above is self-explanatory—we just collate all of our test classes in a suite, and return it. We can now run the JUnit test-suite runner program to run all of the tests in our suite. This is done in the following way: either

```
java junit.swingui.TestRunner mypackagetest.AllTests
```

or

```
java junit.textui.TestRunner mypackagetest.AllTests
```

The test-runner tells us of the first assert statement that fails, giving the exception stack trace so that the assert statement can be identified.

The unit testing frameworks available for other languages work on the same principles (i.e., a function is written for each test, which contains a list of assert

Table 8.5 Test Results Table

Ref.	Test	Expected outcome
1.1	...	...
1.2	...	...
1.2.1	...	...
1.2.2	...	...
1.2.2.1	...	...

statements). The way they differ is in the management of these test functions—JUnit can locate individual test methods automatically using Java's reflection mechanism. Other unit testing frameworks usually don't have this luxury.

8.5.2 Managing Tests

A possible structure for recording is shown in Table 8.5.

The first digit in the Ref. column is the story number. The second digit is a test number and is unordered (i.e., test 1.2 can be carried out before test 1.1). All subsequent digits are test order numbers and indicate that a test x.y.z must be performed after x.y. Tests at the same level are still unordered, so x.y.a is independent of x.y.b. Thus, test 1.2.2 must be performed after 1.2, but is independent of 1.2.1, for example.

8.6 DOCUMENTING UNIT TEST RESULTS

As we saw in Chapter 6, it is vital to maintain a reliable record of what has been done and what needs to be done. This applies as much to testing and debugging as anything. A spreadsheet style record on the tests applied and the debugging done should be a natural part of the project. These details must be available in some shared part of the group's filestore and needs to be kept up to date. The project plan will also need to reflect the progress on the testing and fixing of bugs in the unit code.

To summarize a table such as Table 8.6 is useful for planning the test cases.

As the project continues, it may be necessary to revisit some of these units and their test details. Perhaps there has been a slight change in the requirements, for example, the details of the data to be entered into a method might have been changed subtly in order to achieve some other objective. This may then require the retesting of the unit under slightly different parameter values. These test descriptions will allow you to keep track of these changes. The tables of test cases and results must be updated to reflect the new requirements.

Table 8.6 Unit: PrintAction (Extends AbstractAction)

Method name	Input	Prerequisites	Expected output	Actual output/ action	Status
PrintAction (constructor)	*Name* of type **String** *PrintTitle* of type **String**	Parameters given are initialized	Sets up variables of the action	Constructor sets up variables correctly. Print button shows as required.	Tested Jane (12/03/02)
ActionPerformed	*Event* of type **event**	**ActionEvent** occurs in the **JInternalFrame** returned by clicking the Print button	Shows a *print dialogue*		To do
PrintTableAction (constructor)	*Name* of type **string** *PrintTitle* of type **string** *FrameIn* of type **Component** *TabletoPrintIn* of type **JTable**	All input types valid	Input parameters stored locally	The JButton displays OK and all variables stored.	Tested and debugged Bill (12/03/02)
ActionPerformed	*Event* of type **ActionEvent**	**ActionEvent** occurs in the **JInternalFrame** returned by clicking the *Print* button	The printer job is created and a print dialogue shows. If *OK* then table is printed, if *cancel* then no print.		To do

8.7   REVIEW

The identification of the classes and their implementation will form a major part of the project. If we proceed in the true XP way, we will have written the unit tests first and run these against our code on a very regular basis until we have convinced ourselves that they work as required. This isn't so easy as it sounds.

A principled approach to building unit test sets has been described, but this is still an active area of research. The approach is rather different to the structural or white box technique often used in traditional software development. We have seen that it is not appropriate here as we have to write the tests *before* we write the code. One technique often used in traditional white box testing is to estimate something called *test coverage*. This is a figure that describes how much of the code has been exercised by the tests; it might be defined in terms of what percentage of decision points the test set has exercised, the percentage of branches traversed during testing, and so forth. Sadly, such measures do not tell us much about how well the testing has been done. It merely measures the amount of effort that has been applied to testing. The testing techniques described here can provide complete fault detection if the basic assumptions and design for test conditions are satisfied.

EXERCISES

1. Set up the JUnit system and try it out for a simple program. If you are not using Java, use an appropriate alternative to JUnit. Think up a few test values to apply to the program.

2. Build a simple model of the program written in question 1. Now generate some tests from the model and compare with your earlier list.

3. Apply the techniques to a more complex model with communication and synchronization features.

CONUNDRUM

About 20 years ago, the U.K. government purchased a system to deal with air traffic control over London. It was based on a number of similar systems that had recently been installed in the United States. Unlike the American systems, there were serious problems with the London system. Planes flying over London would suddenly disappear from the screen. Equally alarmingly, planes would suddenly appear as if from nowhere. Extensive testing was carried out, especially on the component of the system that was fed the radar information and dealt with the display of the positions of the planes on the screen. No defects were found, everything was exactly as the requirements demanded.

Why did the system work in the United States but not in London?

REFERENCES

K. BECK. *Extreme Programming Explained.* Addison-Wesley, 1999.

K. BOGDANOV. Testing from object machines in practice. In *Proceedings of UK-TEST'05, Dept. of Comput. Sci.*, Univ. Sheffield, Sheffield, UK, 2005.

W. CUNNINGHAM, K. BECK. A diagram for object-oriented programs. *Presented at Proceedings OOPSLA-86*, Oregon. Sept. 29–Oct. 2.

M. FOWLER. *Refactoring—Improving the Design of Existing Code.* Addison Wesley, 2000.

N. WALKINSHAW, K. BOGDANOV, M. HOLCOMBE, S. SALHUDDIN. Modelling and testing software with X-machines—a case study (submitted).

J. WHITTLE, J. SCHUMANN. Generating statechart designs from scenarios. In *22nd International Conference on Software Engineering (ICSE '00)*, Limerick, June 4–11, ACM Press, 2000, pp. 314–323.

J. YUAN, M. HOLCOMBE, M. GHEORGHE. Where do unit tests come from? In (M. Marchesi, G. Cucci, eds.). *Extreme Programming and Agile Processes in Software Engineering (XP2003)*, LNCS 2675. Springer, 2003, pp. 161–169.

Web Site

www.jhotdraw.org.

Chapter 9

Evolving the System

SUMMARY

Dealing with change

- Changing requirements
- Changing test sets
- Changing code
- Refactoring the requirements, the tests, and the code
- Working with the client
- Integrating the releases

9.1 REQUIREMENTS CHANGE

Change to the requirements is bound to occur, and the way that we deal with it will be a vital aspect of a successful project. We must expect it and be prepared to accommodate it. However, it is necessary to be sensible about things. Large amounts of change bring with them risks, and there needs to be an honest and realistic discussion between the developers and the customers about this. Unnecessary change could delay the project delivery, damage what has already been done, and so on. Are the business benefits sufficiently great to risk this?

There are a number of different manifestations of requirements change, and some are more serious than others. We have been trying to identify those areas of the system that might be subject to change from an early stage in our requirements capture and analysis. Hopefully, we will not be too far wrong, but you can never tell.

We will consider several types of change and how to deal with them. Some are serious and will involve us in redoing a lot of our previous work; some are more easily dealt with and won't affect the project outcome too much. There is always a price to pay if the change is significant, and the client should realize this. The XP approach is to be agile and adaptable as well as to be honest with the client and to talk to him or her frequently. That way we may see the changes coming and prepare for them. We should also explain to the client the costs of the changes, the

Running an Agile Software Development Project. By Mike Holcombe
Copyright © 2008 John Wiley & Sons, Inc.

delays that may occur, the reduction in quality if it isn't thought through properly, and so on. Ask the question: Do you really need this change? If the change is fundamental to the way the client's business or organization is evolving, then we need to embrace it with enthusiasm.

Changes can occur during the discussions about the system or business processes and during demonstrations of software, whether delivered or not. One benefit of an incremental delivery—it might not actually be delivered just demonstrated to the client depending on the context of the relationship between the customers and the developers—is that it gives customers a chance to see what they may be getting and to identify any changes that they may like, including new features. Also, if their business needs have changed, they can then discuss the impact that this may have on your project, in terms of priorities, functionality, and so forth. Not all customers will want to install an increment of the system in their premises. This can be a cause of problems if their computer system differs significantly from that of the development team.

They may also comment on the *look and feel*, on the GUI, and how acceptable that is to their organization and its workers. This may result in a significant change to the user interface—to the presentation in particular. If your metaphor is one where the business logic and the presentation layer are reasonably separate, then this may be something that you can deal with. If the change is due to a significant alteration to the underlying database, then this can also be managed but is likely to have knock-on effects throughout the system because so much of it may need to relate to the database structure.

9.2   CHANGES TO BASIC BUSINESS MODEL AND FUNCTIONALITY

These sorts of changes can occur at almost any stage of the project. Sometimes they are the result of the team not understanding the client's requirements or business processes at the time and are thus a correction of what was originally thought. These changes need to be related to the current state of the project. If the project has developed a requirements document, then the changes may require the introduction or substitution of new requirements statements, and these should be expanded into stories. Then the changes have to be tracked through the development of the project so that, for example, implications for the underlying database, if one is involved, are considered. Then we revisit the integration of the stories into an X-machine model with its accompanying user interfaces and input and output requirements.

The test sets will need to be redefined properly at the systems level. The classes associated with these changes must be identified and the unit tests updated to reflect the new requirements; the code needs to be reprogrammed and tested in the usual way.

It is not always easy to achieve these changes without extra work. If the stories have not yet been implemented, then things are much easier. As always, the later a change is identified, the more expensive it can be. It seems that XP and other agile methodologies are more able to cope with change than are others. If your project is *fixed scope/fixed price*, then there will be times when significant change will not be compatible with the fixed end date for project completion.

Whatever the situation, it is vital that all the new parts of the system are properly documented, so that we have to maintain the key information about the system:

The stories

The models

The system tests

The system metaphor or architecture

The classes and methods

The unit tests

The code

The user manual and maintenance manual

This updating may be accompanied by comments to indicate what has been done.

Finally, the version numbers of the various artifacts listed above must be updated. *Version control* is discussed further in Chapter 10.

9.3 DEALING WITH CHANGE: REFINING STORIES

Now the requirements may change, this is the point of using XP, so how do we deal with this?

Suppose that the client is happy with the initial set of stories and the requirements document. He or she selects some critical stories to implement first. The team begins to think about how to do this (see Chapter 7).

The client then comes back to tell us that there needs to be a change. To decide how to deal with this and what it means for the system testing, we need to consider what sort of change it is.

9.3.1 Changes to the Underlying Data Model

Suppose that the new requirement is to have more information about the customers, perhaps an indication of their creditworthiness or whether they qualify for some discount. This involves changing the internal memory of the model; we can do this quite easily and then introduce a new area of the interface to provide the extra functionality.

Thus we now have:

customer_details:name, address, postcode, phone, fax, email, discount

where *discount* is either yes or no.

The screen is now changed to allow a discount yes/no button to be chosen or a discount flag to be checked.

This will impact on our test sets by requiring the discount data to be present in the tests. We need to identify all these changes on story cards so that they are properly documented and we are in a position to know what to do.

9.3.2   Changes to the Structure of the Interface, Perhaps the Introduction of a New Screen

This will mean altering the state machine model by introducing a new state, for example. To access this state, a new transition together with an accessing function will have to be defined. The activities within this screen and the exiting from it will also lead to new transitions and functions that need to be defined. Each of these will identify a new story, which, in turn, will define a further requirement.

9.3.3   Adding a New Function

Here we are inserting a new transition with its corresponding function into a diagram. Here a similar strategy applies, for every test sequence that gets to the state where this new function originates, we develop a new test sequence that triggers the new function. We then complete each of these new test sequences by creating paths through the machine following on from this function. Again, this will lead us to new test sequences.

9.3.4   Changing the Functionality of a Function

The basic strategy will not be affected here unless there are issues with the preconditions for the function. If the precondition for the operation of the new function is different from that of the replaced function, then the test sets may have to be changed in a more subtle way. In other words, we may need to test for the nonoperation of the function by choosing previous data values and memory values so that the function does not operate. This can only be dealt with on a case by case basis.

9.4   CHANGING THE MODEL

The changes are captured using revised story cards, and now we need to integrate them into our model so that we can see the effect that they have on the system and how they impact the test sets.

The X-machine model is built from the user stories in order to provide a basis for functional system testing. The changes will involve a number of different transformations of the model, which can be considered separately.

9.4.1   Changing a Process

Suppose that we have the model shown in Fig. 9.1. The process EnterOrder is changed in some way, perhaps the information being input is different; thus, this

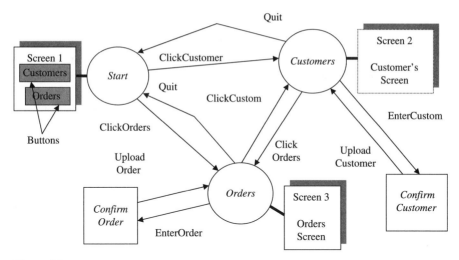

Figure 9.1 A model of part of a system.

needs to be reflected in two ways. The definition of the function is different, and so the interface that provides the user with the capability to input the information will need to be changed. The database will also probably have to change to accommodate the new data being input. An example might involve we need to collect more information about the order, for example the customer's tax number (T-no.). See Figure 9.3.

We should make it clear that this process has changed in the model by amending the diagram at the top level by changing the label to EnterOrder′, as well as altering the lower level diagram where the process is expanded into more atomic processes (Fig. 9.2).

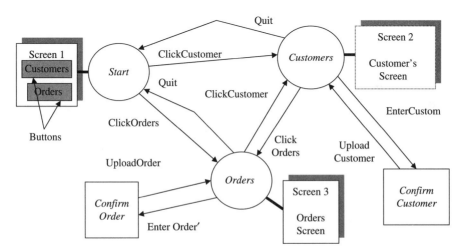

Figure 9.2 An amended model.

The order details diagram also needs to be changed, as follows:

name1, address1, postcode1, phone1, fax1, email1 name2, address2, postcode2, phone2, fax2, email2 name3, address3, postcode3, phone3, fax3, email3	**Order_details**
	Customer_ref3
	Order_ref5
	Order_parts6
	Delivery
	Invoice_ref8
Customer_details	T-no.

9.4.2 Removing States

Here we consider the issues related to removing a state; perhaps the client does not want a particular feature any longer.

If we remove a state, then we must remove all the processes that lead to that state and all those that leave that state. This may interfere with the flow of business

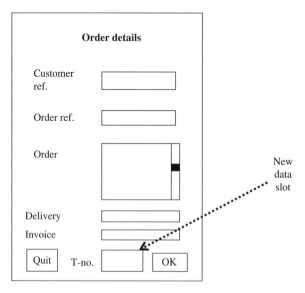

Figure 9.3   A new user interface.

processes, and it is vital that we check this thoroughly before committing ourselves to the new model of the requirements.

All those processes (or transitions) can now be removed from our architecture and the user interfaces associated with them also. It is vital that we then revisit the system tests to see what the implications of this are. Because much of the diagram is unchanged, all the tests that involve sequences that visit this state can be removed also. Take care over this.

It may be necessary to introduce a new process or two to link states before and after the removed state in order to make the whole system work. We look at this next.

9.4.3 Adding States

When introducing a new state, it will also require the introduction of new processes and their transitions. In fact, there is no point in introducing a new state unless there is a process that needs to be dealt with separately. This might be because we decide that a particular case in the business process needs to be dealt with in a separate way, and this might mean designing a new user screen specially for this event. This is often better than trying to cover all the possibilities in one screen. The client will have a view on this. Thus we might then break a process down into several processes with their own states.

The original function is split into two separate functions that target two states instead of one (Fig. 9.4).

As before, we must update the story cards with the new functions and generate new tests to cover the changing model structure.

The interfaces will also have to be changed, and this is important to do at the same time, lest we forget.

The methods implementing the functions will now need different tests, and this is another thing that must be attended to.

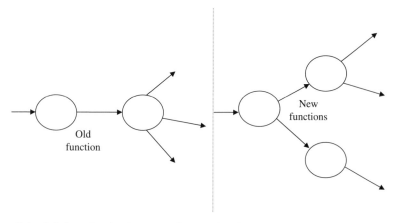

Figure 9.4   Splitting a function from a state into two function to two states.

9.4.4   Adding a Complete Machine

Suppose that the customer wants a major new aspect for the system. This might be of a signiicant size—perhaps a whole new system—and we will have to consider carefully not only how to build the new component but also how to integrate it with the work already done.

Consider the situation with our Customers/Orders system where a new facility is needed that deals with customer returns. Thus we need to develop a system that allows the user to put up a customer's recent orders and then allows them to select those that have been returned and then to give a refund or credit the customer's account. The refunds section will be accessed, probably through the initial screen, by a refunds button, and so this will have to be revised. An XXM diagram can be produced easily (Fig. 9.5).

The rest of the Refunds section needs to be defined in detail—it will contain a number of stories that will be built and integrated together and then built into the existing system—and tested at each stage!

9.4.5   Adding Processes

The final type of change is where we introduce a new process that will operate between two existing states. Here we need to consider, carefully, the way that this process will be triggered from the state; we could easily get into a problematic situation if there is any mistake here. The input to the new process together with

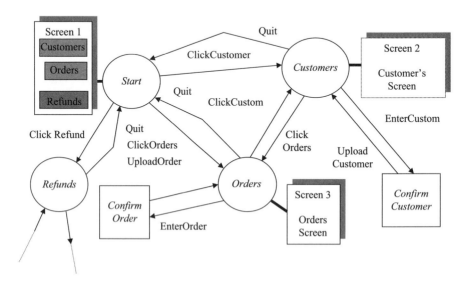

Figure 9.5   An extended diagram with the start of the Refunds section.

the expected memory/database connection at that moment must not interfere with any other process that might already be there.

9.5   TESTING FOR CHANGED REQUIREMENTS

The system testing will now have to take these changes into account. We will either redo the complete system test set—not a good idea because of the work involved—or test the new part of the machine separately and then run a smaller number of integrating tests. These could be developed as shows in Fig. 9.6.

In every test of the form:

$$\ldots g1; \text{ old\_function}; g2 \ldots$$

we create a new test where the function *old_function1* is replaced by a test from the new machine such as:

$$\ldots; g1; \text{ new\_function1}; \text{ func2}; \text{ func3}; g2; \ldots$$

This will lead to a number of new tests. We do all the old tests as well.

The system tests also need updating. Because we have extended the state diagram with a new transition, we need to write tests that will trigger this transition at all possible occasions. This means both legitimate paths through the updated machine, but also we need to try to trigger *process* from every other state to ensure that we have not inadvertently introduced additional, unintended functionality into the system.

In practice, we look at the two models, the original one and the new, revised one and focus on those test sequences that involve the changed parts of the machines. In this way, we can preserve many of our original tests and know that we will not have to retest them. However, if there is any doubt as to whether you should retest, then you should retest!

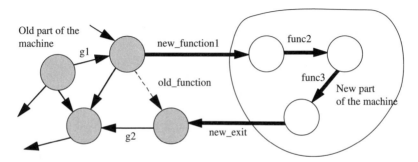

Figure 9.6   Adding new states.

9.6 REFACTORING THE CODE

As the system changes and evolves, the version of the code that represents the current state of the system will undergo a number of changes. Some of the changes will simply be a result of building increments into the existing code, and some will be a result of fixing problems and bugs. Refactoring is the activity of rewriting the code without changing its functionality in order to achieve some specific aim, such as to make the code more understandable for maintenance, to make it compliant with some standards, or to reorganize it in line with changes to the platform or system architecture.

In this section, we will briefly describe some common refactoring techniques; the principle source book for this topic is Fowler (2000), and this should be consulted for the details.

Suppose that you have developed some classes during the early stages of the project, and as you increase the functionality of the system, you develop a new class that uses a method that is already in an existing class. The temptation is to *copy and paste* this method into the new class. This now means that the same method appears in at least two places. It might happen during the course of the system evolution or during maintenance that the method needs changing. The problem now is that you have to remember to change it at all of its locations, and you may forget to do this. The maintenance engineering may not even be aware of all the places where this method belongs. The better way is to create a separate class embodying this method and to refer to this class within the body of the classes that previously used it. This process is called the *extract class refactoring*.

Some methods are very large and thus likely to have behavior that is hard to understand. Rather than spend a lot of time trying to write comments to explain what is going on, it might be better to refactor the method by splitting it up into a collection of simpler methods that are organized in a clearer way. Here the *extract method refactoring* can be used. Take care with variables, however.

Some classes seem to grow out of control, and this might also need dealing with using something like an *extract class refactoring*, which tries to group related variables in a sensible way and perhaps introduce components and subclasses to deal with the complexity of the original class.

Data can be reorganized in more natural ways. We have already seen the architectures that separate data from business logic, and this is another principle that can be applied in the code. Data values can also be replaced by specific objects, which provides a neater structure. Awkward arrays can also be turned into objects.

Conditional expressions can be simplified by extracting the conditional into a method and then dealing with the *then* and *else* parts separately.

Remove confusing flags by using *break* or continue statements.

Because refactoring should not alter the functionality of the code, it is possible to use the test sets to check this. Getting into the habit of continually testing everything as you do it will give greater confidence that you have not broken anything during the refactoring process. This does assume, of course, that your tests are good ones.

There are many more things that can be done, and Fowler's book is an important source of ideas and inspiration.

An issue was raised in Chapter 2 concerning the unit tests and what happens to them when the code is refactored. Ideally, there should be a unit test associated with each class. For some types of refactoring, the overall class structure will not change, and so the tests will still be associated with the right classes. The test sets may need some maintenance, however, especially if there have been changes to variable names, and so forth.

9.7 ESTIMATING THE COST OF CHANGE

Each extra aspect of the system that is identified as we progress with the project will have an impact on the length of time that the project will take. We can estimate this with a quick analysis of the type of change being considered (Fig. 9.7).

In Chapters 5 and 6, we looked at how we might make estimates of simple stories and also use the XXM models to refine these and provide some ideas of time and effort for more substantial parts of the system. This should be done regularly and the overall project plan updated to take account of the changes.

9.8 REVIEW

Coping with changes is something that you will certainly have to do. It makes a big difference if you approach the problem in a systematic and practical way. Panicking is bound to lead to further problems. Stay cool and think through the changes carefully and logically, what they are, how they impact the rest of the system, and how they can

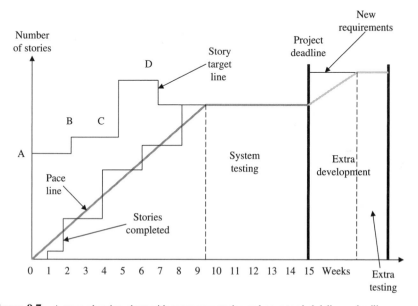

Figure 9.7   A story planning chart with some new stories and an extended delivery deadline.

be managed. The evolution of the test sets is a vital part of the process. XP is totally dependent on the tests for ensuring the quality of the solution; neglecting these will lead to a poor-quality system. Refactoring the code, making it more understandable and more consistent is an activity that will be ongoing as the system evolves and changes. It is important that some effort is made to do this—remember the people coming along behind you who may have to maintain your system. Most university programming exercises do not have this dimension because, in most cases, no one is going to use the software in earnest.

EXERCISES

1. Review the way that you dealt with change. Were you able to revise your test sets to account for the changes in an efficient manner.
2. Did you refactor? What refactoring methods did you use? Could you all agree on what needed to be refactored and why?

CONUNDRUM

The customer was the IT director of a company that produced and sold biological specimens to research laboratories and pharmaceutical companies. The software was to support the entire company activities, which involved the production process (which had to be fully documented to meet government regulatory procedures), the stock contol process, the ordering process, and the invoicing and accounting process.

After working extensively with the customer and delivering a number of incremental versions, the customer was satisfied. A final delivery was made, and at this point the customer invited several personnel from the company to attend the demonstrations. These potential users of the system pointed out many problems with the business concepts upon which the system was based. It became clear that the customer did not understand his company's business process. It was also clear that we would have to reengineer the system. The new requirements were significantly different, there were few areas where the detail was the same, although the overall architecture would be very similar.

Should we start again from scratch or try to adapt what we had already done, reusing and preserving what we could?

REFERENCE

M. FOWLER. *Refactoring—Improving the Design of Existing Code.* Addison-Wesley, 2000.

Chapter **10**

Documenting and Delivering the System

SUMMARY

The purpose of documentation

- Providing maintenance information in the code
- Coding standards
- User manuals
- Online help
- What to deliver
- How to finalize the contract

10.1 WHAT IS DOCUMENTATION FOR AND WHO IS GOING TO USE IT?

One thing that good software engineers and programmers are good at is creating lots of documentation. Poor programmers produce relatively little. However, we should not judge people or organizations by the *amount* of documents generated; *quality* and *relevance* are much more important.

Quality can be defined in many ways, but for our purposes it must mean that the document is fit for its purpose. Thus we need to identify *what it is to be used for*, *who is to use it*, *what they are trying to do*, and to judge the quality of the document on the basis of how it helps them achieve their objectives in the best possible way.

This brings us to our first difficult problem: People are individuals, and whereas a particular document is ideal for one person to use to achieve their task, it may be unsuitable for someone else with a different background and experience carrying out the same task under different circumstances.

Some people like to have the documentation available online and others prefer a book form. This is something that should be confirmed with the client particularly in regard to the user manual for the system.

Running an Agile Software Development Project. By Mike Holcombe
Copyright © 2008 John Wiley & Sons, Inc.

We will consider some of the issues relating to the preparation of documentation and its implementation, either paper based or electronic.

We will look at different types of documents for different uses—documents for programmers and system maintenance, documents for users, and documents for managers.

10.2   CODING STANDARDS AND DOCUMENTS FOR PROGRAMMERS

A vital aspect of XP is that the code is understandable and that those reading it can be in a position to change it, update it, or develop it further as easily as possible. In this section, we will look at coding standards and how the source code should be presented.

The purpose of coding standards is to ensure that all the programmers in a company produce source code to the same standard in terms of how it is structured and presented. Not all software houses will share the same style and standards, but the key point is to get used to working within the constraint of a formalized standards regime. This will be good experience for future careers.

In this chapter, we will present and discuss the standards used in the Genesys Solutions company, a software house run by fourth year students at the University of Sheffield. It is an example of a set of standards that works but is not too burdensome.

XP relies on the clarity and understandability of the code, and this means that we need to take a lot of care over how we write and document this. Remember one day someone may need to maintain your system, and what is obvious to you now may not be obvious to them—or to you in a few months' time!

Maintenance is a vitally important aspect of software engineering. Maintenance can take on many forms from bug fixing (perfective maintenance) to extending or changing the functionality of the system in some way. It is vital, therefore, that the programmers doing the maintenance understand fully what the system does and how it is built. They will not have access to a lot of design information—we have agreed that this is often unreliable and out of date, especially if there have been requirements changes that have not been properly reflected in the designs.

As we mentioned earlier, it is vital that the code is presented in a readable and understandable form. We have emphasized the need to keep things simple and to organize the code in a maintainable fashion. Some of these issues will be discussed in the following chapter. Here, we concentrate on the basics of code documentation and on coding standards.

The language Java has a major facility that will help here, namely the Javadoc system. If Java is being used for the project, then Javadoc should be a mandatory part of the development method. It provides detailed information about the structure and coupling of the program—at the end of the project, a Javadoc print-out (file) should be made available.

We focus here on the issue of coding standards as it is important to address these from the start.

The purpose of coding standards is to establish a common structure and content of object-oriented (or any type of code) that is being developed by a team of programmers. In an extreme programming context, it is vital that everyone abides by the same coding conventions as the task of coding is distributed among the team. Although pair programming can provide some consistency in coding style, it is not enough by itself.

One problem that can occur is that the standards are perceived to be very time consuming and bureaucratic to adhere to. This attitude should be resisted, especially if the grading of the project provides an element related to how well the team adhered to the standards.

We will look at some standards developed for Java within the context of student projects for external clients and comment on why they are the way they are. Standards for other languages can be found, several groups have Web sites with proposals for standards, and these should be consulted where necessary.

10.3 CODING STANDARDS FOR JAVA[1]

10.3.1 Genesys Coding Standard for Java

This coding standard has been adapted from the Web page *Code Conventions for the Java*™ *Programming Language*, which can be found at http://java.sun.com/docs/codeconv/.

10.3.1.1 README

Any directory containing Java Source Files (.java) should also contain a file entitled README. This file should summarize the contents of the directory in which it resides. The summary should be a brief description of what the overall purpose of the file is and not technical details of individual methods, variables, or other implementation-dependent factors.

10.3.1.2 Java Source Files (.java)

Each Java source file should contain a single public class or interface. If private classes or interfaces are associated with a public class, they may be located in the same file. In this situation, the public class must be the first class in the file.

---

[1]These standards were developed by the fourth year students in the student software house, Genesys Solutions, and are used by the second year students in their real projects.

A Java source file has the following ordering (Sections 10.3.1.2.1 and 10.3.1.2.2):

10.3.1.2.1 Beginning Comments
After `package` and `import` statements, and before the main class definition, there must be a block comment of the following format:

```
/*
* Name: The name of the Class
* Author(s): All who contributed to this Class
* Date: Date the Class was last altered
* Version Number: The version number of this update.
* Using the standard major/minor revision system
* Starting from 1.0
* Description: What the Class does. If it becomes too
  long
* consider breaking it down into smaller
* components.
* Changes History: List of changes, referenced by
  version number
* outlining changes from previous version
* i.e.
* 1.1 fixed bug that caused program to
* crash.
* 1.2 added the blah functionality.
*/
```

10.3.1.2.2 Class and Interface Declarations
The following order should be maintained within Class and Interface declarations:

Class (`static`) variables: These should also be sorted into the order `public`, `protected`, package (no access modifier) and finally `private`.

Instance variables: These should be sorted in the same order as for class variables.

Constructors and Methods: These should be grouped by functionality and not by the access modifier that they possess. Each method must have a block comment of the following format:

```
/*
* Name: The method name.
* Author(s): The name of all authors who have
  contributed to
* this method. Only include if there is more than
* one author for this Class.
* Description: Brief description of what the Method
  does. If it
* is too long, consider decomposition.
* Parameters: List of input parameters.
* Output: The relevance of the returned value. Only
* include if the return type is not void.
*/
```

Four spaces should be used as the unit of indentation. This avoids excessive horizontal spread across the screen in deep sections of source code.

Comments should not be enclosed in large boxes drawn with asterisks or any other characters. Also, consider that many people believe that frequency of comments sometimes reflects poor quality of code. If you are about to add a comment, take a moment to see if you can rewrite the code to make it clearer.

10.3.2 Blank Lines

Blank lines should be used in the following circumstances:

Between methods.

Between the local variables in a method and its first statement.

Before a block or single line comment.

Between logical sections within a method that will increase readability.

Table 10.1   Naming Conventions for Identifiers

Identifier type	Conventions	Examples
Class	Should be nouns in mixed case with the first letter of each internal word being a capital. Do not use all capitals for acronyms.	`class Person;` `class PageCreator;` `class HtmlReader;`
Interfaces	Follow the conventions for *Class*	`interface Storing;` `interface PersonDelegate;`
Method	Should be verbs in mixed case with the first letter being lowercase, and the first letter of each internal word being a capital.	`run();` `getBackground();` `findPerson();`
Variable	Should be mixed case with the first letter being lowercase, and the first letter of each internal word being a capital. Names should be designed to indicate their intended use to a casual observer. One-character variable names are allowed for one-time-use throw-away variables. For integers use i to n; For characters use c to e.	`int i;` `char c;` `String personName;`
Constant	Should be all uppercase and words separated by an underscore.	`static final` ` int MIN_WIDTH = 4;` `static final` ` int MAX_WIDTH = 99;`

Table 10.1 outlines the conventions that should be used when naming an identifier. These are essential for readability and quickly determining what the function of an identifier is.

10.3.2.1 Block Comments

These should be indented to the same level as the code it is referring to and preceded by a single blank line. To aid setting it apart from the actual code, each new line in a block comment should start with an asterisk as shown in the example below:

```
/*
* This is a block comment.
* Each new line, like this one, starts with an asterisk.
*/
```

10.3.2.2 Single Line Comments

These should also be indented to the same level as the code it is referring to and be preceded by a single blank line. If the comment cannot be written on a single line, then the block comment style should be used.

```
if (condition)
{
// This is a single line comment.
```

10.3.2.3 Trailing Comments

These can be located on the same line as the code they are describing. However, they must be short and should be shifted to the far right. If there are multiple trailing comments in a given method, they should be aligned with one another. The use of the comment delimiter // to comment out chunks of code is preferred over a block comment style because of the ease of un-commenting individual lines at a later date:

```
if (foo > 1)
{
// int i = 0;
// i++;
// foo = i;
return TRUE; // explain why here
}
```

10.3.2.4 Comment Format

To allow for easy determination of who has altered pieces of code and to ascertain when the changes were made, the following format should be adopted for all comments:

```
// XYZ - The following will do something new - DD/MM/YY
...
/*
* XYZ - DD/MM/YY
* This needed some extra explanation...
*/
```

where *XYZ* are the initials of the programmer who has added the comment and *DD/MM/YY* is the current date/month/year.

10.3.2.5 Number Per Line

There should be no more than one declaration per line as this encourages the use of trailing comments to describe the purpose of the variable. It is also recommended to indent the names of variables in a block of declarations to the same level to enhance the readability of the code:

```
int percentageComplete; // how much the project is
  complete
int daysRunning; // how many days the project has run
int i, j; // AVOID!
Object currentProject; // the current project
```

10.3.2.6 Initialization

Where possible, all variables should be initialized upon declaration. The only time that this cannot be done is when some computation is required before the initial value of the variable is known.

10.3.2.7 Placement

Declarations should only appear at the start of a block (or clause) of code (this meaning a group of statements surrounded by { and }). You should not wait until their first use to declare a variable. However, for one-time "throw-away" variables in a for loop, they may be declared as part of the statement:

```
public void aMethod()
{
int int1 = 0;
...
if (condition)
{
int int2 = 0;
...
}
for (int i = 0; i < int1; i++)
{
...
}
}
```

If variable foo is still in scope, new variables should not be named using this same name, which would hide the declaration of foo at the higher level.

10.3.2.8   Class and Interface Declarations

When coding Java classes and interfaces, the following formatting rules should be adhered to:

> No space should be left between a method name and its opening parenthesis (which starts its parameter list).
>
> The open brace { should be located on the next line down at the same level of indent as the method or class name.
>
> The closing brace } should start a new line on its own and be indented to the same level as the open brace }. This ensures that paired braces are at the same indent level and are easy to spot.
>
> Methods should be separated by a single blank line.

10.3.2.9   Simple Statements

Each line should contain at most one statement:

```
argc++; // OK
argc++; argv++ // AVOID!
```

10.3.2.10   return Statements

A return statement that includes a value should only use parentheses if this aids the clarity of the statement:

```
return;
return anObject.aMethod();
return (size? size:  defaultSize); // adds clarity!
```

10.3.2.11   if, if-else, if else-if else Statements

The following format should be adopted for these statements:

```
if (condition)
{
statements;
}
if (condition)
{
statements;
}
else
{
statements;
}
if (condition)
{
statements;
}
```

```
else if (condition)
{
statements;
}
else
{
statements;
}
```

Note that in the situation where `statements` is in fact a single `statement`, the following is permitted:

```
if (condition)
statement;
```

10.3.2.12   for Statements

The `for` statement should be formatted like this:

```
for (init; condition; update)
{
statements;
}
```

10.3.2.13   while and do-while Statements

The `while` statement should have the following form:

```
while (condition)
{
statements;
}
```

Similarly, the `do-while` statement should look like this:

```
do
{
statements;
} while (condition);
```

10.3.2.14   switch Statements

A `switch` statement should have the form shown below. Notice that each time a case falls through (i.e., there is no break command), there should be a single line comment to warn of this. This helps prevent simple errors upon later revisiting the code. Every `switch` statement must have a `default` case.

```
switch (condition)
{
case ABC:
statements;
// falls through!
case DEF:
```

```
statements;
break;
case XYZ:
statements;
break;
default:
statements;
}
```

10.3.2.15 try-catch Statements

A `try-catch` statement is shown below. Notice that it is not essential to provide a `finally` clause.

```
try
{
statements;
}
catch (ExceptionCase e)
{
statements;
}
```

10.3.2.16 Blank Spaces

Blank spaces should be used in the following circumstances:

A blank space should appear after commas in argument lists.

A binary operator should be separated from its operands with a blank space. A unary operator should not be separated from its operand.

A blank space should appear after the semicolons in the for loops expressions.

Casts should be followed by a blank space.

10.3.2.17 Referring to Class Variables and Methods

Avoid using objects to access a class (`static`) variable or method. Instead, use a class name:

```
classMethod(); // OK
AClass.classMethod(); // OK
anObject.classMethod(); // AVOID
```

10.3.2.18 Constants

Numerical constants should not be coded directly except for −1, 0, and 1, which can appear in, for example, for loops as countervalues.

10.3.2.19   Variable Assignments

Avoid assigning multiple variables to the same value on a single line or using embedded assignments:

```
foo1 = foo2 = 2; // AVOID!
/*
* The following should be:
* a = b+c;
* d = a+r;
*/
d =(a = b + c) + r;
```

Do not use the assignment operator where it can be easily misinterpreted as the equality operator:

```
if (c++ = d++)
{
...
}
```

10.3.2.20   Parentheses

Ensure that the use of parentheses is very liberal. Always prefer to include parentheses as opposed to allowing possible operator precedence problems. This is still the case even if you think the operator precedence appears clear to you—it may not be so clear to another person!

```
if ((a == b) && (c == d)) // We prefer this...
if (a == b && c == d) // ...to this
```

10.3.2.21   Returning Values

Think twice about returning values dependent on certain criteria.

```
if (booleanExpression)
return false;
else
return true;
// The above is equivalent to the following!!!
return !booleanExpression;
// Here is another example!
if (condition)
return x;
else
return y;
// Again, the above is equivalent to the following!!!
return (condition ? x:  y);
```

10.3.2.22 ?: Operator

If there is a binary operator in the condition before the ? in the ternary operator ?:, use parentheses:

```
return ((x >= 0) ? x:   -x);
```

Other languages have standards recommendations and should be consulted where appropriate. Among the useful Web sites available are those for PHP (http://www.phpcodingstandards.com/) and C# (http://weblogs.asp.net/lhunt/pages/CSharp-Coding-Standards-document.aspx).

10.4 MAINTENANCE DOCUMENTATION

Your system will be the subject of maintenance, assuming that it gets used at all. Someone will have to deal with the support of the system and possibly the further development of it. In your professional career, maintenance will often play a large and important role, and it is usually regarded as an unpopular activity. We should aim to make it as easy and as painless as possible. Much maintenance carried out in industrial and commercial contexts is seriously hindered by a lack of documentation that prevents the engineer from fully understanding the system and what it is supposed to do. In the past, the popular belief was that large amounts of design documents would be the resource that was the most effective basis on which to carry out different types of maintenance. In reality, this is rarely the case as we discussed in an earlier chapter. The design documents may not fully reflect the source code; these designs may not have been updated as the requirements changed or as implementation problems drove the design away from the theoretical position adopted at the beginning. We have to provide some basic information relevant to the maintenance team that is reliable, understandable, and complete, as far as is possible.

It is assumed that the requirements documents and user stories will be available. These are numbered and organized in a systematic way. The system metaphor and overall software architecture should also be present and should match the actual system. This is easier to achieve than trying to relate everything to a large design that may not have been updated during the development of the system because of the need to solve unforeseen problems in implementation, the changes to the requirements, and so forth.

The code should be consistent with the coding standards and the comments useful and complete. They should refer to the other parts of the document so that we can trace how different parts of the code relate to the user stories.

The test sets that were used to demonstrate compliance with the requirements should also be available so that they could be rerun for retesting or parts of them used for regression testing (testing that checks that the overall system works properly when parts of the system have been changed).

Testing documents should be available from the project. We discussed how these should be designed, using tables and spreadsheets to describe the tests and the test results. All this information should be preserved and included in the system documentation for future maintenance.

10.5 USER MANUALS

User manuals are vital parts of the system, at least as important as the code in the sense that a poor manual will compromise the success of the system: people can't or won't use it properly, it fails to assist users in carrying out their tasks, and so on.

What makes a good user manual, and how can we write one?

We need to go back to think about the purpose of the system. This has already been encapsulated in the user stories, the user characteristics of the system, and in some of the functional and non-functional requirements documents.

The document should start with a brief review of the purpose of the system and then provide a structured basis for carrying out all the tasks commonly expected. This should be written in simple, jargon-free language with plenty of screen shots and other simple diagrams to explain the processes described. A good *index* is vital as well as a *glossary* of the terms used.

Look at a few examples of user manuals for systems that you have used and ask yourself how good they were for you. Generally, user manuals are written by technical people, often programmers in the project team; they are often written at the end of the project, and they are often written poorly. In an XP context, it is likely that some of the manual cannot be written until the end but quite a lot can be done beforehand, especially if the system is being delivered incrementally. In this case, the manual will have an incremental structure.

Some may take the view that the system is so intuitive to use that no manual is necessary. This may be the case with some Web-based systems, perhaps an e-commerce development or an information system based around a Web browser. Do not make any assumptions about this. If you think that your system is intuitive and it is obvious how to use it, then you should prove this. Choose some typical users and ask them to use it and observe them. You will probably be surprised at the difficulties some people have even with the *simplest* system. Many of the unpopular and unusable software systems of the past (and present) have been built under the assumptions that the use of them is obvious to all.

The requirement stories had estimates of the change likelihood, and this will give you an indication of when parts of the manual can be written. Some authors, notably Weiss (1991), suggest that the manual should be written first, before the code, so that it provides clear information to the programmers and could be used as a basis for testing. We have essentially adopted this position here with the use of X-machines as the basis for the specification of the test sets. The user manual could be a simplified version of the paths through the X-machine written in everyday language. As the requirements change and mature, they will be reflected in the X-machine structure and thus the structure of the user manual.

The user manual, like everything else in the project, needs to be reviewed and tested with users or representatives of the type of people likely to be users. Creating a simple questionnaire for users to fill in as they use the manual to operate the finished system will provide helpful feedback; this can be used to show your client that you have tested the system thoroughly and that it is ready for acceptance.

One question that needs to be answered by the client is what type of user manual is needed. Should it be a paper booklet or an online system? There are advantages and disadvantages for both. One advantage with a small paper manual is that it can be easily flicked through and read prior to using the system. The online manual is easier to use when searching for information.

Some examples of a user manual produced by student teams using XP is in the Appendix.

10.6   VERSION CONTROL

One important practical issue that arises in the course of developing any software system is that there will be a number of versions of different documents created. These documents will include requirements documents, source code, test sets, and user manuals at the very least. All will be available in different versions as they will have been developed and revised over a period of time. Many of these will refer to aspects of the system that change as the development proceeds. Members of the development team will have to refer to these documents and will need some way of ensuring that at any given stage they are consulting the correct version. This may not be the most up-to-date version. We have therefore a *version control problem*. We need to keep track of what version each document has reached and which version we need to consult or change. In an XP development, where all team members are interchanging their roles and sharing the responsibilities for the entire project, it is vital that we avoid the situation where an individual is working on a version of a document that the others do not know about.

It is natural that some members will need to work away from the laboratory, perhaps on their own machine, and it is vital that they regularly update their colleagues with what they have done. At any rate, there should always be two people involved in any part of the development whether it is on the university machines or on an individual's machine.

This problem is made worse by the fact that for some systems, there may be a number of different configurations of the software that need to be produced, for instance to contain different special features for particular clients, or to run with different hardware or operating systems. Thus, along with versions created at different times in the history of a system, there may also be different versions in parallel for different configurations of the software, and these need to be managed properly. This involves the task of *configuration management*. Furthermore, as a system develops, there are likely to be different versions of each configuration of it that are released to the clients at different times: these different versions are often referred to as different releases of the system. Thus, in principle, there are three aspects to be managed: the different versions of components, the different configurations, and the different releases.

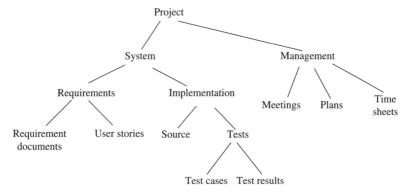

Figure 10.1 Project archive structure.

10.6.1 The Project Archive

We need to set up a proper archive for the project in a systematic way and develop some conventions and protocols for its use. There are tools available that can help with this. One, CVS, is widely and freely available. It is worth investigating and asking for it or something similar to be installed on your machines.

The simplest approach is a shared directory on a network where the team has privileged access to this directory.

In this archive, we will be putting documents of various types: requirements documents, story cards, test plans, source code, ancillary material, manuals, as well as management information such as minutes of meetings, plans, and other material. One way to structure this is shown in Fig. 10.1.

Within each basic component, the archive will be organized in terms of versions and date of creation. It is sometimes useful to have a spreadsheet that describes what state each document is, for example whether it has been reviewed and confirmed as an acceptable product or whether it is still under development. The authors of the documents and the time of its creation and review are also useful to help everyone know what is going on.

Although XP stresses minimal bureaucracy, we cannot use this as an excuse for an unprofessional approach; remember there are people, your clients, who are depending on the outcome of your work, and being sensible about how you organize things is vital.

10.6.2 Naming Conventions

A scheme for naming documents and components of the system should use sensible and descriptive names for the document, explaining, if possible, its nature as well as the relationships that will exist between it and other documents. There will be different versions of each document, and these might also involve different releases and configurations of the whole system.

In terms of the version control, the usual basis is that the different releases will usually be numbered in a linear sequence involving a two-level scheme with major and minor releases. Each XP release should be given a new initial number. Then each release number will change when there are major changes to the functionality of the system such as new stories implemented and then integrated into a working system. Internal, minor release numbers will be used during the development of new stories to describe the various versions that are being developed prior to integration.

In traditional software development, it is common that for each release there will be an alpha version (built for internal testing only), a beta version (built for release to a small number of selected clients for them to test), and then the final version, which is released generally to all clients, so that the minor release numbers also need to identify whether this is an alpha, beta, or full release of the system. In XP we hope to avoid the subsequent issue of patched or corrected versions by delivering in well-tested increments and getting feedback from the client.

The scheme for naming documents (and other components of the system) is then based on this numbering scheme for releases, so that versions of these are given new numbers whenever they need to change in order to match the new release of the system. In practice, though, the naming scheme for documents will also need at least a third level of numbering, as it is likely that the updating of a document to match the development of a new release may happen in several stages, as new versions are inspected and corrected before finally being accepted.

10.7 DELIVERY AND FINALIZATION

These are the procedures for handing over a project to the customer in Genesys.

Please note that as part of your handover procedure, you will be required to produce a copy of the following for the management.

1) Readme.txt - giving the version of the application, file listings etc.

2) A document giving a brief technical spec. & user guide - describing what the application does and how (for support and maintainability) - max of 2 pages.

3) A document describing the Installation Procedure & System Requirements (eg hardware, operating system, version of browser etc).

4) A CD containing a copy of the application.

5) A Genesys delivery note (a Genesys template

available from marketing) acknowledging the delivery/
installation of your working solution, which must be signed
by your client.

You will also be required to give a brief presentation
to the Genesys management demonstrating all the major
features of your working solution.

The reason for this information is the need to be prepared for any after-sales
service or maintenance requirements; the team who did the project may not be available, and others will have to sort out any further issues.

10.8   REVIEW

We have discussed the different types of documents associated with a software
system, who reads them, and what they are for. We have discussed the two main
forms of documentation: paper based and on line. The project archive is considered
as a key resource and a mechanism for preventing the project from descending into
chaos. The issues of version control and configuration were also covered.

EXERCISES

1. Read through the user manual in the Appendix. Is it clear? Could you use the system by
following it? How could it be improved?
2. Each team pair should review another pair's code to see if it meets the coding standards. They
should report back their findings to the whole group. If necessary, the code should be refactored.
3. The group should review all of the software being developed and identify what stage it is at,
the connection between the stories and the classes, the status of the code in terms of whether
it passes all of the unit tests, what has been integrated and delivered, and where any new
requirements may be needed. All of this should be documented carefully.

CONUNDRUM

When should the user manual be written: at the end when all is completed or much earlier?

REFERENCE

E.H. WEISS, *How to Write Usable User Documentation*, 2nd ed. The Oryx Press, 1991.

Chapter 11

Reflecting on the Process

SUMMARY

- What has been learned
- What will be useful for projects in the future
- How has XP been used
- How can XP be improved and adapted to different circumstances
- Assessment and self-assessment

11.1 SKILLS AND LESSONS LEARNED

The satisfaction gained from delivering a high-quality product to a grateful client is hard to beat. It makes much of the struggle and the hard times worthwhile. It is one of the attractive aspects of being a programmer and software engineer—solving people's problems using sophisticated and powerful technology.

In the course of doing this, however, you will find out a lot about software development, about programming, about writing good documentation, and about quality assurance. You will also learn about working and communicating with a business client—an invaluable experience—and how a team operates. There will have been problems; problems of working with people, of trusting them, and of being trusted. All of these experiences will be important in your development as a professional in the field.

You will also improve your programming skills and your knowledge of different languages and systems greatly. It is much better to do a real project with a team like this than to do any number of small programming exercises in traditional programming courses.

At the beginning, a skills audit was suggested as a way of identifying what your abilities were before starting on this program. It is a good idea to revisit this and see how you may have developed. Bear in mind, however, that as your skills become more sophisticated, so do your expectations. Where once you believed, say, that you were an average programmer, you may still believe that is still the case, but what you can do now will be vastly improved compared with what you could do

Running an Agile Software Development Project. By Mike Holcombe
Copyright © 2008 John Wiley & Sons, Inc.

then. Try to estimate the improvement in terms of what aspects of the language you can now deal with easily and which were once hard or unknown.

Look at the way you manage things and each other and how you plan your time. It might not have been plain sailing but there are many things that you would do differently in a future project. Note these down.

11.2   THE XP EXPERIENCE

Here is an opportunity to reflect on the XP process. You will have found that it is quite hard to stick to all of the 12 practices. The four general principles of XP (communication, simplicity, feedback, and courage) should have directed our efforts. How did it turn out? What was good and what was less useful about XP?

Did you find that writing tests first was hard? Was pair programming something that you enjoyed or hated? Was the relationship with the client good, did you communicate well, obtain feedback that was timely and helpful? Are you satisfied with the documentation that was produced? Did you get the balance right between recording useful and necessary information rather than producing material for the sake of it?

How did you get on with your teammates? Did everyone put in the same amount of effort? How could team working skills be improved?

How would you adapt XP to the sort of projects that you might be involved with in the future?

Does XP work or is it another case of theory being out of step with reality? Can only highly motivated and skilled programmers make XP a successful approach to software engineering?

These questions will be answered in the fullness of time. Your experiences may help to guide the process of finding better ways of building software in a fast-changing world.

11.3   PERSONAL AND TEAM ASSESSMENT

In many organizations, there is a regular process of staff evaluation. Often this is tied to promotion and performance evaluation and can thus lead to salary raises and advancement within the organization.

In the book by Jenkins and Coens (2000) there is a well-argued critique of the usual approach to personal assessment that takes place in most companies. In many organizations, this involves managers assessing their staff through a defined process involving one-on-one review sessions and the production of reports based on structured forms and performance measures. In many organizations, the assumption is that a standard process can be applied to many different personnel working in widely different roles. The assumption is that a standard process is fair and transparent and is also important in the cases where some legal action occurs. There is significant doubt about the effectiveness of the process in terms of its effect on work performance and morale and its value in subsequent court cases.

In the context of an XP or agile development, the issue of personal and team appraisal becomes an important one. If the philosophy of agile development is based on individual responsibility and trust, then this should extend also to appraisal.

One approach to this issue is to combine a number of techniques that are based on self-appraisal with a broader approach. This might invole what is termed *360° appraisal*.

11.4 REVIEW

Reflecting on your experiences with the XP approach (Even though you might not have been able to follow all the practices completely) will enable you to understand an alternative approach to software engineering to the traditional design-led approach. Dealing with a real client with a real business need should have also transformed your understanding of the business of software creation.

The references at the end are just a sample of the rapidly growing number of books on extreme programming; they are often fairly accessible and provide a useful insight into many aspects of XP, both theoretical issues and experiences of XP in industry.

EXERCISES

1. Write down your experiences of the project and of XP. What have you learned? How enjoyable was it? Did XP deliver? How can XP be improved?

2. Look at some of the other books on extreme programming and see how they suggest an XP project should work and compare these accounts with your own experiences.

11.5 CONUNDRUMS: DISCUSSION

Chapter 1: The Internet is opening up, and many businesses are now connected. Banks are beginning to consider if they could provide online access to their business customers. One bank considers two strategies.

(A) The bank's IT director suggests that they put together a *quick and dirty* Web site that allows customers to submit transactions through their browser, to get this up and running, and to try to develop a connection with the "back-office" legacy mainframe database system.

(B) The bank also gets a report from some outside consultants that suggests they should reengineer the legacy back-end and build an integrated Web front-end to provide a powerful, user-friendly e-banking system engineered to a high standard.

Which strategy would be best and why?

Answer: The IT director is right but probably for the wrong reasons. His priority is to protect his department, he wants to be involved in the software development, he hasn't the resources for a big new development, but he could do something that would work up to a point. He doesn't want external consultants taking over and saddening him. He doesn't yet know how to connect the Web front-end to the transaction system but is confident that they can fix something.

In this case, the right reasoning is based around business pragmatics. What the bank actually did was to get the Internet site and front-end working quickly and to commission it. At the time there was no connection with the legacy transaction system, so a large number of typists were employed who printed off the Internet transactions and typed the details into the mainframe system. This was initially expensive but effective. This bank grabbed 70% market share of this new business. This then generated the income to allow them to build an integrated system involving a newly engineered back office produced by their consultants.

Meanwhile, the rival banks were building integrated solutions before going live; they never ever captured market share from the first bank.

Our bank demonstrated *agility* in both its business planning and in IT deployment. Using people for the data entry instead of a software alternative also demonstrated a *low-risk* approach as the alternative was, at the time, an untried technology. This illustrates that business considerations as well as technical ones are vital; neither should dominate the other. In an ideal world, the business leaders should have a deep and realistic knowledge of IT, and the IT specialists should have an informed and pragmatic understanding of business realities and the fundamental need to be able to make money, to maximize market share, and to deliver quality products and services. Agile methodologies need to be compatible with these objectives.

Chapter 2: Your client has already built a prototype system and wants you to develop it further so that he can then market it. He needs to demonstrate something fairly soon to his business backers in order to persuade them to put more money into the development of the system.

The original system is very poorly written, the database is badly structured, the code is all over the place, and it is going to be a nightmare to maintain.

Should you:

(A) Carefully document the functionality of the system and start reengineering it before adding new functionality?

(B) Carry on building the prototype based on what has already been done?

Answer: Your client may have a very good reason for wanting something quick; there may be more business benefit in doing so. Our scenario relates to the business person's need to be able to demonstrate a piece of working software to the business backers who will decide on putting further money into the project. Showing something working, even if it did not have all the functionality required or was a little unreliable, to these backers was much more important than doing a good software engineering job. If the extra funding becomes available, then the proper engineering of a reliable and maintainable system would probably become a priority. This also illustrates that the link between the business context and the software development process is fundamental. Traditional software engineering textbooks discuss approaches that are dominated by technical issues and the pursuit of quality without looking at how the real business pressures can force the way things have to be done. Although XP provides a number of practices that can guide us toward building high-quality and relevant software solutions, they shouldn't prevent us to respond to real business needs in favor of some abstract notion of how things should be done properly.

Chapter 3: Your project involves programming in a language that is familiar to only one member of your team. Two others have a slight knowledge of the language but have never written anything serious in it. You are trying to do pair programming, but the "expert" is getting frustrated because whenever she is paired with another team member, progress is very slow (because much of the time is taken up with explanations of what she thinks is obvious). She believes that it would be better if she worked on her own on the program and the other team members did other things, such as writing documentation and testing.

Answer: First we need to review the objectives of the project. Sure, we all want to deliver a great system for the client. But we also want to learn more about programming, particularly in this new language, we want to learn how to work in an XP team, and we want to learn how to manage a real project and work with our client. The team needs to discuss all of these things in a rational and calm manner.

Let's look at a possible way forward. We need to look at the project plan. It will contain a number of ongoing tasks, liaising with the client, writing code, working on stories, and so on. We need to include among these the need to learn the new language. Schedule some sessions where the expert gives a tutorial to the others. Of course, this may seem like wasted time because no productive code is being generated, but the benefits will come later. The expert should identify with the others small pieces of code that they can produce in pairs. Meanwhile the expert looks at some other issues such as story analysis and the definition of both functional tests and unit tests. While this is being done, the others are getting up to speed a little. After 2 or 3 weeks, if everyone works hard and with a positive attitude, we might get to a position whereby any pair can program together in a reasonably effective way and they will get better all the time.

Chapter 4: Your team is in trouble. The client has not been in touch with her feedback on the proposed system. She doesn't have much IT experience and only has a rather vague idea of what she wants. There are no similar systems known to you that you can show her. You need to start getting some requirements identified and some initial stories prepared.

Do you:

(A) Wait until she has thought further about the system she wants?

(B) Build a simple prototype using your imagination and background research in order to show her something that might stimulate her ideas?

Answer: Choose option (B). The delay may be caused by the client not knowing how to proceed and lacking in confidence; it may be their first experience as a client, and their knowledge of IT is minimal. Some good suggestions from you could be a lifesaver for them. Even if they don't like your ideas, these may stimulate them into suggesting things that are suitable. It also gives you an opportunity to be creative instead of just sitting around waiting.

Chapter 5: The company wanted an *intranet* that provided support for many of their business activities and also their personnel management. The site would contain information about the various company activities, a diary system, and templates for administrative tasks such as the submission of illness and absence forms. The users would be able to log on remotely to carry out tasks as well as from within the company offices. The customer was able to maintain a very close relationship with the development team and had a clear idea of what the company needed. There were three teams using XP working on this project, each competing with all the others. Initially, all the teams thought that the project would take 10 weeks. It didn't quite work out like that. When the first team delivered their first increment, they discovered something important that had not emerged from the planning game. The company had a service agreement with a third-party network solutions company that provided the computer system and the Internet connection for the customer. This led to a serious problem for some of the teams and resulted in some failing to meet the 10-week deadline despite the careful planning.

What might have been the problem?

Answer: The network service provider had an important policy on the type of technology that they supported. Not all the teams were using a compatible approach. The customer did not know about the technicalities of this side of the project. The early delivery of a functioning piece of software brought the issues to light when the team tried to install it. The customer was then asked to negotiate with the network supplier to introduce the required support. This was eventually achieved but some teams still, unfortunately, used an unsupported technology, and so, though their solutions were good, they did not work for this customer.

It is important to investigate all aspects of the customer's situation, including the services used and the constraints that may apply. Getting an early release installed at the customer's site can help to identify problems like this.

Chapter 6: Two leading supermarket chains introduced their first Internet ordering system at around the same time. Their e-commerce sites, although superficially looking similar, fared rather differently. One saw a much greater growth in business than did the other. Yet the technology used and the warehousing and delivery systems were comparable. Customers just didn't like using one of the sites.

What could have been the differences between the two user interfaces that made this happen? (It was nothing to do with the look and feel of the Web pages or the way that the orders were managed or the price of the goods.)

Answer: One company relied on graphic arts specialists to design the Web pages; the other used a combination of graphic artists and computer scientists. In the unsuccessful Web site, there were lots of attractive graphic images featuring a popular TV chef in the home pages. The other site had attractive graphics, too, but these had been optimized in terms of their memory size without any obvious loss of image quality. This meant that the pages downloaded much faster, especially over slow modems.

The other site took much longer, and many prospective customers gave up waiting and switched to the other site. (Note that in the United Kingdom, local telephone charges can be significant.) Thorough testing under all likely conditions should have identified this problem—it shows that some non-functional requirements can be critical.

Chapter 7: A local retailer specializing in luxury goods commissioned an e-commerce system. This was completed and installed satisfactorily. The shop gave the job of printing out the Internet orders and processing them through the orders system to one of the sales assistants to do at the end of their shift. This worked well at the beginning as the numbers of orders gradually grew.

After a few months of steady growth, the sales figures of orders placed through the Web suddenly collapsed to nothing. Initially, it was thought to be a software fault, but no problems were found when we investigated.

What could have gone wrong?

Answer: Initially, it was thought that the volume of orders was too great for the database system chosen for the application. This hypothesis was soon rejected. Other thoughts focused on the architecture of the system and on the connection between the interface, business, and database layers. Again, no problems were uncovered here. We then looked more carefully at how the system was operating in the business. The reason for the problem was found to be because the increase in the number of orders was not accompanied by a corresponding increase in the people dealing with the orders. The assistant became increasingly frustrated at the volume of work that had to be done at the end of their shift. The desperate solution taken was to delete all the Internet orders instead of dealing with them.

This indicates that the system must be designed to include the human dimension as well as the computer. A management strategy should have been designed alongside the introduction of the computer system so that it could adapt to the needs of the business as these changed.

Chapter 8: About 20 years ago, the UK government purchased a system to deal with air traffic control over London. It was based on a number of similar systems that had recently been installed in the United States. Unlike the American systems, there were serious problems with the London system. Planes flying over London would suddenly disappear from the screen. Equally alarmingly, planes would suddenly appear as if from nowhere. Extensive testing was carried out, especially on the component of the system that was fed the radar information and dealt with the display of the positions of the planes on the screen. No defects were found; everything was exactly as the requirements demanded.

Why did the system work in the United States but not in London?

Answer: The system used latitude and longitude positions to track the planes. These were treated as real positive numbers. Now the problem is that London lies on the Greenwich Meridian, which is longitude $0°$, and so planes would be moving across this line. Planes moving from West to East would have their longitude value reduce from a positive number through 0 to negative values. The system had not been designed to deal with negative numbers so they were ignored. Similarly, planes coming from the East had negative longitude and were also invisible. Of course, there is no situation like this in America and so the problem was not considered during the development of the system.

The problem ultimately showed up during unit testing after the initial system test failed. The moral is to think the unthinkable, question all the assumptions, and to do this make sure that they are all documented. Then, in problems like this, someone may realize that what might have been true under certain conditions may not be true under others.

Chapter 9: The customer was the IT director of a company that produced and sold biological specimens to research laboratories and pharmaceutical companies. The software was to support the entire company activities, which involved the production process (which had to be fully documented to meet government regulatory procedures), the stock control process, the ordering process, and the invoicing and accounting processes.

After working extensively with the customer and delivering a number of incremental versions, the customer was satisfied. A final delivery was made, and at this point the customer invited several personnel from the company to attend the demonstrations. These potential users of the system pointed out many problems with the business concepts upon which the system was based. It became clear that the customer did not understand his company's business process. It was also clear that we would have to reengineer the system. The new requirements were significantly different; there were few areas where the detail was the same although the overall architecture would be very similar.

Should we start again from scratch or try to adapt what we had already done, reusing and preserving what we could?

Answer: Genesys started out trying to adapt the system to the new requirement. Initially, this seemed to involve redesigning some of the screens, altering the database, and retesting the system. This took a number of months, but progress was held up by problems with system quality. Whenever we thought that we had tested and debugged a section, we discovered more problems with it afterwards. After a while, the decision was taken to start again. Because of the previous work on the system, the new build was very rapid, and a complete working system was delivered within a relatively short time to a quality that the customer and his colleagues were happy with.

Should we have started on a complete rebuild immediately after we found out that the requirements were wrong? It is difficult to answer this. Trying to adapt the original system did help us to capture and understand the new requirements, and this enabled us to build the final system quickly. Perhaps this was the best strategy.

Chapter 10: When should the user manual be written, at the end when all is completed or much earlier?

Answer: Traditionally, it is done at the end. It is often done by a junior member of the development team and is rarely tested with potential users.

Why not start thinking about it when we are creating the stories? A simple page or two giving the outline *script* for a user can be developed in tandem. As the stories get changed, then the draft manual will also be changed. The development of the system metaphor's interface will create the framework for the user manual, and the final screen shots can be inserted into the document when they are ready.

11.6 A FINAL WORD

We hear a lot about failed software projects, failure to deliver, failure to deliver something usable, failure to deliver something of value. Extreme programming and other agile development approaches are an attempt to try to improve matters. Whether they do provide a better way will be determined over the next few years. What is clear; however, are two basic points:

1 Software development methods, including XP, will continue to evolve to try to meet the challenges of tomorrow.

2 We cannot afford to ignore the complete environment of any software solution: the clients and customers, the users, the business process, and the marketplace all will impact on the success of whatever we build.

The stories that were discussed in the *conundrums* are all real examples of situations that you might face in the future. Adopting XP and ignoring any of the stakeholders in item (2) above may still result in failure.

There is still much research to be done on XP and the agile approach. What is certain is that many of the principles articulated by these ideas will stay with us. Your experiences trying to apply them in a real project in a professional way will provide you with a firm foundation for a future career in software development. It is not easy applying all these ideas; it needs discipline and perseverance, as you have probably discovered. Doing it well will, I am sure, leave you with a great sense of achievement.

Being agile might be hard, but it's worth it!

Appendix to Chapter 11

Genesys Solutions' Students 2007/8: Initial Self-Assessment Form.

Name:

Team:

Consider the following statements about the sort of things that you have been doing. If you can answer YES to all of them then that would indicate a high mark for some of the criteria below.

Note that people doing different roles should make their return based on what their role entails.

Group A: Leadership and Company Processes

"The suggestion and implementation of company processes and resources to enhance and improve company operation"

(1) Making suggestions for improving the efficiency and quality of what the company does.

(2) Taking a lead in your project and getting the best out of your colleagues

(3) Promoting the company and providing a professional image to customers and others

Group B: Development

"The production of software to meet a customers needs"

(1) Test First – evidence that the member has produced and run extensive unit tests, and ntegration tests

(2) Documentation, to describe the software on the Wiki. Video presentations to describe the key technology used

(3) Adherence to XP practices, with evidence

(4) The delivery of a working system on time and within budget

Group C: Specification

"The production of a specification to describe a customer's needs"

(1) Documentation present on Wiki: continuously updated documentation to reflect the current and actual requirements agreed with the customer

(2) Meeting minutes present in the management tool

(3) A formal contract produced and signed off

(4) A project plan, which plans in detail for the next fortnight (tasks via management tool), and less detail for the remainder of the project (milestones via management tool)

Group D: Marketing

"The capture of business, and the promotion of Genesys"

(1) Accurate client profiles on the Wiki

(2) Meeting minutes via Sheffield Management

(3) Maintain the company diary via Sheffield Management

(4) Update the website with client profiles

Group E: Management

"The company board meeting and the Wiki are where we all learn about what the company is doing"

(1) To present to the board some aspect of another teams work

(2) To update your Wiki every week

(3) To be aware of other projects details from their Wiki

(4) To provide sensible and accurate estimates of the time for the tasks and the project to be completed

Group F: Admin

"To ensure the network is maintained"

(1) All PCs should be kept in a working state

(2) The services (website/email etc) should be running

(3) Installation of new software carried out promptly

(4) Installation and maintenance of servers, backup processes etc. done seamlessly

1 Individual Qualities and Achievements

(Your personal self-assessment on a scale 1(low)-5(high))

Evidence of leadership skills:

1 2 3 4 5

Why? ....

Evidence of working towards team and company goals:

1 2 3 4 5

Why? ....

Evidence of planning and organisational ability:

1 2 3 4 5

Why? ....

Evidence of involvement in quality control activities:

1 2 3 4 5

Why? ....

Evidence of technical achievement:

1 2 3 4 5

(relative to abilities at start of course)

Why? ....

Evidence of skills in customer liaison:

1 2 3 4 5

Why? ....

Evidence of skills in document production and management:

1 2 3 4 5

Why? ....

2 Assessment of team members: estimate their overall contribution to the team on a 1...5 scale.

Name:　　　　**Grade**

1 2 3 4 5

Why? ....

Name:　　　　**Grade**

1 2 3 4 5

Why? ....

Name:　　　　**Grade**

1 2 3 4 5

Why? ....

Name:　　　　**Grade**

1 2 3 4 5

Why? ....

3 Comment on the following:

3.1 Objectives of your team (refer to each project you had)

3.2 Achievements

3.3 Failures

3.4 Your role in the team (what your part was)

3.5 What deliverables the team produced

3.6 Your view on communication/cooperation in the team (& ways of improving it)

3.7 Assess your contribution to the project(s) in the 1st semester (compared with the other team-mates)

3.8 Ways of improving Genesys:

Chapter 12

Lifestyle Matters

SUMMARY

The impact of lifestyle on software development performance

- Exercise and relaxation
- Holistic approaches to well-being
- Diet, music, and problem solving

This chapter is a slightly unusual contribution to an important issue that is rarely addressed in textbooks like this. Although not a specialist in the field, I think it is still possible to appreciate some of the most recent research and draw some useful conclusions about how we should bring into the world of software development aspects pertaining to how we live our lives at work. If in doubt about any aspect of this subject, it is best to consult a specialist.

There is more to being a productive and effective software developer than just technical knowledge, intellectual ability, and the use of appropriate processes. We have looked into issues such as personality and psychology generally and have seen how these can impact the social activity of agile software development.

But what about the whole person, the physical aspects of life? Many lifestyle choices can affect one's ability to carry out one's duties, and this is rarely appreciated.

The food you eat, the exercise you take, and the ways you relax can make an enormous difference to your overall performance.

This chapter will take a look at how lifestyle choices can be made that will enhance your life as an agile software engineer.

Professional sportsmen and sportswomen have a carefully designed diet and exercise regimen. This is based on the latest research into physiology and sports science. Such athletes need to be at their peak when performing, and a great deal of effort and planning is devoted to this aspect of life.

In team sports such as soccer, football, baseball, rugby, and so forth, the players need to be agile, fast, strong, creative, aware, and trained up in tactics, roles, and many different planned routines of play. All of these issues are relevant to agile development. Although the athletes do not always have a managed program of intellectual

Running an Agile Software Development Project. By Mike Holcombe
Copyright © 2008 John Wiley & Sons, Inc.

training, there is no reason why agile software developers should ignore the physical aspects of their work.

These could range from suitable working environments (the position of screens, height of chairs, etc.) to diet and types of exercise undertaken.

Our brains are complex and highly evolved machines that have developed over thousands of years in circumstances very different from today where we enjoy a rich variety of food, many types of entertainment and leisure activities, and where physical exercise can be avoided. The proper functioning of our brains is based on a complex interaction of many types of chemicals, much of which is not fully understood. The overindulgence of some types of food and drink, the lack of exercise, and the inability to relax all have an impact on the way our bodies, including our brains, function. By taking a more holistic approach to our lifestyles, we will be able to train ourselves to perform better as well as to live longer and happier lives.

Too many software developers pay little attention to these issues. They often slump at their desks, take little physical exercise—playing computer games may be as far as they go—survive on large quantities of coffee and junk food, high levels of alcohol, tobacco, and, possibly, recreational drugs. Lack of a balance in these activities may lead to long-term health troubles but they may also affect software development projects. You may not be very effective as a team player or be able to be as creative and productive as you could be if you are in poor shape.

12.1 KEEPING FIT

In the main, programming is a sedentary activity, sitting for long hours at a keyboard and peering at a screen. Many people who have a career that involves the use a computer suffer from a variety of physical ailments. The most serious and painful are back pain and repetitive strain injury (RSI). For young, healthy people, the prospect of suffering from these problems may seem a long way off. However, it can strike people at a relatively young age—several of my students in their early twenties have had quite serious cases of both back pain and RSI.

It makes sense to think about how these might be avoided—be smart about your working practices and help yourself to avoid problems in the future.

One thing that needs to be made clear throughout this chapter is that everyone is different. Two individuals working in the same way may experience very different outcomes: one may suffer from RSI, whereas the person alongside them may not.

Scientific and medical research tries to understand the root causes of medical problems and to produce recommendations that will apply to as wide a sample as possible; however, they are generalizations and have to be subject to that realization.

There are many Web sites and other publications that provide advice about ergonomic issues relating to the extensive use of computers.

Here is a list of useful sources:

Correct sitting position: http://www.clevelandclinic.org/health/health-info/docs/0300/0359.asp?index=4485

Correct sitting position: `http://www.bbc.co.uk/health/conditions/ back_pain/preventionback_posture.shtml#`sitting_properly

RSI: `http://www.local-10.com/RSIEXERCISES.html`

General well-being and ergonomics: http://ergo.human.cornell.edu/ergoguide. html

Let's think about posture first.

You will spend many hours sitting at a terminal and how you do this will determine whether you could suffer from posture-related problems such as back pain of various types.

12.1.1 Correct Sitting Position

Consult suitable sources such as http://www.clevelandclinic.org/health/health-info/docs/0300/0359.asp?index=4485, from which this advice is summarised.

1 Sit up with your back straight and your shoulders back. Your buttocks should touch the back of your chair.

2 All three normal back curves should be present while sitting. A small, rolled-up towel or a lumbar roll can be used to help you maintain the normal curves in your back. Here's how to find a good sitting position when you're not using a back support or lumbar roll: Sit at the end of your chair and slouch completely; draw yourself up and accentuate the curve of your back as far as possible. Hold for a few seconds; release the position slightly (about 10 degrees). This is a good sitting posture.

3 Distribute your body weight evenly on both hips.

4 Bend your knees at a right angle. Keep your knees even with or slightly higher than your hips (use a foot rest or stool if necessary). Your legs should not be crossed.

5 Keep your feet flat on the floor.

6 Try to avoid sitting in the same position for more than 30 minutes.

7 At work, adjust your chair height and work station so you can sit up close to your work and tilt it up at you. Rest your elbows and arms on your chair or desk, keeping your shoulders relaxed.

8 When sitting in a chair that rolls and pivots, don't twist at the waist while sitting. Instead, turn your whole body.

9 When standing up from the sitting position, move to the front of the seat of your chair. Stand up by straightening your legs. Avoid bending forward at your waist. Immediately stretch your back by doing 10 standing backbends.

And from http://www.bbc.co.uk/health/conditions/back_pain/preventionback_ posture.shtml#sitting_properly, this advice on sitting properly:

- Use an upright chair that supports your lower back.
- Try supporting the small of your back (the bit that curves in above your hips) with a small cushion or rolled-up towel.
- Get up and stretch every 20 to 30 minutes.

When pair programming, don't forget these simple rules.

The type of chair that you use can be a problem—it is important to use one that encourages healthy sitting. Make sure that it is at the right height for you and that the desk or table that you are using is also suitable.

For pair programming, you both need to have convenient access to the keyboard and mouse. It is easy to stretch across a partner and strain your back. Using a wireless keyboard and mouse can be a useful way to address this.

Periodically stand up and stretch your body and arms upwards with your arms raised over your head.

With your arms held behind your back, stretch your neck forward and to the right and hold for a few seconds, and then to the left. Repeat three times.

Gently pull your elbow across your chest toward your opposite shoulder and hold for 5 seconds. Repeat with the other arm.

12.1.2   Combating RSI

Regular exercises of your hands, wrists, and arms are essential if you are going to counteract the repetitive actions that programming can involve.

It is a good idea to get into regular habits and to do some exercises frequently, so before you start and at periods during the day, do the following:

Stretch your hands out wide and stretch your fingers in and out for 5 to 10 seconds.

Rotate your hands with your fingers outstretched to exercise your wrists; repeat with your hands half closed and finally closed.

Drop your hands to your sides and shake them for 5 to 10 seconds.

Press you hands (palms) together.

Stand up, put your hands behind you, and interlace your fingers; keeping your chin tucked and your body straight lift your hands away from your body and hold this positions for 15 seconds.

The above information was taken from http://www.local-10.com/RSIEXERCISES. html, where more exercises can be found. See also http://www.ucsf.edu/sorehand/.

Juggling can also help; this not only keeps your wrists supple but also develops your hand–eye coordination and helps you to relax and at the same time to concentrate more—it could be a good start to the day.

12.2 GENERAL WELL-BEING

During the day, it is important to take regular breaks; every 30 minutes is a good idea. Get up from your desk and walk around, look at something in the distance to give your eyes a break from focusing on something close such as a computer screen.

Have a drink of water or some fruit.

When it comes to a meal break such as lunch, then avoid taking it at your desk. Find somewhere where you can relax and take some light exercise—walk around but avoid strenuous exercise. Concentrating on your work during mealtimes can be counterproductive and may not lead to the best solutions.

Guidelines such as these are widely promoted by employers and universities, see for example http://ergo.human.cornell.edu/ergoguide.html.

After work, it is important to manage your leisure—this does not mean that you should avoid any work-related activity. There are benefits to engaging in social activities with colleagues working on your project. In more relaxed surroundings, there could be opportunities to discuss things about the project that will help it. There are many cases where key information is shared or important insights obtained when out for a meal or other activity with project colleagues.

Organizing a social event with your colleagues can also help to build team cohesion and spirit—many management training companies develop elaborate activities with this in mind. Of course, it could lead to arguments and have a negative effect as well so be aware of the risks.

A "friendly" game of ping-pong (table tennis) or something similar can often help to relieve tension arising from unresolved feelings of tension or aggression.

Some highly energetic sports such as squash can be dangerous if you don't train properly because they expose the body to sudden stresses that can cause long-term damage. Jogging, if done sensibly, may be beneficial but it has to be a regular activity if it is to be beneficial.

My particular enthusiasm is for gardening. This involves many different physical activities and promotes general physical well-being. Most of your muscles are involved, and the body will be more supple as a result although back pain caused by a poor stance when digging or lifting heavy objects is a danger to be looked out for. Not everyone has a garden, but there are often public amenity gardens in many neighborhoods that are usually pleased to recruit volunteers. However, extreme weather conditions can interfere with regular gardening activity. Another activity that might be considered is conservation volunteering.

If you are suffering from pain and discomfort caused by work or leisure, then see a healthcare professional—don't try to be a hero and put up with it. Your advisers, tutors, and other colleagues could help with advice on who to see.

12.3 MENTAL PREPARATION

Sometimes you need to do some mental exercises to really tune up for an intensive burst of mental activity in a project. Athletes would never consider starting a race without warming up; neither should you. For most people, the warm-up involves checking one's e-mails. This can be okay but it really depends on what you get— some may be project related or of a more social nature, some may make you angry or frustrated, some may make you feel good. With such a mixed bag of possibilities, it is probably worth thinking about how you may be able to prepare better for work.

Here is some advice from Kent Beck (personal communication, 2007):

> *Timed writing. I find it soothing to just write a stream of consciousness for a set amount of time or set number of pages. The goal of the exercise is to never stop moving your pen (I do this with pen and paper, which works better than typing for me). At first my thoughts are around random topics, then whatever is bothering me about my life, and then eventually I start thinking about work. When that happens I'm ready to program.*

12.4 DIET

What you eat affects both your physical and mental states. There is a lot of research about this, and we will review some of it.

First, we will review some of what is known about the impact of diet on brain function, cognition, and problem solving.

Bear in mind that there are two types of experimental work: there is psychological research, which involves humans, and there is the more detailed biological work that tends to focus on experiments involving rats, mice, and other animals. The validity of generalizing from the latter to humans is something that needs to be considered, and for the former types of experiments there may be doubts about the actual effects observed in the absence of a clear molecular mechanism to explain the phenomena.

12.4.1 Diet and Brain Function

Diet is known to affect brain function in a number of ways. Although some research in this area is based on studies of rodents, recent work with human patients and modern brain scanning technologies are confirming much of this work. It is worth considering how this research applies to everyday life, but it shouldn't be used as a basis for some obsessive dietary regime.

Bourre (2006a) discusses the role of nutrients and brain function. Vitamins B9, B6, and B12 all have roles in cognitive performance and memory, synthesizing neurotransmitters and preventing memory loss. Vitamin D has a role in the prevention of neuroimmune diseases. Cobalamin improves cerebal and language function. Elements like iron, lithium, magnesium, zinc, and iodine all contribute to healthy brain function as people with deficiencies in these trace chemicals suffer a variety of problems. Essential micronutrients such as polyphenols are involved in protection against free radicals.

Macronutrients are potentially more important. The polyunsaturated omega-3 fatty acids and ALA (alpha-linolenic acid), are involved in many aspects of brain structure and function along with polyunsaturated omega-3 and omega-6 carbon chains.

Diets with a low glycemic index (GI) improve intellectual performance (Bourre, 2006b). GI diets focus on the use of foods that break down into glucose slowly and they thus reduce the desire for more food—hence they seem successful for many people who are overweight as well.

Chalon (2006) also looks at the role of omega-3 fatty acids in monoamine neurotransmission. Subjects with a history of diets low in these suffer from a number of neurotransmission system problems. The biochemical basis of this is being uncovered. Rectifying the diet to include these fatty acids improved the general biochemical activity but not the neurochemical factors.

Puri (2006) has developed noninvasive scanning techniques and demonstrated major improvements in brain function and structure, mental performance, and behavior in patients with a history of poor diet through the incorporation of omega-3 and omega-6 fatty acids into the diet.

Essential fatty acids (EFAs) are a key set of nutrients found in nuts and oily fish and have a measurable effect when incorporated in a balanced diet.

Omega-6 is found in nuts, sunflower seeds, and sesame seeds; omega-3 is contained in soya beans, flax seeds, and oily fish (sardines, salmon, pilchards, herrings, mackerel, etc.). But life is not quite as simple as this. Some people lack the ability to process EFAs efficiently and derivatives such as EPA (eicosapentaenoic acid) provide the benefits more effectively.

12.4.2 Summary of Dietary Information

Knowing what foods are high in the beneficial components is important.

Table 12.1 describes the GI of common foods. This is not to say that only low-GI foods should be eaten but rather that high GI foods should be eaten less often than the others.

Meat: Choose lean meats and poultry in preference for those high in unhealthy fats. Fast foods such as burgers and French fries (chips) are thought to affect brain function—certainly in children—and to encourage obesity. Research indicates that such foods have a very high energy density, which has the effect of fooling people into consuming more than their body needs (Prentice, 2004). The biochemical basis (chemicals such as leptin and galanin) is now becoming clear and provides evidence for the addictive properties of such foods.

Alcohol: The message, again, is moderation, and the occasional glass of wine—especially red wine—is thought to be beneficial. However, large quantities of alcohol can have a serious effect on both brain function and the body generally.

Tobacco: Medical researchers analyzing the brains of smokers and drug users have detected significant changes that have taken place in the brain structure (Naqvi, 2007). Some of these regions seem to be implicated in the addictive behavior of smokers. Thus it looks as though the addictive properties of some drug abuse are derived from structural changes the abuse triggers in the brain. Tobacco also has many other serious side effects that are well-known. Tobacco is often used as an

Table 12.1   GI of Common Foods

	Low GI	High GI
Fresh fruit	Apples, pears, oranges, grapefruit, plums, strawberries, peaches, grapes	Dates, watermelon
Vegetables	Broccoli, cabbage, lettuce, onions, mushrooms, peppers, pulses generally (lentils, beans)	Parsnips, potatoes, cooked carrots, broad beans, pumpkin
Fish	Oily fish (sardines, salmon, pilchards, herrings, and mackerel)	Breaded fish and battered fish
Nuts and seeds	Some nuts and seeds (if not allergic)	
Bread and pasta	Rye bread, pasta, noodles, brown basmati rice	White bread, baguette, bagel
Cereal	All bran, muesli	Cornflakes, Rice Krispies, Shredded Wheat
Drinks	Low-fat Yogurt, milk, custard	Soft and fizzy drinks, sugary foods, cakes

antidote to stress and other pressures, but it is not the best way to handle these problems. Medical guidance should be taken if they become serious.

Stimulants: Again the consumption of coffee, tea, and other stimulants should not be excessive—"moderation in all things"! Coffee can enhances alertness, concentration, and mental and physical performance in some, but not all, people. There are known antioxidant substances in coffee (e.g., chlorogenic acid) and tea (catechins), and these might have a health benefit.

12.5   MUSIC AND WORK

This section deals with an issue that is not fully understood and can be seen as being somewhat controversial.

Many people find that music can help them relax and to be more productive in work.

A study by Rauscher, Shawn, and Ky (1995) found that playing music by Mozart to university students helped them to perform a number of mental and dexterous tasks better.

This was followed up by an investigation into the effect of music training (keyboard lessons) on school children and the benefits this gave them in spatiol-temporal reasoning (Rauscher et al., 1997). The belief is that long-term modifications occur in neural circuitry in regions not specifically concerned with music appreciation. Some experiments have shown that does up-tempo music has a more marked effect than does slow music

This research is controversial, and some have expressed doubts about the existence of this effect [see Waterhouse's (2006) critical review]; however, recent work has tended to confirm it. For example, Jausovec and colleagues (2006) came to the conclusion that Mozart's music, by activating task-relevant brain areas, enhances the learning of spatio-temporal rotation tasks. Similar results have been found concerning Bach's music (Schellenberg, 2007).

Another investigation (Furnham, 1999) studied the effects of vocal and instrumental music upon the performance of introverts and extraverts on three cognitive tasks. "There was a trend for the introverts to be impaired by the introduction of music to the environment and extraverts to be enhanced by it, particularly on the reading and coding tasks. There was a condition effect on the logic task with subjects doing best in the presence of instrumental music."

Whatever the current state of science, many people like to listen to music while they work. In the context of an XP team, it can cause problems if there is a disagreement about what sort of music should be available. When two people are pair programming, then the presence of music can be a distraction—how can you discuss the issues easily if you are wearing headphones. If the music is broadcast throughout the room, then it has to be agreed among all the programmers as to what will be chosen.

My personal preference is for some music (my particular favorites are Bach and Purcell), and I think that it helps me to concentrate and to solve problems better. Some believe that instrumental music is best for writing text and songs for programming.

Why not carry out some experiments with different types of music and see which works best?

12.6 REVIEW

There is clear evidence that a balanced diet rich in fatty acids, fruit, and with a low GI is both generally healthy and promotes significantly enhanced brain function.

Naturally, if you suffer from allergies, such as nut allergies, then you cannot adopt all of these recommendations, and you should see your doctor to discuss ways to deal with this.

Keeping fit with regular exercise is also thought to be beneficial for all walks of life.

Extensive use of a computer brings with it new risks that can be a precursor for a number of painful ailments. Taking some precautions about posture, undertaking some simple regular exercises, avoiding long periods of concentrated working, and being sensible about one's work–life balance will all be beneficial.

It should be stressed, however, that the opinions of experts for specific problems is something that we should seek before these problems get out of hand.

This chapter provides some suggestions on how to avoid problems, some information about recent scientific research into some relevant issues, but our knowledge is growing all the time, so it is best to keep alert and take appropriate precautions to avoid trouble in the future and to maximize one's ability to contribute to projects and to enjoy one's professional life.

REFERENCES

J.M. Bourre. Effects of nutrients (in food) on the structure and function of the nervous system: Update on dietary requirements for brain. Part 1: Micronutrients. *Journal of Nutrition Health and Aging*, **10**(5):377–385, 2006.

J.M. Bourre. Effects of nutrients (in food) on the structure and function of the nervous system: Update on dietary requirements for brain. Part 2: Macronutrients. *Journal of Nutrition Health and Aging* **10**(5):386–399, 2006.

S. Chalon. Omega-3 fatty acids and monoamine neurotransmission. *Prostaglandins, Leukotrienes and Essential Fatty Acids*, **75**(4–5):259–269, 2006.

A. Furnham, S. Trew, S. Sneade. The distracting effects of vocal and instrumental music on the cognitive test performance of introverts and extraverts. *Personality and Individual Differences*, **27**(2):381–392, 1999.

N. Jausovec, K. Jausovec, I. Gerlic. The influence of Mozart's music on brain activity in the process of learning. *Clinical Neurophysiology*, **117**(12):2703–2714, 2006.

N. H. Naqvi, D. Rudrauf, H. Damasio, A. Bechara. Damage to the insula disrupts addiction to cigarette smoking. *Science*, **315**(5811):531–534, 2007.

A. Prentice. Storing up problems: The medical case for a slimmer nation. *Clinical Medicine*, **4**(2):99–101, 2004.

B.K. Puri. Proton and 31-phosphorus neurospectroscopy in the study of membrane phospholipids and fatty acid intervention in schizophrenia, depression, chronic fatigue syndrome (myalgic encephalomyelitis) and dyslexia. *International Reviews of Psychiatry*, **18**(2):145–147, 2006.

F.H. Rauscher, G.L. Shaw, K.N. Ky. Listening to Mozart enhances spatial-temporal reasoning: Towards a neurophysiological basis. *Neuroscience Letters*, **185**:44–47, 1995.

F.H. Rauscher, G.L. Shaw, L.J. Levine, E.L. Wright, W.R. Dennis, R. Newcoinb. Music training causes long-term enhancement of preschool children's spatial-temporal reasoning abilities. *Neurological Research*, **19**:1–8, 1997.

G.E. Schellenberg, T. Nakat, P.G. Hunter, T. Tamoto. Exposure to music and cognitive performance: tests of children and adults. *Psychology of Music*, **35**(1):5–19, 2007.

L. Waterhouse. Multiple intelligences, the Mozart effect, and emotional intelligence: A critical review. *Educational Psychologist*, **41**(4):207–225, 2006.

Appendix

Some examples from second-year student projects, Software Hut 2008.

Requirements document

Storycard

Tests and test results

Running an Agile Software Development Project. By Mike Holcombe
Copyright © 2008 John Wiley & Sons, Inc.

Requirements document 07/03/08

From hut01's Wiki

Contents

Background Information

The client is The School of Health and Related Research (ScHARR), a multidisciplinary school within the faculty of Medicine at the University of Sheffield. They require an automated system to replace the current manual Excel spreadsheets used to plan and record data relating to the scheduling of teaching, and the calculation of each staff member's weighted teaching hours (see glossary).

ScHARR have somewhere between 80 and 100 modules, spread over approximately 10 degree programmes. Planning for this number of modules each year requires a lot of work, and due to the manual nature of the current system this can take a long time. The client has requested a database application with an internet browser based front end that will allow them to perform the task more easily.

The client has identified the key features that they would like implemented, as well as several additional optional features, that are shown in the stories section of this document.

Stories

Mandatory

1. Users should be able to log in to the system at one of two levels (administrator/basic user) by supplying a username and correct password to the login screen.

2. Produce user interface for page that will allow a module coordinator to enter the details for a particular module.

3. Designing and implementing an underlying database for the system. This will contain login details and schedule information, as input through the system interface.

4. Administrator users should be able to create staff/administrator users.

5. Administrator users should be able to edit existing staff/administrator users in the system, including password, user type and disabled status.

6. Administrator users should be able to amend weightings for teaching sessions.

7. Administrator users, or specified course directors, should be able to add/edit courses.

8. Staff users should be able to enter module details for any modules they co-ordinate.

9. Users should be able to view submitted module details for their own modules (or administrators can view all), including learning sessions etc.

10. Users should be able to view module timetables.

11. Administrators should be able to edit any modules' details.

12. Administrator users should be able to add/edit modules.

13. Administrators should be able to view and print reports for modules that show all of the associated sessions for a particular semester.

Desirable

14. Users should be able to retrieve forgotten passwords.

15. Users should be able to view Staff Detail reports, which include their hours, weighted hours, timetables, and any associated modules. Administrators can view all staff reports, whereas a staff can only view their own.

16. It should be possible to roll forward module run details to the next year to avoid unnecessary work re-entering data.

Optional

17. Users should be able to query the database for timetables at a particular period. Administrators should see all details, whereas staff can only see details for modules they are associated with.

18. Administrators should be able to find out what staff members are available (not lecturing) in a specific time period (week, day, time, length) to identify staff that could fill in gaps.

Non-Functional Requirements

- Consistent interface.
- Interface that displays correctly across different operating systems.
- Interface that displays correctly across different internet browsers.
- It should be clear where to enter data, and how to save it.
- It should take less than 3 steps to get to the page to perform any given function.

- Clear and concise error messages.
- Pages should load within a maximum of 10 seconds.
- System should be available for multiple users simultaneously.

Glossary

- Administrator - A user who has full access rights and control to change any option in the system.
- Course - A degree course which will consist of many modules controlled by (usually) one Course Director.
- Course Director - A staff member responsible for an entire course.
- Distance Learning - A session of teaching for "distance learning" – in other words, learning where students do not attend classes. Might not have scheduled times.
- Guest - A user who cannot log into the system. Used for staff members who are either barred from accessing, or not allowed to access.
- Lecture - A formal lecture session on a module. Can be new or repeat (which will only change how the session is reflected in the weights).
- Module - A learning unit provided on a course.
- Module Co-ordinator - The staff member responsible for entering their module details.
- Module Run - An instance of a module related to a semester in a year. Each module will likely have multiple module runs.
- Online Tutorial - A session for a tutorial performed online. Might not have scheduled times.
- Seminar - A session, scheduled with a day and time in a week.
- Session - Modules will be made up of many sessions – these include lectures, seminars, tutorials and distance learning. *There could be more than one session in a week.
- Session Staff - A staff member who is associated with a session.
- Staff - A user who only has limited access rights, and should only be able to edit any data first associated with them.
- Tutorial - A session, scheduled with a day and time in a week.
- User - A staff member on the system. Can be an Administrator. Staff or Guest.
- Weightings - Different types of learning sessions will have different weights, which contribute to a weighted total of hours for a module.

Retrieved from "http://vt.shef.ac.uk/sm/wiki/2007/hut01/index.php/Requirements_document_07/03/08"

- This page was last modified 14:38, 7 March 2008.

Storycard 346

From hut01's Wiki

Process Followed

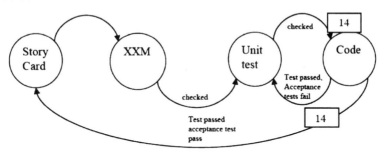

The story card has been written and checked, no errors were found. The XXM was written, and no errors were found. Once correct a unit test was written. The unit test was checked, and found to be OK, then the code was written to satisfy that test. The test ran successfully and another test was written. In all fourteen tests were written to implement the storycard in turn, adding the code at each point before the acceptance tests passed. The story was then signed off.

Sheffield Management 2007: hut01 - Storycard

ID	2059(1)	Priority	0
Description			
Users should be able to log in to the system at one of two levels (administrator/basic user) by supplying a username and correct password to the login screen.			
Tests			
Entering no username and/or no password results in error. Entering a username that doesn't exist (regardless of the entered password) results in error. Entering an invalid password with an existing username results in error. Entering an existing username and valid password results in success, with the user being taken to the main screen with the correct privileges. User can only login if their user account has not been disabled.			
Nonfunctional Tests			
Acceptance or rejection is within 10 seconds. Text boxes are clearly labeled. An appropriate message is shown in case of error.			

Tasks for this story

():

Entry:

Comments:

():

Entry:

Comments:

Date	Type	Time	Description	Problems	Users
19/02/2008 13:50	Writing a test		0.16666667	Producing test cases	aca06se@sheffield.ac.uk, aca06lm@sheffield.ac.uk
19/02/2008 14:50	Checking a test		0.66692525		aca06se@sheffield.ac.uk, aca06lm@sheffield.ac.uk
12/03/2008 16:20	Testing some code		2.6641731	System testing login functions	aca06se@sheffield.ac.uk

Testing

- Testing

Retrieved from "http://vt.shef.ac.uk/sm/wiki/2007/hut01/index.php/Storycard_346"

- This page was last modified 11:31, 2 May 2008.

Tests SC 346

From hut01's Wiki

Test results for Storycard 346
(Users should be able to log in to the system at one of two levels (administrator/ basic user) by supplying a username and correct password to the login screen.)

Contents

Unit Tests

Test results (22/02/2008 15:15)

```
1..14
TestSuite "UserManagerTest"  started.
Ok 1 - testUserEmptyFields  (UserManagerTest)
Ok 2 - testUserEmptyPassword (UserManagerTest)
Ok 3 - testUserEmptyUsername (UserManagerTest)
Ok 4 - testUserInvalidPassword (UserManagerTest)
Ok 5 - testUserValidPassword (UserManagerTest)
Ok 6 - testSessionEmptyUsername (UserManagerTest)
Ok 7 - testSessionEmptyPassword (UserManagerTest)
Ok 8 - testSessionValid (UserManagerTest)
Ok 9 - testLoginNoInputNoSession (UserManagerTest)
Ok 10 - testLoginUsernameNoPasswordNoSession (UserManagerTest)
Ok 11 - testLoginUsernamePasswordNoSession (UserManagerTest)
Ok 12 - testLoginInvalidUserNoSession(UserManagerTest)
Ok 13 - testLoginNoInputSessionsValid (UserManagerTest)
Ok 14 - testLoginNoInputSessionsInvalid (UserManagerTest)
TestSuite "UserManagerTest" ended.
```

System Testing

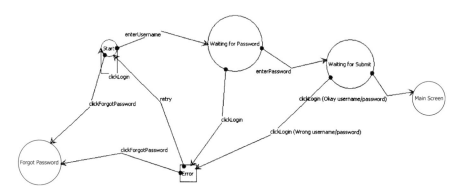

Test 1

ID	Action Performed	Expected Result
1	enterUsername	Usernamed entered, system waiting for password
2	enterPassword	Password entered, system waiting for submit
3	clickLogin (okay username/password)	System takes user to main screen

Results

Test No	Date	Pass/Fail	Comments
1	14:20 11 March 2008	Pass	Attempted to access page when logged out

Test 2

ID	Action Performed	Expected Result
1	enterUsername	Username entered, System waiting for password
2	enterPassword	Password entered, System waiting for submit
3	clickLogin (wrong username/ password)	System presents "Cannot login" error
4	retry	System shows login form again
5	enterUsername	Username entered, System waiting for password

Results

Test No	Date	Pass/Fail	Comments
2	14:22 11 March 2008	Pass	

Test 3

ID	Action Performed	Expected Result
1	enterUsername	Username entered, System waiting for password
2	enterPassword	Password entered, System waiting for submit
3	clickLogin (wrong username/ password)	System presents "Cannot login" error
4	retry	System shows login form again
5	clickLogin	System takes user to the Forgotten Password screen

Results

Test No	Date	Pass/Fail	Comments
3	13:25 11 March 2008	Fail at Step 4	System works, doesn't login, but XXM should just take user to login form again, not show the error. The XXM has been updated to reflect this.
3	13:31 11 March 2008	Pass	Works as expected, and exactly to XXM spec

Test 4

ID	Action Performed	Expected Result
1	enterUsername	Username entered, System waiting for password
2	enterPassword	Password entered, System waiting for submit
3	clickLogin (wrong username/ password)	System presents "Cannot login" error
4	retry	System shows login form again
5	clickLogin	System shows login form again
6	enterUsername	Username entered, System waiting for Password

Results

Test No	Date	Pass/Fail	Comments
4	13:33 11 March 2008	Pass	

Test 5

ID	Action Performed	Expected Result
1	enterUsername	Username entered, System waiting for password
2	enterPassword	Password entered, System waiting for submit
3	clickLogin (wrong username/ password)	System presents "Cannot login" error
4	retry	System shows login form again
5	clickLogin	System shows login form again
6	enterUsername	Username entered, System waiting for Password

Results

Test No	Date	Pass/Fail	Comments
5	13:37 11 March 2008	Pass	

Test 6

ID	Action Performed	Expected Result
1	enterUsername	Username entered, System waiting for password
2	enterPassword	Password entered, System waiting for submit
3	clickLogin (wrong username/ password)	System presents "Cannot login" error
4	retry	System shows login form again
5	clickLogin	System shows login form again
6	clickLogin	System shows login form again

Results

Test No	Date	Pass/Fail	Comments
6	13:38 11 March 2008	Pass	

Test 7

ID	Action Performed	Expected Result
1	enterUsername	Username entered, System waiting for Password
2	clickLogin (wrong username/ password)	System presents "Cannot login" error
3	clickForgotPassword	System takes user to the Forgotten Password screen

Results

Test No	Date	Pass/Fail	Comments
7	14:42 11 March 2008	Fail at Step 2	Error message not shown
7	14:52 11 March 2008	Fail at Step 3	Forgot Password not yet implemented
7	13:41 12 March 2008	Pass	Forgot Password link added

Test 8

ID	Action Performed	Expected Result
1	enterUsername	Username entered, System waiting for Password
2	clickLogin	System presents "Cannot login" error
3	retry	System shows login form again

Results

Test No	Date	Pass/Fail	Comments
8	14:44 11 March 2008	Fail at Step 2	Error message not shown
8	14:53 11 March 2008	Pass	

Test 9

ID	Action Performed	Expected Result
1	enterUsername	Username entered, System waiting for Password
2	clickLogin	System presents "Cannot login" error
3	clickForgotPassword	System takes user to the Forgotten Password screen

Results

Test No	Date	Pass/Fail	Comments
9	14:44 11 March 2008	Fail at Step 2	Error message not shown
9	14:44 11 March 2008	Fail at Step 3	Forgot Password not yet implemented
9	13:44 12 March 2008	Pass	Forgot Password link added

Test 10

ID	Action Performed	Expected Result
1	clickForgotPassword	System takes user to the Forgotten Password screen

Results

Test No	Date	Pass/Fail	Comments
10	14:46 11 March 2008	Fail at Step 1	Forgot Password not yet implemented
10	13:45 12 March 2008	Pass	Forgot Password link added

Test 11

ID	Action Performed	Expected Result
1	clickLogin	System presents "Cannot login" error

Results

Test No	Date	Pass/Fail	Comments
11	14:46 11 March 2008	Pass	

Retrieved from "http://vt.shef.ac.uk/sm/wiki/2007/hut01/index.php/Tests_SC_346"

- This page was last modified 13:29, 29 April 2008.

Bibliography

S. Syed-Abdullah, M. Holcombe, M. Gheorghe. Practice makes perfect. *Extreme Programming and Agile Processes in Software Engineering*. Lecture Notes in Computer Science, Vol. 2675. Springer, 2003.

S. Syed-Abdullah, M. Holcombe, M. Gheorge. The impact of an agile methodology on the well being of development teams. *Empirical Software Engineering*, **11**(1):143–167, 2006.

S. Adler, A. Berglund, J. Caruso, S. Deach, T. Graham, P. Grosso, E. Gutentag, A. Milowski, S. Parnell, J. Richman, S. Zilles. Extensible Stylesheet Language (XSL), Version 1.0, 2001 Available at http://www.w3.org/TR/xsl/.

A.J. Albrecht. Measuring application development productivity. Presented at *SHARE/GUIDE/IBM Application Development Symposium*, Monterey, CA, 1979.

S. Ancha, A. Cioroianu, J. Cousins, J. Crosbie, J. Davies, K. Ahmed, J. Hart, K. Gabhart, S. Gould, R. Laddad, S. Li, B. Macmillan, D. Rivers-Moore, J. Skubal, K. Watson, S. Williams. *Professional Java XML*. Wrox Press, 2001.

S. Ambler. *Agile Modeling*. John Wiley & Sons, 2002.

R. Banker, R. Kauffman, C. Wright, D. Zweig. An empirical test of object-based output measurement metrics in a computer-aided software engineering (CASE) environment. *J. Management Information Systems*, **8**:127–150, 1992.

K. Beck. *Extreme Programming Explained*. Addison-Wesley, 1999.

K. Beck, C. Andres. *Extreme Programming Explained*. Addison-Wesley, 2005.

R.M. Belbin. *Management Teams: Why They Succeed or Fail*. Butterworth-Heinemann, 1981.

B. Boehm. *Software Engineering Economics*. Prentice-Hall, 1981.

B. Boehm, et al. *Cost Models for Future Life Cycle Processes: COCOMO 2*. Balzer Science, 1995.

K. Bogdanov. Testing from object machines in practice. In *Proceedings of UK-TEST'05*, Sheffeld, University of Sheffield, 2005.

R.P. Bostrom, K.M. Kaiser. Personality differences within systems project teams: Implications for designing solving centers. In *Proceedings of the 18th Annual Computer Personnel Research Conference*, ACM Press, 1981, pp. 248–285.

J.M. Bourre. Effects of nutrients (in food) on the structure and function of the nervous system: Update on dietary requirements for brain. Part 1: Micronutrients. *Journal of Nutrition Health and Aging*, **10**(5):377–385, 2006.

J.M. Bourre. Effects of nutrients (in food) on the structure and function of the nervous system: Update on dietary requirements for brain. Part 2: Macronutrients. *Journal of Nutrition Health and Aging*, **10**(5):386–399, 2006.

T. Bray, J. Paoli, C. Sperberg-McQueen, E. Maler. *Extensible Markup Language (XML) 1.0*, 2nd ed. 2001. Available at http://www.w3.org/TR/REC-xml.

S. Brown, R. Burdick, J. Falkner, B. Galbraith, et al. *Professional JSP*, 2nd ed., Wrox Press, 2001.

T. Buzan, B. Buzan. *The Mind Map Book*. Pearson, 2006.

S. Chalon. Omega-3 fatty acids and monoamine neurotransmission. *Prostaglandins, Leukotrienes and Essential Fatty Acids*, **75**(4–5):259–269, 2006.

P. Coad, J. de Luca, E. Lefebre. *Java Modelling in Color*. Prentice Hall, 1999.

A. Cockburn. *Agile Software Development* (A. Cockburn, J. Highsmith, eds.). Addison-Wesley, 2001.

D.L. Cooperrider, S. Srivastva. Appreciative enquiry in organisational life. *Research in Organizational Change and Development*, **1**:129–169, 1987.

Running an Agile Software Development Project. By Mike Holcombe
Copyright © 2008 John Wiley & Sons, Inc.

P. Costa, R. McCrae. Four ways, five factors are basic. *Personality and Individual Differences*, **13**:653–665, 1992.

A.J. Cowling, J.S. Karn. An initial observational study of the effects of personality type on software engineering teams. In *Proceedings of the 8th International Conference on Empirical Assessment in Software Engineering (EASE 2004)*, University of Keele, UK, 2004, pp. 155–165.

A.J. Cowling, J.S. Karn. An initial study of the effect of personality on group projects in software engineering. *Department of Computer Science Research Report CS-04-01*, University of Sheffield, 2004.

W. Cunningham, K. Beck. A diagram for object-oriented programs. Presented at *Proceedings OOPSLA-86*, Portland, OR, Nov. 1986.

B. Curtis. Techies as non-technological factors in software engineering. In *Proceedings of the 13th International Conference on Software Engineering (ICSE 1991)*, Austin, TX, ACM Press, 1991, pp. 147–148.

S. Eilenberg. *Automata, Machines and Languages*, Vol. A. Academic Press, 1974.

J.J. Elam, D. Walz. A study of conflict in group design activities: Implications for computer supported cooperative environments. In *Proceedings of the Twenty First Annual Hawaii International Conference on Decision Support and Knowledge Based Systems Track*, ACM Press, 1988, pp. 247–254.

M. Fowler. *Refactoring—Improving the Design of Existing Code*. Addison-Wesley, 2000.

L. Fernando-Capretz. Personality types in software engineering. *International Journal of Human-Computer Studies*, **58**:207–214, 2003.

A. Furnham. The big five versus the big four: the relationship between the Myers-Briggs Type Indicator (MBTI) and NEO-PI five factor model of personality. *Personality and Individual Differences*, **21**:303–307, 1996.

A. Furnham, S. Trew, S. Sneade. The distracting effects of vocal and instrumental music on the cognitive test performance of introverts and extraverts. *Personality and Individual Differences*, **27**(2):381–392, 1999.

T. Gilb. *Principles of Software Engineering Management* (S. Finzi-Wokingham, ed.). Addison-Wesley, 1988.

L. Hatton, A. Roberts. How accurate is scientific software? *IEEE Transactions on Software Engineering*, **20**(10):785–797, October 1994.

L. Hatton. Does OO sync with the way we think? *IEEE Software*, **15**(3):46–54, 1998.

L. Hull, K. Jackson, J. Dick. *Requirements Engineering*. Springer, 2002.

M. Holcombe, F. Ipate. *Correct Systems–Building a Business Process Solution*. Springer-Verlag, 1988. Available at http://www.dcs.shef.ac.uk/~wmlh/correct.

J. Hughes, J. O'Brien, T. Rodden, M. Rouncefield, I. Sommerville. Presenting ethnography in the requirements process. Presented at the *Second IEEE International Symposium on Requirements Engineering (RE'95)*, Delhi, India, 1995.

W.S. Humphreys. *A Discipline for Software Engineering*. Addison-Wesley 1995.

D. Hunter. *Beginning XML*. Wrox Press, 2000.

D. Janzen, H. Saiedian. Test-driven development concepts, taxonomy, and future direction. *Computer*, **38**:43–50, 2005.

N. Jausovec, K. Jausovec, I. Gerlic. The influence of Mozart's music on brain activity in the process of learning. *Clinical Neurophysiology* **117**(12):2703–2714, 2006.

R. Jeffries. XP Installed. Available at www.xprogramming.com.

C.B. Jones. *Systematic Software Development Using VDM*. Prentice Hall, 1986.

C.G. Jung. *Psychological Types*, Vol. 6. Harcourt Press, 1923.

J.S. Karn, A.J. Cowling. A study of the effect of disruptions on the performance of software engineering teams. In *Proc. ISESE2005*, IEEE, 2005, pp. 417–427.

J.S. Karn, A.J. Cowling. A follow up study of the effect of personality on the performance of software engineering teams. Presented at *Proc. ISESE2006*, Rio de Janeiro, Sep. 21–22, 2006.

F. Macías, M. Holcombe, M. Gheorghe. A formal experiment comparing extreme programming with traditional software construction. In *Proceedings of the Fourth Mexican International Conference on Computer Science (ENC 2003)*, IEEE, 2003, pp. 73–80.

D. MARTIN, I. SOMMERVILLE. Patterns of cooperative interaction: Linking ethnomethodology and design. *ACM Transactions on Computer-Human Interaction* **11**(1):59–89, 2004.

R. MILLER. When pairs disagree, 1-2-3. In *XP/Agile Universe 2002* (D. Wells, L. Williams, eds.). Lecture Notes in Computer Science, vol. 2418. Springer-Verlag, 2002, pp. 231–236.

G. MYERS. *The Art of Software Testing*. John Wiley & Sons, 1978.

I.B. MYERS, P.B. MYERS. *Gifts Differing: Understanding Personality Type*. Mountain View, CA: Daves Black Publishing, 1987.

N.H. NAQVI, D. RUDRAUF, H. DAMASIO, A. BECHARA. Damage to the insula disrupts addiction to cigarette smoking. *Science* **315**(5811):531–534, 2007.

J. NAWROCKI, A. WOJCIECHOWSKI. Experimental evaluation of pair programming. Presented at *European Software Control and Metrics (Escom)*, 2001. Available at http://www2.umassd.edu/SWPI/xp/pairprogramming/Nawrocki.pdf.

J. NIELSEN. *Usability Engineering*. Academic Press, 1993.

A. PRENTICE. Storing up problems: The medical case for a slimmer nation. *Clinical Medicine* **4**(2):99–101, 2004.

R.S. PRESSMAN. *Software Engineering: A Practitioner's Approach*. McGraw-Hill, 2005.

B.K. PURI. Proton and 31-phosphorus neurospectroscopy in the study of membrane phospholipids and fatty acid intervention in schizophrenia, depression, chronic fatigue syndrome (myalgic encephalomyelitis) and dyslexia. *International Reviews of Psychiatry*, **18**(2):145–7, 2006.

F.H. RAUSCHER, G.L. SHAW, K.N. KY. Listening to Mozart enhances spatial-temporal reasoning: Towards a neurophysiological basis. *Neuroscience Letters*, **185**:44–47, 1995.

F.H. RAUSCHER, G.L. SHAW, L.J. LEVINE, E.L. WRIGHT, W.R. DENNIS, R. NEWCOINB. Music training causes long-term enhancement of preschool children's spatial-temporal reasoning abilities. *Neurological Research*, **19**:1–8, 1997.

R.H. RUTHERFORD. Using personality inventories to help form teams for software engineering projects. In *ACM SIGCSE Bulletin, Proceedings of the 6th Annual Conference on Innovation and Technology in Computer Science Education*, ACM Press, vol. 33, 2001, pp. 9–13.

G.E. SCHELLENBERG, T. NAKAT, P.G. HUNTER, T. TAMOTO. Exposure to music and cognitive performance: tests of children and adults. *Psychology of Music* **35**(1):5–19, 2007.

B. SCHNEIDERMAN. *Designing the User Interface*. Addison-Wesley, 1998.

K. SCHWABER, M. BEEDLE. *Agile Software Development with SCRUM*. Prentice Hall, 2002.

I. SOMMERVILLE. *Software Engineering*, 8th ed. Addison-Wesley, 2006.

J.M. SPIVEY. *The Z notation: A Reference Manual*, 2nd ed. Prentice Hall, 1992.

S. ST. LAURENT, E. CERAMIE. *Building XML Applications*, McGraw-Hill, 1999.

J. STAPLETON. *DSDM: The Dynamic Systems Development Method*. Addison-Wesley, 1997.

K.T. STEVENS, S.M. HENRY. Using Belbin's leadership role to improve team effectiveness: An empirical investigation. *Journal of Systems and Software*, **44**:241–250, 1999.

M. STEPHENS, D. ROSENBERG. *Extreme Programming Refactored: The Case Against XP*. Apress, 2006.

J. TEAGUE. Personality type, career preference and implications for computer science recruitment and teaching. In *Proceedings of the Third Australasian Conference on Computer Science Education (ACSE 98)*, ACM Press, 1998, pp. 155–163.

C. THOMSON, M. HOLCOMBE. Applying XP ideas formally: The story card and extreme X-machines. In *Proceedings of the 1st South-East European Workshop on Formal Methods*, South-East European Research Centre, 2003, pp. 57–71.

C. THOMSON, M. HOLCOMBE. Using a formal method to model software design in XP projects. In *Proceedings of the 2nd South-East European Workshop on Formal Methods*, Ohrid, FYR of Macedonia, AMCT, SEERC, Thessaloniki, Greece, **1**(3), 2005.

C. THOMSON, M. HOLCOMBE. A design change metric derived from extreme X-machines. Presented at *Proceedings of the 3rd South-East European Workshop on Formal Methods*, 2007. Available at http://www.seefm.info/seefm07/PDFs/15_212-226.pdf.

N. WALKINSHAW, K. BOGDANOV, M. HOLCOMBE, S. SALHUDDIN. Modelling and testing software with X-machines—a case study (submitted).

L. WATERHOUSE. Multiple intelligences, the Mozart effect, and emotional intelligence: A critical review. *Educational Psychologist* **41**(4):207–225, 2006.

E.H. WEISS. *How to Write Usable User Documentation*, 2nd ed. The Oryx Press, 1991.

J. WHITTLE, J. SCHUMANN. Generating statechart designs from scenarios. In *22nd International Conference on Software Engineering (ICSE '00)*, ACM Press, 2000, pp. 314–323.

L. WILLIAMS, R.R. KESSLER, W. CUNNINGHAM, R. JEFFRIES. Strengthening the case for pair programming. *IEEE Software*, **17**:19–25, 2000.

J. YUAN, M. HOLCOMBE, M. GHEORGHE. Where do unit tests come from? In *Extreme Programming and Agile Processes in Software Engineering (XP2003)* (M. Marchesi, G. Cucci, eds.). LNCS Vol. 2675. Springer, 2003, pp. 161–169.

Web Sites

http://www.XProgramming.com
http://www.junit.org
http://www.dcs.shef.ac.uk/~nw/Files/testSets.html
http://www.dcs.shef.ac.uk/~nw/statechum.html
http://www.borland.com/together/
http://www.hacknot.info/
http://www.issco.unige.ch/projects/ewg96/node13.html
http://www.jhotdraw.org
http://www.useit.com/papers/heuristic/heuristic_list.html
http://www.poppendieck.com
http://jeffsutherland.com/scrum/SutherlandDistributedScrumHICSS2007_v6_7_Jun_2006.pdf
http://www.clevelandclinic.org/health/health-info/docs/0300/0359.asp?index=4485
http://java.sun.com/docs/codeconv/
http://ergo.human.cornell.edu/ergoguide.html
http://www.phpcodingstandards.com/
http://weblogs.asp.net/lhunt/pages/CSharp-Coding-Standards-document.aspx
http://www.humanmetrics.com/cgi-win/JTypes1.htm
http://www.rubyonrails.org/
http://www.symfony-project.org/

Index